NEW STRATEGIES, TECHNIQUES AND TECHNOLOGIES
TO WIN THE CUSTOMERS YOU WANT AND KEEP THEM
FOREVER

RELATIONSHIP
MARKETING

IAN H. GORDON

John Wiley & Sons Canada, Ltd

Toronto • New York • Chichester • Weinheim • Brisbane • Singapore

John Wiley & Sons Canada, Ltd
22 Worcester Road
Etobicoke, Ontario
M9W 1L1

Canadian Cataloguing in Publication Data

Gordon, Ian
  Relationship marketing : new strategies, techniques and technologies to win the customers you want and keep them forever

Includes index.
ISBN 0-471-64173-1

1. Relationship marketing. 2. Customer relations. I. Title.

HF5415.55.G67 1998   658.8   C97-932667-2

Production Credits:
Cover design: Christine Kurys, RGD
Text design: JAQ, RGD
Printer: Tri-Graphic Printing Ltd.

Printed in Canada
10 9 8 7 6 5 4 3 2 1

DEDICATION

Joanne, Lauren and Evan
For whom my heart beats

CONTENTS

ॐ

No man is an island, entire of itself;
every man is a piece of the continent, a part of the main.
John Donne

This book is about business relationships and how the marketer can create new value for its customers, suppliers, employees and investors by managing these relationships. Although the focus of this book is on business, the concepts can also be used by government and not-for-profit organizations, such as charities and foundations, to manage their relationships for mutual advantage with their stakeholders.

The fundamental thesis in this book is that relationships are the only real asset of the enterprise — not the machines that make the products, the products themselves, or even the intellectual capital inherent in people, patents or know-how, important though all these might be. Traditionally, an "asset" has been seen as that which affects the short-term revenue generating potential of a company. A relationship, in contrast, provides the company with long term, lower risk revenues and the opportunity to grow both revenue and profit, in many ways.

A relationship does not come in a single size. Relationships mean different things to different customers. The buyer of a box of detergent will value different aspects of their relationship with

Procter and Gamble than will a buyer of a car from Ford. Relationships need to be formally understood and the process needs to be effectively managed for supplier and customer to continuously derive mutual value from the relationship. This then is what Relationship Marketing is about: the ongoing process of creating and sharing value with the customers that the company chooses to serve. Seen this way, Relationship Marketing recognizes the importance of learning with customers to create the value each wants, although that does not necessarily mean that the value created for individual customers must be unique. Of course, in some cases, customers do want unique value, but in others, that may not be feasible, affordable or even required.

I don't want unique value from my Tide detergent. I just want the detergent to clean my clothes and do this at a fair price. Other than occasional feedback or the resolution of unexpected problems, I don't really want unique services from P&G. But, I place a very high value on my relationship with Ford. This relationship includes a requirement that Ford pay some attention to helping my peers view Ford positively, even if they themselves choose to not own a Ford. This helps assure me that there will not be a line-up of neighbors pointing their fingers and controlling their chortles as I drive my new Ford into the driveway. I also want from Ford a car with features important to me, ones that work. I want any reasonable amount of service tailored to my vehicle's problems and my personal convenience. And I want Ford to help me buy new cars and get rid of old ones in a professional and friendly way, throughout my purchasing lifetime. Do this well, Ford, and I will promise you hundreds of thousands of dollars in business over my remaining years.

If relationships are the key assets of the enterprise, then all its efforts should be geared to building them. While all businesses have sought to build relationships with their customers, many have viewed the development and maintenance of the relationship as strictly the territory of sales, with the associated processes being owned by sales. But the relationship neither starts nor ends with sales. Relationships are the business of the whole company and must involve the entire enterprise. The goal of the company and its leaders, then, should be to enhance the value of its relationships. And this value will come from enduring relationships not just with customers, but with all those who together contribute to the continuity of the customer relationship.

This means that everyone from suppliers, to employees, customers and others, including retailers and other members of the distribution channels, investors and the board of directors, need to be forged into a "chain of relationships" that will add ever increasing value to the end-customer relationship. The relationship the company forms with end-customers will be only as strong as the weakest link in the chain; all are needed to maintain and deepen the relationship with the end-customer. Therefore, relationships need to be forged and nurtured with every one of those who contribute to the customer relationship. Relationship Marketing seeks to create and share new value with each of these individual stakeholders, as each wishes to relate to the company over the long term in a partnership where many interests are common and aligned.

Relationship Marketing affects virtually every person, technology and process in the enterprise. It is not about isolated concepts such as database marketing, predictive modeling, data warehousing, one-to-one marketing, relationship selling, mass customization, customer intimacy or bonding, although each of these and others may have important roles as components of the overall concept of Relationship Marketing. Relationship Marketing seeks to align the enterprise with the expectations of certain customers and to deliver the value these customers want, continuously.

A meaningful relationship starts, as in a more private way, when supplier and customer see that it is in their interests to get together for the long term. This means a supplier needs to take stock of the customers it serves and decide which ones will receive special and continuing attention. Which customers are the most profitable now? Which can be made more profitable? Which are very important to the company's future? Which customers should be fired? Which customers want a relationship with us and which want to buy on price alone? Relationship Marketing requires that organizations consider issues such as these and choose the customers on which it will focus, develop meaningful insight and predict the behaviors of chosen customers, formulate strategies for individual customer relationships and build the abilities within the company to deliver the value customers want. Companies asking themselves these questions may find that they have more work within the company to assess customers' profitability, strategic value and perceptions of the company and its competitors. Some companies may need to build better databases about their customers. Others may need to focus many areas of the their companies on the customer relationship, in part by organizing their companies with relationships in mind, and in part by integrating people, process, technology and knowledge systems to bring about a deepening of customer bonding.

It is management's role to define and shape the basis for the end-customer relationship and to align all aspects of the enterprise with the customer. It is also the purpose of management to recognize and address the importance of the relationships that contribute to the end-customer relationship. For the end-customer relationship to endure, management may often need to rethink aspects about the company's internal and external relationships. For example, are salespeople compensated to be "hunters" or "farmers"? Are call center personnel rewarded for the number of calls they process or the satisfaction of the caller? Does marketing focus on developing new products or on the current and future profitability of its customers? Do investors include patient capitalists who favor growing the business or capricious venture capitalists with an inclination to pillage?

This book discusses a number of considerations for management to profitably improve customer relationships. In Chapter 1, we review changes in the practice of marketing including the profound impact of technology on virtually every aspect of marketing and the company. Chapter 2 extends this discussion and explores how Relationship Marketing can be considered the central umbrella under which the diverse initiatives of the company can be linked and aligned. Spending on Relationship Marketing will depend, as for all business initiatives, on the quality of the business case that is advanced in support of this approach. Chapter 3 describes selected issues which can help advance the business case for Relationship Marketing in the company. Chapter 4 reviews how the company is bonded with its customers, and the importance of setting objectives to advance the customer relationship one step at a time. Chapter 5 notes that relationships companies form with businesses differ materially from relationships with consumers. This chapter describes the differences in the relationships between the two types of customers, and reviews selected implications. In Chapter 6, the book presents a process for the planning of customer relationships. The main building blocks of the plan are described in this chapter, and the next three. Chapter 7 describes selected developments in technology that have important implications for the Relationship Marketing company and how these advances can help companies bond more tightly with their customers. Chapter 8 reviews issues and processes for making individualized products and services, and how this mass customization links to advancing customer relationships. Chapter 9 discusses the importance of deepening relationships with every category of stakeholder the company needs to contribute to the end-customer relationship, and presents strategic considerations for advancing this so-called "chain of relationships." Chapter 10 offers suggestions for companies wishing to design customer relationships into their organizations, while focusing management on Relationship Marketing.

Before Relationship Marketing can be adopted by most companies, a number of internal barriers will need to be overcome. Some of these relate to widespread skepticism of new strategic initiatives. Others may simply stem from insufficient review of the subject matter or genuinely important priorities other than Relationship Marketing that cannot be deferred, such as business survival. Returning to the matter of skepticism, companies have become used to "flavor of the month" management initiatives. We all laugh at Dilbert cartoons when they reflect absurdities back to us. We are used to the boss who goes to a seminar or conference and then manages as though this were the only way. Many companies have introduced a wide array of fragmented initiatives without strategic linkages, each of which is urgently pursued and some of which are poorly implemented. A few years ago, management was focused on reengineering, then customer intimacy, then product simplification and now perhaps one facet or another of technology adoption. The challenge for management is to provide coherence and strategic linkages for all major initiatives. So, for example, call centers, Internet marketing, real-time marketing, data warehouses or delayered distribution channels need an overall umbrella. This book is about creating and managing that umbrella and how Relationship Marketing, applied throughout the company, can create new value to build the firm for the long term.

Of course this will not be easy. Enduring business triumphs rarely are.

ACKNOWLEDGEMENTS

ॐ

*I*n writing this book, I would like to acknowledge and deeply thank those who have made this possible:

- To clients, thank you for seeing in me one worthy of your time, your support, guidance and friendship, for the opportunity to learn with you and to continue to add value to your company. Thanks for the opportunity to be relevant. My particular thanks to Al, Ann, Brooke, Francine, Gary, Kurt, Larry, Ted, Terry and Sandra.
- To my partners at TCI Convergence Management Consultants, Toronto — Richard, Roger, Lorne, Jon, Steve and Greg. I appreciate daily the opportunity to work with the best marketing and business minds, people who know the value of concepts and the greater value of character. You know that Relationship Marketing is not just between this firm and its clients, but between partners.
- To friends and associates, including Alex, Bill, Bob, Chris, David, Elisabeth, George, Mark, Mike, Peter, Rob and Vijay, thanks for your friendly support, guidance and insight, and particularly to John, with whom core ideas presented in this book were conceived in 1988.

- To Gladys, who everyone loves, none more than your children, who gave me context, judgment and will.
- To Louis, who taught that integrity, humility, learning and gentle humanity are for all seasons and that there is much value in taking the long view.
- For Joanne, who knows that a relationship starts with values — strong, resolute and absolute, and grows when attended by trust, thoughtfulness and attention.
- For Lauren, who makes my heart dance and for Evan, my total joy. Listen, think and learn to create new value that you can be proud to share.
- My thanks to the professionals at John Wiley and Sons, and particularly to Karen, who, as editor, has patiently, kindly and with great intelligence, guided this project to completion, while serving as your advocate.
- Importantly, my thanks to you for investing your time in this book. I have worked hard to create value for you. I hope you will find it worthwhile. Please let me have your views by contacting me at the following e-mail address: rel82ian@aol.com. I look forward to hearing from you.

CHAPTER ONE

&

Marketing is Dead — Long Live Marketing

All for one, one for all, that is our device.
Alexandre Dumas, *The Three Musketeers*

The role of marketing has been under siege for over a decade. Management wants more revenue impact from marketing, more immediate "bang for the marketing buck." In addition, marketing is bearing the political brunt of enterprises not fully adopting the marketing concept, while still holding the marketer responsible for delivering volume. But marketers have also suffered from difficulties of their own creation, such as applying unmodified the principles they learned at business school in the 1970s and 1980s. Marketers have been slow to add to their marketing tool kit, so competitors increasingly have been adopting similar principles and have been achieving similar performance.

Busy attending to the practice of marketing, marketers may not have noticed that marketing is, for all practical purposes, dead. (Marketers may prefer to say it is in the declining phase of its life cycle!) Today, marketing attracts neither interest nor patience from the investor community, except to the extent that basic marketing skill must be demonstrated by the enterprise. Marketing rarely achieves its promise of differentiating and developing enduring, competitively superior, value. Marketing has barely recognized the dramatic changes in technology that provide all in the enterprise, including the marketer, with entirely new strategic capabilities, such as those associated with data warehousing and mining, the Internet and Intranet and computer-telephony integration (CTI). Today, technology, driven by declining costs of memory, processing, bandwidth and storage, is offering new opportunities for marketers to create new business value by:

- Helping customers to be more satisfied with the purchase experience, by addressing any of their concerns or complaints in real time, before they have a chance to become dissatisfied. "Your car is taking longer to repair than we expected. You previously took one of our sport cars for a test drive. Can we lend you one as a loaner for the next day or two?"

- Broadening the range of products or services available to the customer by expanding the scope of the enterprise, perhaps by cross-selling or distributing the products and services of others. "Your term investment will come due in two weeks. Should we reinvest it in a similar manner for you, or would you like to review other investment alternatives that could provide a better yield?"

- Deskilling the selling process by providing customer, product, inventory and selling and other know-how to the sales staff "just in time" to influence the customer. "Usually we take samples of your business forms back to our offices to do a detailed analysis and provide a quotation. Today, I can quote immediately on your forms' requirements, using this laptop, and then send your order in via modem. You'll have the fastest possible turnaround."

- Focusing promotional activities to those customers likely to be most influenced by specific offers when they are ready to buy. "We have just sold the home of a friend of yours. She said you may be interested in moving to a larger home. Your friend tells me you are concerned about the cost of moving. We have taken a careful look at that, and we and our associate firms can move you for two-thirds of what most people pay. Can I send you information about our approach today?"

- Tailoring all aspects of communications to the information needs and media preferences of customers, using mass customized communication and media selection. If you take in information best via e-mail, companies wishing to sell to you should know this and do so.

Technology, wherever it has been adopted, has resulted in processes being changed to accommodate, manage and tend the technology. Marketing was one area that resisted integration into technology-led change. Rather than drive the change, marketing management often opposed it, seeing the technologies as restrictive on their spans of control or creativity. But the technologies are going into companies with or without the support of marketers, and marketers now often find themselves in the uncommon role of reacting to, rather than driving change. It is not too early to recognize that marketing needs new thinking, direction and application.

The Marketing Challenge: The Relationship Marketing Solution

Relationship Marketing may be a very practical and appropriate approach for marketers to regain their edge as the company's strategic driver. Not only is the current practice of marketing under siege, but many specific components of marketing are being questioned. Some of these represent significant opportunities for marketers to review and revise their approach to marketing, setting the stage for marketers to lead change throughout organizations and renew their role as customer advocates.

Some of the main challenges faced by marketers include issues associated with a shortening time horizon of business in general and for marketers in particular, changes in approaches to market segmentation, designing individual preferences into products and services, compressing time frames for researching markets and customers, communicating with individuals, proactively servicing customers as they wish to be served over their lifetimes and customer participation in pricing decisions. These issues are discussed next.

1. Time Horizon

The time horizon available for marketers to achieve results in many companies has shrunk. Increasingly, marketing has been losing power in companies to those in the financial stream. Now, venture capitalists, impatient investors and financial managers have dramatically reduced the time frame available for building revenues and margin. Yet, the market place may mean that selling cycles and internal challenges, such as product development cycles, may remain long. In addition, customers have no patience for suppliers that take the money and run. Many want to work with their suppliers over the long term to build new business value. Marketers who remain focused on transactions rather than relationships will miss these opportunities. However, those focused instead on relationships know that customers want a longer-term association with the company and/or its brands. By accepting that many customers want an association over a longer time horizon, the marketer will first need to develop internal support for developing enduring alignment with customers to the advantage of both supplier and customer.

This is important. A relationship that exists only as an imperative of the vendor will certainly flounder. The challenge is to identify meaningful ways for customer and supplier to associate in the long term and build strategic value together — value from which both benefit.

This means that organizations should shift from a transaction to relationship orientation, and that they must recognize that, in many cases, they simply do not know the full extent of their profitability by customer. An early issue for the marketer is to decide with which customers they want relationships, with which they do not, and what type of relationships to encourage. It is often the customers the firm values most that may be the ones with which they should no longer do business. The marketer will have two roles in this: to identify the customer base with which the firm is to maintain and deepen relationships, and to champion the changes needed within the company for this to happen. This is a vital role for marketers, which puts them back on the center stage of the enterprise, this time as Relationship Managers.

2. Market Segmentation

In addition, the marketer needs to accept the fact that market segments no longer exist the way they were taught. Whether considering customers demographically, psychographically, attitudinally or by lifestyle, it is becoming increasingly hard to categorize buyers. They seem to do unusual things. Some "scrimp and splurge," saving their money or deferring spending in some areas and then buying heavily in others. Some customers within a historically defined segment are much more sensitive to some media than others. Some are sensitive to price, others to service. And so on. If the only categorization that is meaningful is actual buyer behavior — what people or businesses buy, rather than the underlying drivers of that behavior — then *there are no more market segments, just individual customers.*

While business-to-business marketers have long recognized the importance of relationships unique to the purchase decision, consumer marketers have focused more on segment-based marketing principles. The traditional market segmentation paradigm required aggregation of customers with like — but not identical — needs into segments to ensure that, generally speaking, customers would benefit by receiving more appropriate goods and services than had they been in a single mass market. Thankful for this, customers were supposed to shell out more than their mass market counterparts, sufficient for the seller to more than cover the higher costs of serving this segment. Or so the thinking went. Yet, no matter how small the segment, it always seemed that competitors were prepared to target a yet smaller segment, and do so without fully pricing out the apparently higher costs associated with the more highly tailored marketing mix. Frustrating though this has been, most marketers would rather have endured declining market share and even profitability than commit almost certain career hara-kiri by attempting to serve uniquely individual consumers. The economics were just not there.

So, the requirements of individual customers, although relevant to the customers, have been largely ignored because most purchasers simply could not be economically profiled, tracked, anticipated, managed and served uniquely — at least not until the declining costs of existing technologies, the advent of new technologies and Relationship Marketing principles made this possible. And it is now possible, if not always economic, for every enterprise to consider. Some consumer non-durables, such as packaged foods, do not usually create enough new value, even when considered over the buyer's lifetime of purchasing, to warrant the investment associated with customization of product, service, communications and pre- and post-sale attention. But some apparently do. The British division of Heinz, the ketchup to baby food company, markets its products directly to the over 4.6 million consumers it has on its database.[1] It

---

[1] "Down the Data Mine We Go," *The Economist*, August 23, 1997, p. 48.

sends a free copy of its *At Home* magazine to these households to promote its products, a strategy also adopted by Harry Rosen, the Canadian upscale menswear retail chain, which publishes a fashion magazine for its customers.

3. Product or Service Design

For products and services where the lifetime volume and margin warrant it, individual customers can and should be considered in every aspect of the business, including the processes that drive new product and service design. This act recognizes that customers are not equal — they want different things in different amounts at different times — and the profit derived from each will vary. The key challenge for the marketer is to identify the core strategic value that will be delivered to the customer and the elements that the customer can change, allowing the buyer to be firmly in charge assembling the value she wants. For most organizations, mass customization requires a material shift in current practice. Again, the marketer can lead the charge.

4. Market Research

Marketers used to rely on market research approaches to help identify issues and assess consumer responses to hypothetical solutions. But market research can take more time than the marketer has available, not only for the reasons discussed above, but because market conditions are changing so fast that a company addressing current research findings may actually be dealing with yesterday's issues. This was actually the main reason for the Edsel failure and marketers have not always learned the lesson.

How is the marketer to guide the company's relationship with its customers without timely and relevant knowledge about them? Now marketers need to devise knowledge systems to learn more about individual customers so that firms can create the value each customer wants and be ready to serve the customer with this value when he is ready to buy. Market research needs to give way to customer knowledge. And the marketer needs to help the company provide the systems and know-how to implement the gathering, storage, intelligence, retrieval and reporting needed to make this happen.

5. Marketing Communications

Previously, marketers relied on broadcasting their message. No longer. Today the marketer has an opportunity to communicate with individual customers according to the media each prefers, with the message most relevant to the individual in a time and manner most likely to have influence. Perhaps I prefer receiving timely information via e-mail. The marketer's message could inform, remind or persuade me directly at my e-mail address, with a tailored communication geared to the preferences or interests revealed by my buying behaviors.

The customer should be engaged with relevant and timely communications, which seems to become even more so as the vendor learns more about the customer and applies this knowledge.

The challenge for the marketer is to apply technology judiciously to facilitate this relevant, timely, personalized and customized communication, learn individual preferences of customers and engage them as to their needs and preferences, satisfaction, dissatisfaction, favorability and intent with regard to future purchases.

One-way communications typically employed by marketers with their customers, such as mass advertising, promotional offers, manuals, price lists, product literature and warranty response cards, must be replaced with two-way communications to involve the customer much earlier in all matters which affect their future purchase behaviors. The challenge for the marketer is again to work with IT managers to design processes and incorporate technologies to engage the customer collaboratively at appropriate times for both the customer and the company. In this way, the company can become more relevant, without driving costs through the roof.

6. Customer Service

The old adage is that the customer is always right. Certainly the customer service department has always tried to operate according to this maxim. Make customers happy when they complain. Engage them positively. Offer restitution. But this approach is the equivalent of making bad cars and delaying the day of reckoning by having the dealer make the repairs. When customers complain, it is a signal of a broken process somewhere in the business. Perhaps the broken processes have to do with understanding and shaping customer expectations or delivery to these expectations. Whatever the case, an organization that works collaboratively with customers throughout the value chain should have limited need for a customer service department, at least not in the conventional sense.

Today, the customer service department is the front line where it engages the irate, disappointed or ill-informed. But this role is miscast, as it provides service after the customer has already had an unpleasant experience, a little like having waiters offer you daiquiris as your voyage aboard the Titanic takes a turn for the worse. You appreciate the service, but see it as a little irrelevant in the broader context. Perhaps recast as the customer information center geared to anticipating customer issues, the service role assumes new importance. The customer information center could proactively engage customers, ensure lifetime customer satisfaction and be the leading edge of the marketing communications changes referred to above.

7. Pricing

Customers want to participate in decisions regarding the value they receive and the prices they pay. Give them a standard offering and they will expect to pay a single price. But offer them options in the product and they will want some more than others, and will pay more for these. Give them a chance to have an even more tailored solution and they might pay more again. Give them options they don't want and they will expect these to be removed and deleted from the price. If the clothes don't fit, don't charge for alterations — just make clothes that fit.

This does not apply just to companies selling to consumers. Business-to-business customers in the pharmaceutical industry, for example, buy quality control services from Contract Research Organizations (CRO) and expect to pay for each test performed on their behalf. As the tests may take some time to schedule and perform, they want to see the progress of the tests on-line at their computer screen and, once the results are available, to quickly release incoming ingredients to speed up the production of their pharmaceuticals. Customers consider this on-line access important because it accelerates their production processes and they will pay more for this benefit. They still want to purchase and pay for individual tests. The CRO recognizing both the information content and the preference for paying by the test has an opportunity to develop even more value from the information obtained conducting tests for their customers. For example, the CRO could develop a data warehouse of all comparable tests, allowing customers to see if results from a certain test fall within the norms of prior tests, how results compare with others from the specific supplier and how this supplier stacks up with others in the industry. These results and other company-specific information could be accessible over the Web.

What is Relationship Marketing?

Relationship Marketing is the ongoing process of identifying and *creating new value* with individual customers and then *sharing the benefits* from this over a lifetime of association. It involves the understanding, focusing and management of ongoing collaboration between suppliers and selected customers for mutual value creation and sharing through interdependence and organizational alignment.

Relationship Marketing draws from traditional marketing principles, yet is quite different. Marketing can be defined as the process of identifying and satisfying customers' needs in a competitively superior manner in order to achieve the organization's objectives. Relationship Marketing builds on this, but has six dimensions that differ materially from the historical definition of marketing. Taken together, these differences have the potential to transform a company's view of the marketing it undertakes and almost everything about the enterprise, from the work it does to the technology its employs to the products it produces to the structure by which it achieves its objectives.

Relationship Marketing:

- Seeks to create *new* value for customers and then *share* the value so created between producer and consumer.

- Recognizes the key role *individual* customers have not only as purchasers, but in *defining* the value they want. Previously, companies would be expected to identify and provide this value in what the company would consider a "product." With Relationship Marketing, the customer helps the company provide the benefit bundle that the customer values. Value is thus created *with* customers, not *for* them.

- Requires that a company, as a consequence of its business strategy and customer focus, *design and align* its business processes, communications, technology and people in support of the value individual customers want.

- Is a continuously cooperative effort between buyer and seller. As such, it operates in real time.

- Recognizes the value of customers over their purchasing *lifetimes,* rather than as individual customers or organizations that must be resold on each purchasing occasion. In recognizing lifetime value, Relationship Marketing seeks to bond progressively more tightly with customers.

- Seeks to build a *chain of relationships* within the organization to create the value customers want, and between the organization and its main stakeholders, including suppliers, distribution channel intermediaries and shareholders.

This has a number of important implications. With Relationship Marketing, the company now focuses on six areas: technology and individual customers, scope of the business, selecting and rejecting customers, a chain of relationships, rethinking the 4 Ps of marketing and using relationship managers to help companies build new value with others.

1. Using Technology to Communicate with and Serve Individual Customers

If there are no more market segments, customers need to be served as individuals. Companies can give individual customers, or logical groups of customers (where serving the individual uniquely makes no sense to either customer or supplier) the value each wants, by using technology appropriately and throughout the value chain. Often this means taking apart existing business processes and inserting technology into the process. For example, when the Internet is used for on-line ordering, the process for purchasing has been redesigned and technology has been injected to "disintermediate" the process for introducing technology between customer and supplier (which can result in distribution channel intermediaries being bypassed), and to mass customize. Companies doing this have the potential not only to get closer to their individual customers, but also to gain competitive advantage, a particular opportunity for the innovator.

amazon.com was a pioneer in selling books over the Internet. This virtual bookstore carries 2.5 million titles, has over 600,000 customer accounts and annualized sales are running in excess of $80 million. Now there are a host of competitors, some large, such as Barnes and Noble and Book Stacks Unlimited, and others quite specialized, such as canadabooks.com and cvbookstore.com, both of which deal most-ly in Canadian books. The challenge for these firms is no longer to demonstrate that product can be sold on the Internet, but that signif-icant returns on investment can be made. For example, amazon.com is experiencing mounting losses, in part the result of high advertising expenditures, thin margins, lesser publisher discounts than super-stores and chains and processes which require frequent ordering, in mostly single units, from publishers and wholesalers.

Physical bookstores are finding the Internet can be a profitable channel to distribute product since it expands their audience and increases their inventory turns. For example, The City of Books is a huge, independent new and used book retailer in Portland, Oregon with a national reputation. When City of Books computerized its inventory and went on the Web in 1996 as powells.com, it found that sales grew and kept growing at about 20% per month. Cus-tomers around the world are discovering the phenomenal range of titles available from this site and the company is prospering while other independent bookstores, being pressured from many sides, from superstores to Web-based retailers, are floundering and failing.

2. Growing Through Scope and Partnering

Companies serving customers as they wish to be served may find they have to do something they have never done before to serve cus-tomers as they wish to be served. Some companies may need to expand the scope of their products or services, providing customers with more than just what the companies make. In the process, firms increasingly will distribute the products or services of others, or work with companies with stronger or more relevant customer relation-ships to distribute their own products or services. This represents a marked departure in strategy for those companies that have built their businesses through economies of scale. It may also require that firms reorient their relationship focus, from serving customers to see-ing other firms as their primary customers or as their collaborative partners.

This is a component of Relationship Marketing. It means that firms may have to form non-traditional alliances and partnerships, perhaps even with their competitors, so that customers are better or more completely served.

3. Customer Selection and Rejection

Employing this principle, firms will focus on customers appropriate to their strategy and reject others that no longer fit. A major accounting/consulting firm has recently been through an account review and has decided to focus on a limited subset of companies, narrowing its worldwide priority focus customer list from several thousand firms to under 200. Although the move initially met stiff opposition among the firm's partners, it is now achieving record sales and profits.

4. Chains of Relationships

Many companies consider how to improve their supply chains, configuring processes to supply products and services within specific time, quality and cost guidelines. It may be more appropriate for companies to consider how the needs and behaviors of customers can drive procurement, production and logistics, among other considerations. For this to work effectively, the firm needs to develop and align a chain of relationships to provide for changing demands. This chain comprises stakeholders such as resellers and retailers, employees, suppliers, bankers and investors. Each of these will have different needs and each will want to benefit from the creation and sharing of the value developed by the company with its end-customers. This is a reversal of traditional thinking in the area of supply chain management and will be discussed at greater length in Chapter 9.

5. Rethinking the 4 Ps of Marketing

Below, we discuss the impact of Relationship Marketing on the 4 Ps of marketing: product, price, promotion and placement/distribution.

Product

Relationship Marketing, when appropriately implemented, results in products being cooperatively designed, developed, tested, piloted, provided, installed and refined. Products are not developed in the historical way, with the company conceiving of product concepts, researching these with customers and then engaging in various research and development initiatives, leading to product roll-out some time later. Rather, Relationship Marketing involves real-time interaction between the company and its priority customers, as it seeks to move more rapidly to meet customer requirements. The product is therefore the output of a process of collaboration that creates the value customers want for each component of the product and associated services. Products are not bundles of tangible and intangible benefits the company assembles because it thinks this is what customers want to buy. Rather, products comprise an aggregation of individual benefits customers have participated in selecting or designing. The customer thus participates in the assembly of an unbundled series of components or modules that together comprise the product or service. The "product" resulting from this collaboration may be unique or highly tailored to the requirements of the customer, with much more of their knowledge content incorporated into the product than was previously the case. Consider how General Electric works with airframe companies such as Boeing, from the outset of the concept for the plane, to make jet engines capable of meeting Boeing's specifications. GE's engines for one Boeing plane differ from another, in part because Boeing's knowledge and direction is incorporated in the design and development process.

Price

Traditional marketing sets a price for a product and offers the product/price set in the market, perhaps discounting the price in accordance with competitive and other market-place considerations. The price seeks to secure a fair return on the investment the company has made in its more-or-less static product. With Relationship Marketing, the product varies according to the preferences and dictates of the customer, with the value varying commensurately. So, when customers specify that a product should have specific features and that certain services should be delivered before, during and after the sale, they naturally want to pay for each component of the value bundle separately. Just as the product and services are secured in a process of collaboration, so too will the price need to reflect the choices made and the value created from these choices.

Business-to-business marketers, especially for larger capital goods and installations, have typically engineered the products and services to customer requirements, and negotiated the prices of their services. But customers have not often been involved in all aspects of the value chain and the price-performance trade-offs that vendors have deemed necessary. Relationship Marketing invites customers into the pricing process and all other value-related processes, giving customers an opportunity to make any trade-offs and to further develop trust in the relationship.

Promotion

Traditional marketing sent smoke signals for all within a specific market segment to see. "Buy me," the signals said to all who could see them. Relationship Marketing instead gives an individual customer an opportunity to decide how they wish to communicate with the enterprise, using smoke signals or another media, how often and with whom. Mass promotion becomes support to build equity in the firm or brand, rather than a means to influence purchase directly. So, when Motorola sponsors a racing car, it has the opportunity not only to claim that its on-board telemetry was an important ingredient in the vehicle's success, it can develop the multiple impressions of its umbrella brand to an audience which may include customers for each of its individual products.

Technology can make promotion become communication because technology can engage individual customers when and how they wish to relate. For the producer of capital goods, this communication may involve opportunities for supplier and customer to interact at the strategic level — considering each others plans, customers, strategies and initiatives — so that both can consider how best to be interdependent over the planning horizon. It may also tie in the customer's and supplier's information and communications systems, letting staff in each firm feel as though they work with the other in an integrated way. In this way, the lines between supplier and customer can be further blurred. For the producer of consumer products, they could relate and communicate in much the same way with their channel intermediaries, such as the retailers. And now, with technology, individual end-customers can be interactively and uniquely engaged. Using technologies such as the Internet, computer-telephony integration at call centers, intelligence at point-of-sale, kiosks, smart cards and interactive voice response, companies can give customers a host of options to communicate with the company and have information on hand to engage, inform and direct each customer with complete knowledge as to their preferences and behaviors.

Placement/Distribution

Current marketing thinking focuses on distribution channels as the mechanism to transfer a product or its title from producer to consumer. That is, marketing sees distribution as the channel that takes the product from producer to consumer. In the case of the computer industry, Dell sees distribution as a direct sales approach, primarily using telephone sales and order placement, while IBM uses many approaches to distribution, including its own stores, a direct sales force and retailers that resell the firm's personal computers. Relationship Marketing instead considers distribution from the perspective of the customer who decides where, how and when to buy the combination of products and services that comprise the vendor's total offering. Seen this way, distribution is not a channel but a *process*. The process allows customers to choose where and from whom they will obtain the value they want. Continuing the computer example just mentioned, the customer can choose whether to buy one off-the-shelf from a reseller and take it home immediately, order one that is built to individual preference at the factory and shipped within a week or so, or have one configured in-store and available within a few days. It thus may be more accurate to think of distribution as "placement," giving the customer choice with regard to location at which they will specify, purchase, receive, install, repair and return individual components of the products and services. That is, while traditional marketing considered a product as a bundled package of benefits, Relationship Marketing unbundles the product and service and allows the customer to initiate a placement decision for each element.

6. Using Relationship Managers to Manage the Relationship

The Relationship Marketing company looks to engage the customer interactively in the many steps of creating value, looking for innovative ways to unlock new and meaningful benefits for the customer. And then, the company will want to share in the value of the benefits newly created for the customer, whether it relates to choice of features or functionality, rapid product and service delivery, timely communications or any other aspect of the benefit bundle. The role of managing the relationship includes the responsibility of listening to and with the customer and integrating communications, technologies, people and processes collaboratively with a customer counterpart. This role falls now to the Relationship Manager, a new title in many companies. The Relationship Manager will be there for the customer and work with him to ensure that both get the value they seek. The Relationship Manager will also lead an internal process of review and value creation with all those who deal with the customer using the technology and business processes put in place by the firm for this purpose. This is how Ernst and Young did business prior to the KPMG merger, and many other firms are following this approach. In general, by applying the principles of Relationship Marketing, each person within the company communicates and creates value with its customer counterpart, with the Relationship Manager guiding overall. So the president communicates with the customer's president, IT with IT, R&D with the users, and so on. The Relationship Manager works with the decision makers and influencers who are part of the collaborative process by which customers are involved in the purchase, including specifiers within customer organizations and those within the company that communicate with customers and create the value they want.

ᎧᏪ

This book will show how each of these issues can be addressed to transform your company and change materially the role of marketers within the company. Employing the principles in this book, marketers now have options other than maintenance of the status quo, occasional breakouts and Kevorkian marketing (attending at the business suicides of their companies as they try to compete in positions that are progressively less tenable in the market place).

Relationship Marketing offers an opportunity for the company and the marketer to break out of existing frameworks and to glue the firm into its customers' minds and wallets. And Relationship Marketing offers marketers a chance to help the company to grow in a competitively challenging environment. The firm will surely appreciate marketers again seizing strategic control to grow the firm.

A company embracing Relationship Marketing has the potential to become fundamentally different. As shown in Figure 1, the Relationship Marketing company is less concerned about selling what they make. Rather, they are more likely to take a closer look at their business model and consider whether they could be more profitable by building scope, sizing their production to the scale demanded by customers, and focusing on customer rather than product profitability. Enabled by new technologies, Relationship Marketing finally provides the marketer with the tools needed to serve individuals as they wish to be served, throughout their specification, purchasing and consumption lifetimes.

Companies that are first to adopt Relationship Marketing principles in their industries and to apply the concepts with vigor, have the

FIGURE 1: Relationship Marketing and the Role of the Relationship Manager

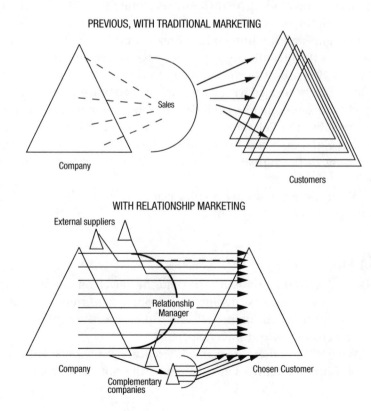

PREVIOUS, WITH TRADITIONAL MARKETING

Sales

Company

Customers

WITH RELATIONSHIP MARKETING

External suppliers

Relationship Manager

Company

Complementary companies

Chosen Customer

potential to gain a first-mover advantage difficult for competitors to emulate. Importantly, this means that companies have the potential to gain a pre-emptive position with the best customers and to ensure that the needs of these customers are well addressed long before competitors try to copy and target these same individuals or companies.

What Relationship Marketing is NOT

The words Relationships and Relationship Marketing are in increasingly wide currency. Some people mean favorable disposition, when they use the term Relationship. Some use Relationship Marketing interchangeably with Marketing, Relationship Selling, Database Marketing, Loyalty Marketing, One-to-One Marketing, Partnering or almost whatever it is that the marketer is pursuing.

Relationships are about favorable disposition and more, as Relationship Marketing includes terms such as the above. Relationship Marketing is fundamentally different from existing management approaches because it invites the customer into the company throughout the value chain. It blurs the lines between where the customer begins and the firm ends, it organizes the company differently, changes the incentive systems and seeks to change virtually every other existing aspect of the company to enable the firm to become more intensely bonded with its customers. Relationship Marketing is *not* what most companies do today, although, some may undertake parts or subsets of Relationship Marketing. Additionally, few companies have gone beyond the informal consideration of Relationship Marketing to the formal objectives and strategies suggested in this book.

We previously considered what Relationship Marketing is. Now let us reflect on what it is not.

Marketing

Relationship Marketing is not just another layer on the marketing onion; it is a brand new discipline that offers marketers new opportunities to achieve breakthroughs and to create new business value for their customers and shareholders.

As we will see, there are many differences between marketing and Relationship Marketing. One of these is the notion that marketing targets segments while Relationship Marketing creates value with individual customers. One targets competitors, not customers. Targeting customers sounds like a military strategy, and no customer wants to be the casualty of a business war.

The executive marketer, the champion of an organization of Relationship Managers, leads the process associated with customer value creation. As such, the marketer is not just the customers' advocate inside the company, but the advocate of the *process* by which value is created for customers. However, there will be opponents to any major process change in the company. Finance will likely oppose the cost of any change, sales and production will oppose the implied focus and IT will consider the changes to be of lower priority than whatever initiatives are now under way. A key challenge for the marketer is to develop broad support for the revised processes that will touch just about everything the company does throughout its value chain.

Relationship Selling

Relationship selling is most typically employed in business-to-business selling, and is the responsibility of the sales force. Sales has long sought to understand buyer behavior and the associated decision-making process in major clients and how these can be influenced to advantage. Relationship selling seeks to ensure that the needs of individual decision makers and the decision-making unit as a whole are understood, anticipated and satisfied throughout the typically lengthy purchase process. It has the potential to be oriented more to the needs of the seller than the buyer in that it may focus on persuading customers of the value in purchasing a product already on the market, rather than for their unique requirements. In the extreme, relationship selling can be focused on helping the company avoid price competition, rather than creating the value customers want and are happy to pay for.

Relationship Marketing may involve relationship selling to develop the initial impetus for the opportunity, but Relationship Marketing is focused on continuously creating new value to share with customers. It is thus oriented to the needs of the *process*, not the buyer or seller alone.

Database Marketing

Relationship Marketing includes the gathering and analysis of individual customer data, contact histories and transaction information to facilitate an ongoing two-way communication in order to keep their customers and to enhance their loyalty. Database marketers have been among the first to embrace selected principles of Relationship Marketing and some view Relationship Marketing and database marketing as interchangeable concepts. They are not. Few database marketers have focused more broadly on strategic marketing imperatives, let alone on all the Relationship Marketing issues associated with their company's strategy and customer interfaces — aligning their firm's business processes with the value customers seek, working to develop the IT infrastructure to support the business processes and building the organizational commitment and culture needed to support the changes. Rather, database marketers have been focused more on issues such as customer profiling, predictive modeling and other analysis to guide direct marketing. These are valuable components of Relationship Marketing but nevertheless do not fully describe the broader and more all-encompassing concept.

Loyalty Marketing

Loyalty programs typically result in another piece of plastic in your wallet in order to encourage more customer patronage. Whether you belong to a frequent flier program with an airline, frequent buyer program with a retailer, frequent fryer program with a restaurant, frequent kibitzer program with a telephone company or frequent snorer program with a hotel chain, all seem to be offering you incentives for using them and buying often. But these are just components of Relationship Marketing, not substitutes for it.

Partnering

Companies forging partnerships with customers, suppliers, channel intermediaries or competitors often practice Relationship Marketing principles in a number of key dimensions. They may align their people, processes and information technology and perhaps their business strategies, but rarely all four simultaneously. For example, in the aerospace industry, Sperry teamed with RCA to provide the computer software and specialized computers for the Aegis battlegroup defense systems, estimated to have eventually cost US taxpayers upward of a trillion dollars with the full commissioning of cruisers, destroyers and other Aegis-class vessels. Yet, even in the face of this very lucrative contract, both RCA and Sperry employed business strategies that were unaligned with one another. (Ultimately, GE acquired RCA and merged its aerospace group into the comparable capability within GE.)

ᎣᏣ

Relationship Marketing focuses on processes and whatever else is needed to advance the customer relationship, not just front-line involvement with the customer. Relationship Marketing recognizes that the traditional 4 Ps of marketing — product, promotion, price and placement/distribution — change fundamentally in a world in which technology can mass customize all these aspects in virtually infinite variation at close to mass-marketing costs. Relationship Marketing seeks to change the company into one that is more comfortable with managing as a digital enterprise in which the traditional "laws" of marketing are very much passé. In this digital world, customers are individually

FIGURE 2: Selected Relationship Marketing Elements

important, and served that way, with mass-customized and -personalized products, services and communications processes.

Figure 2 on page 21 displays the various areas of Relationship Marketing discussed in the course of the book and shows how many marketing techniques or principles fit into the larger context of Relationship Marketing.

The Eight Components of Relationship Marketing

Relationship Marketing comprises eight main components:

1. Culture and Values

2. Leadership

3. Strategy

4. Structure

5. People

6. Technology

7. Knowledge and Insight

8. Process

The goal of Relationship Marketing is to align all these aspects of a company with its chosen customers and stakeholders. This view of Relationship Marketing is illustrated in Figure 3 on the following page. Each of the components presented in this figure represents a challenge for the Relationship Marketer.

Figure 3 applies particularly to companies marketing to or through other businesses, which is the case for most business-to-business marketers and consumer product companies using channel intermediaries. Additional considerations for consumer marketers and other firms going directly to their customers are described and illustrated in Chapter 5. Now let's look at each Relationship Marketing component. (Subsequent chapters will consider many of these issues in greater depth.)

1. Culture and Values

Companies with dissimilar cultures can create value together, but the similarities and differences between cultures need to be understood at the outset. Extremes of cultural difference can work against the

FIGURE 3: Relationship Marketing

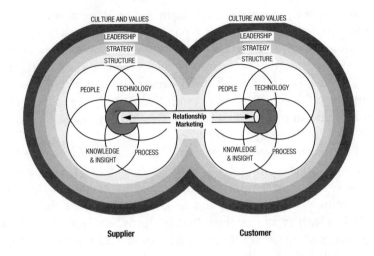

formation and maintenance of a relationship. For example, where the culture and values of one company is to maximize the value of today's transaction and use whatever combination of competence, guile and cunning to achieve its ends, it is unlikely that an enduring relationship can be formed with a company geared to building genuine, longer-term value. Deal-making companies do not typically co-exist happily with companies categorized as patient builders.

The message: The customer's culture and values must be conducive to the formation of an enduring relationship.

2. Leadership

The leaders within your company *and* those of your customers must be prepared to focus on the value that can be unlocked through Relationship Marketing and on the mutual interests of individual customers and suppliers. Leadership, both customer and supplier, must be prepared to choose those companies with which each will engage. And both must be prepared to forego certain types of customers/suppliers and the possible value they will create if they are to focus their firms on just one type of relationship. They must then align their companies in support of this type of relationship.

Nypro, one of the largest plastic injection molding companies in the world, is a quality focused company determined to bring uniformity to its processes. It has narrowed its customer base to only those with which it chooses to do business. In 1987, the company had 800 customers. In the next ten years, they jettisoned 750, explaining with care its strategy to these "fired" customers. Nypro wanted to do business with large purchasers that themselves wanted a relationship and valued both quality service and the provision of solutions, rather than just products. By September, 1997, Nypro had sixty-five customers after cutting the rest. Sales had grown from less than $50 million in 1987 to over $450 million a decade later. Only strong leadership could have caused this focusing to be considered and to be implemented successfully.

Importantly, no organization will successfully implement a Relationship Marketing initiative as long as the leadership in the company is focused on winning at the expense of others. In some companies, executives try to ensure that they maximize the value of each deal with every customer. In these firms, it is regarded as smart to sweep all the chips to their side of the table. Companies trying to forge relationships with this underlying approach to customers will find, for obvious reasons, that customers have no interest in long-term bonding with such suppliers. The opportunity to continuously create new and mutual value over time will go to competitors more amenable to sharing.

Companies with greater bargaining power than their customers and suppliers have a special role. They have an obligation to lead both their own firm and those of their customers and suppliers to a higher state of relating, one in which new value can be created and shared rather than the more traditional model of a zero-sum game in which players bargain to cut a bigger slice from the pie.

The message: Leadership must view sharing as a virtue and understand the real meaning of a relationship before committing the company to Relationship Marketing. Where companies have bargaining power relative to customers and suppliers, it is their role to initiate Relationship Marketing in the interests of their firm, customers and suppliers.

3. Strategy

Strategy needs to occur at multiple levels, as will be reviewed in the next chapter. This includes customer strategy and strategies to develop the underlying capabilities needed to advance the customer relationship. The customer — not the product, research and development or other competencies — must be central to the business strategy if the firm is to implement effectively Relationship Marketing. Many companies remain locked into the product management era, applying the principles of consumer packaged goods to their industries. In an era of sophisticated customers choosing from products with limited differentiation, product management strategies have less value than strategies geared to creating the value customers want. And they may not always see the product as central to the value they want their vendors to create. If timely, responsive service, for example, is a key dimension of the value they seek, then the company would do well to consider organizing around individual customer relationships in a "customer-centric" strategy rather than by product.

Strategy also needs to be aligned between the company and its customers to ensure that both understand the direction of the other, enabling each to assess the other in its role as long-term partner, and to create the value each wants. Over time, this means that the supplier must become very familiar with its customer's customer, and be in a position to advance initiatives proactively, perhaps even before its customer does.

The message: Strategy needs to be customer-centric, with relationship objectives and strategies geared to individual customers.

4. Structure

The structure of a company should facilitate its strategy. In fact, the easiest way to see if a company has strategy problems is to review how often they reorganize. Companies that reorganize frequently, without strategic context and rationale, often have difficulty defining and implementing a winning strategy.

Relationship Marketing, impacting as it does the entire firm, can result in an entirely different way to structure a company. A company organized according to Relationship Marketing will have managers who own a specific category of relationship, such as that of current customers, new customers, employees, suppliers, investors and so on. So, rather than having a sales and marketing department, for example, it may have a department to create new value with current, important customers, while another may be charged with gaining new customers whose profile matches the firm's best customers.

In addition to management of relationship categories, the Relationship Marketing company will have executives in charge of improving and focusing the capabilities that advance relationships, such as people, process, technology and knowledge and insight.

The message: Go beyond considering traditional organizational structures such as business units organized by product or market. Consider organizing by relationship and capability. Have managers in charge of each material category.

5. People

People are key to any relationship. Business is still people, but now these people must be supported by technologies and processes to multiply their capabilities and make them even more effective. In the prior marketing era, market and customer knowledge was centralized and the marketer sought to involve others in the company in strategic marketing programs. Now customer information is pushed to the front line where customers and the company interact. The people at the front lines should have the ability to communicate with customers in a manner that recognizes them, remembers their contact history, understands the current customer issues, predicts anticipated behaviors and suggests appropriate responses, solutions or suggestions. Increasingly, the front-line people are becoming consultants, working with customers to add value to their company. This is a marked departure from historical practice and requires recognition, reward and incentives that support this redirection.

And when the people serving the customer on your behalf are not directly controlled by your firm, human resource systems become even more complex. This is the typical case of companies selling their products through distribution channel intermediaries, such as retailers and dealers. We have recently helped a car manufacturer/assembler to recognize and reward individual salespeople in dealerships. We compared what other car and consumer durable companies do to link their customer relationship strategies with the way salespeople perform. Dealers often pay more attention to moving units than engaging with customers to create new and mutual value. The car companies reward this practice in their internal measurements and in the way they recognize and reward dealers. The salesperson who sells the most units goes to Hawaii. The customer relationship has received secondary attention and is not fully considered over his purchasing lifetime. Thus, dealers have specific initiatives geared to improving service, leasing, sales of new and used cars, but there is little evidence of the car companies facilitating an integrated approach to the customer relationship that applies the principles described in this book. For example, while all car companies have programs that recognize the performance of the dealer's sales staff, none link reward and recognition effectively to the overall business and marketing objectives of their companies, such as customer retention objectives and associated activities.

Many, if not most people in a company focused on Relationship Marketing should move from being functional experts to being *process owners for specific categories of relationships*. Their role is to work with others within the company, its customers and suppliers to develop the new value which customers want. In the Relationship Marketing era, selling, marketing, servicing and supporting customers become integrated processes incorporating the eight dimensions of Relationship Marketing discussed here. The Relationship Marketing process owner must be geared to being the integrator and rewarded and recognized for successful integration.

But how do we measure success? Specific people can be measured according to the extent to which they advance the objectives of the firm with each category of customer. If the objectives are to bond more tightly, this can be defined and measured. Measurements can include long-term revenues and profit. Ask customers regarding their *favorability* towards the company, not their *satisfaction* with the firm. Customers that are merely satisfied with their suppliers may not buy from them again, a finding which has challenged more than one marketer. They may be even more satisfied with a competitor. If they favor a firm, they are more likely to buy again. Find out what your share of business is with each customer and what the trend of this share is. Establish what the role of your firm will be in the customer's strategic initiatives. This can help establish your share of their future business.

The message: Train, develop and grow people into owners of a process which seeks to build customer bonding and purchase favorability.

6. Technology

Technology can serve multiple roles within a company and between a company and its customers, including:

- External Communications
- Internal Communications
- Computing
- Content

External Communications

- facilitating two-way interaction between individual customers and the company about every aspect of their requirements such as collaboration in product or service design, product codevelopment, pilot testing, ordering, reviewing the inventory levels in one another's warehouses and account status information;
- providing a more rapid or informed communication than was possible with manual intervention;
- opening new approaches to communicate with customers such as Interactive Voice Response (IVR), Electronic Data Interchange (EDI) with customers and distribution channel intermediaries and using the Internet to communicate with customers, channel members and other partners;
- communicating with other stakeholders including investors, board of directors, employees, management, suppliers and distribution channel intermediaries.

Internal Communications

- removing "stove-pipe" functionality from the many individual internal processes and technologies that face the customer, including call centers, Internet access, order, shipping, billing, field sales forces, dealer sales, direct mail and mass advertising so that the customer relationship can receive clearer attention;
- tying together diverse communications systems, call centers, communications channels and databases so that the company becomes a more informed supplier with whom it is easier to do business.

Computing

- The role of computing in Relationship Marketing is to provide organizational memory for customer relationships, a predictive ability and current content needed by Relationship Marketers to add value to the account.

- Computing is used primarily to facilitate storage and retrieval of huge amounts of data which provides the history of a number of factors important to the advancement of the customer relationship.

Content

- Content includes customer information, customer context, customer behaviors and customer profitability.

- Customer information includes data describing customer demographics, locations, usage patterns, order frequency, favorability and preferences.

- Customer context captures information to describe the priorities the customer emphasizes, the decision-making unit, criteria for buying and the purchase processes.

- Customer behaviors captures information reflecting interactions before the sale, during and post sale; the number, nature and scale of orders; and other behavioral information.

- Customer profitability tracks the financial performance of the account with a costing methodology that recognizes all the costs and time associated with selling to, servicing and financing a customer, not just the cost of goods sold.

In the early 1990s, Wal-Mart required that their customers, even fairly small ones, begin to take and send orders on-line. Even companies with minimal experience in this form of electronic interaction found that their investment paid off. After catering to the needs of Wal-Mart, suppliers were able to leverage the investment with other retailers. Cedar Works, an $18 million manufacturer of bird feeders and mailboxes, was able to improve both cash flow and customer satisfaction as a result of complying with Wal-Mart's leadership.[2]

---

[2] Joshua Macht, "Are You Ready for Electronic Partnering?," *Inc. Technology*, No. 4, 1995, p. 43.

The message: Deploy technology to provide a better customer memory. Give customers the communications options they want to help them repeat the purchase experience.

7. Knowledge and Insight

- Technology must enable the Relationship Marketer to develop new knowledge and insight about the customer relationship and facilitate action on the information. The challenge is to do this economically, of particular interest to companies with widespread customer databases and modest margins.

- Software, modeling and reporting tools can help add value to the underlying data and even predict what an individual customer will do, helping the marketer to be proactive in customer management.

- A key challenge to the marketer is to secure resources for investment in individual customer knowledge and insight over the longer term. Digital Equipment has elaborate customer knowledge and insight systems. The firm acknowledges that "managing upward" can be a real challenge in securing needed resources at a time in which overall resources available within the company can be scarce indeed and when management and structure of the company is in a state of flux. Yet Digital has continued to make progressive investments, incrementally, rather than in one master plan, to advance the cause of its customer knowledge and insight.

- Fingerhut Companies (annual revenues of $1.9 billion) is a database marketing company that sells a broad range of products and services, through catalogs, telemarketing, television and other media. Fingerhut has six terabytes (a million/million bytes) of customer information, the equivalent of almost 100 pages for each of its customers. Through good times and bad, Fingerhut has maintained its investment in customer databases and it has recently been reaping considerable reward.[3]

---

[3] For the thirteen weeks ended March 28, 1997, Fingerhut's sales declined by 2% to $350 million, but net income was up to $2.6 million compared with a loss of $2.1 million in the same period.

The message: Invest in customer knowledge and insight, and do it through thick and thin.

8. Process

Reengineering, applied as it has been over the last decade, excluded the customer and the individual customer relationship as the core around which the business should be engineered. Firms struggling for survival may have found a reengineering effort productive, but others may now find that reengineering cuts off their feet. They are now being asked to run in a different race than that originally intended — for profitable revenue growth. Relationship Marketing requires that processes be engineered around the customer, which may require essential changes to existing processes. For example, communications processes may currently be developed to broadcast to a market segment, when interactive or narrowcast communications may be used instead. Current selling processes may adopt the traditional view of the sales person as a combination of hunter and artist, to be left alone to bring back the big game. Perhaps sales force automation processes have been attempted, and perhaps they are not achieving their desired ends. Why? Because the role of the sales person as historically defined is of value only when the company wishes to bring onboard new customers. However, it has less merit when the company is focused on creating value for existing customers, and having the relationship managed in an integrated way, tying together the various processes, people and technologies with which the customers can relate.

The message: Focus processes around existing customers, giving each the value they want and communicating as every one wishes to be engaged by the company.

زغ

It may be easier to align processes throughout the chain of relationships, and even to align people and technology, as companies such as Wal-Mart and General Motors have done with their suppliers. It is quite feasible to create knowledge systems to deliver relevant content throughout the organization as and when required, as companies such as IBM and Digital have done. It is much harder to align strategy with chosen customers since it forces the company to make uncomfortable choices such as whether it will serve some customers and not others within a competitive industry. And it is much harder to align culture. Fundamentally, there may be cultural clashes that cannot be aligned and the company will need to consider whether it should do business with a firm that is not culturally aligned. Consider the "take-no-prisoners" culture of a company geared to profit by any means and the culture of a supplier wishing to forge a relationship and manage that relationship for mutual value over the long term. Even if all the Relationship Marketing factors are brought into alignment, the relationship will likely fail because the cultures will clash. This is a real situation we encountered which taught us that the potential for cultural conflict must be recognized early before too much is invested by the party wishing to forge the relationship.

The Enablers of Relationship Marketing

A Relationship Marketing initiative should start with the recognition that technology now enables companies to understand, motivate and serve the individual customer as never before. In a previous marketing era, companies carved up the mass market into market segments. They then targeted specific segments because this enabled more value to be created for customers in each segment than had they been treated as members of a mass market. This might be termed the analog era, where customers were viewed as belonging to a group, and appeals were made to the group in order to influence the individual.

Enter the digital era. Now segmentation can continue until the company satisfies the individual customer. Three enablers need to be successfully addressed if customers are to be served and managed uniquely over their purchasing lifetime:

1. Manufacturing Technology
2. Customer Knowledge
3. Customer Access

1. Manufacturing Technology

Most manufacturers have engineered design and manufacturing processes for intermediate or long production runs, not for the customization of production, service, delivery, ordering, shipping and billing. Design and manufacturing processes currently employ the principles of Total Quality Management (TQM), and cycle-time reduction, not mass customization. The rapid development of technology and the declining cost of memory, processing, storage and communication has made possible what few thought was feasible just a few years ago: production and delivery of products and services unique to the customer at prices affordable by both customer and supplier. The 1980s was the decade in which quality moved from being available to just a few to the mass market (from Rolls Royce and other high-end quality cars for the affluent to Ford, Toyota and Acura for the average working person). But the 1990s is the decade in which product and service application has moved (and is moving) from a good fit to the needs of most customers in a market segment to a perfect fit to the needs of each individual customer.

The equipment and processes previously employed typically could not achieve economical design, development or production in short production runs, let alone "runs" of one. If you needed a suit designed for your size alone, you had to be prepared to go to a tailor who made one for you specifically and pay much more than for one of those off-the-rack suits. Today, intelligence has been introduced into the design and development processes, and manufacturing equipment allows flexible production in much smaller batches. Now, the run length can be as little as a single unit, and the costs of production can be similar to mass production costs. In fact, Japanese suit manufacturer and retailer Melbo[4] has done just that, offering Givenchy, Daniel Hechter and Nina Ricci designer suits custom fitted to individual measurements and delivered anywhere within a week.

Another example is Levi's Personal Pair jeans which are now available in Levi's stores across North America. Consumers can order jeans made to their personal measurements. The jeans are made on the same production line as the regular Levi's jeans and shipped to the customer within a few weeks. The cost to the customer is within sight of a pair of jeans produced for the mass market. Actually, average costs for mass-customized products can go down because short runs, production-to-order or configure-to-order can drive inventory levels down substantially.

Mass-customized production is no longer just for capital-intensive products such as automobiles or jet engines. Examples abound of

---

[4] R. Westbrook and P. J. Williamson, "Mass Customization: Japan's New Frontier," *European Management Journal*, v11n1, March, 1993, pp. 38-45.

companies using technology throughout the value chain — from design through order, production, shipment to payment — to provide customers with the unique benefits they seek. Andersen Windows of Bayport, Minnesota has a program called the "Window of Knowledge." They equipped 387 Andersen dealers with personal computers for customers to design and order the very specific windows they want. Customers enter data on their individual window requirements and the order is sent to Andersen's plant for immediate production. General Electric, on a formerly uniform production line, now produces electric meters in over 2,000 permutations and combinations so that customers get the ones they want, when they want them.

At the same time as the market place is fragmenting into individual consumers, so too is technology enabling individuals to be addressed and served uniquely. As Figure 4 illustrates, now two-way interaction facilitates mass-personalized and -customized marketing and production at mass-production and mass-marketing costs.

FIGURE 4: Market Fragmentation and Interactivity of Technology

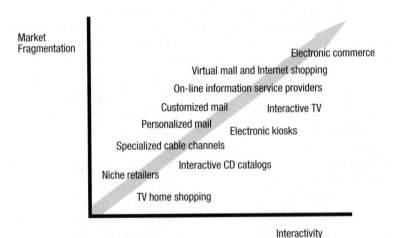

2. Customer Knowledge

The ability of companies to know their customers and serve them the way they wish to be served has been a limiting factor in segmentation. Marketing Information Systems now in place in most companies are typically geared to market segments, including customer needs, customer satisfaction and competitive intelligence, not to the needs of individual customers. That would be fine if the objective of business were to satisfy segments, but it is not. Segments do not spend money; customers do. Yet the information systems of most companies cannot tell the marketer much more than a basic profile of customers and their purchases with the organization.

If you go to your favorite shoe store, tailor or hairdresser, the better proprietors will know your name, engage you in conversation that carries over from prior visits, be aware of your purchase preferences and perhaps do something unexpected, such as throw in a free shoe horn, tie or hair spray with your purchase. But if you go to a local mass merchandiser, you can expect that they will not know your name, that they will not engage you in meaningful conversation nor do much of anything for you other than take your money. Even then you may have to wait in long lines and deal with a sales clerk who is new on the job or stopped caring some years ago. So the smaller enterprises have a service advantage over the bigger ones. And since all companies are, to a greater or lesser extent, in the service industry, the larger ones are potentially at a disadvantage. However, technology now allows these companies to put more information in their organizational memory about each and every customer than the corner stores have. Technology can turn the tables for the large operator. Now the potential exists for mass merchandisers to anticipate the needs of individual customers. When they throw open their doors in the morning, they can anticipate who will be coming through. And they can have a process to serve each of these customers as they individually wish.

Consider the case of Ukrop's, a twenty-three store supermarket chain based in Richmond, Virginia. Unlike all the other supermarkets in the area, Ukrop's does not advertise in the weekly newspapers. Rather, Ukrop's advertises to their Value Customer cardholders. They focus on increasing loyalty and decreasing cherry pickers — those customers who buy on price alone. So customers that do not have a Value Customer card can only see store specials by visiting the store itself. Ukrop's can do this because they have a sophisticated customer database guiding their marketing. Of course, use of a sophisticated database by itself does not guarantee high performance marketing initiatives. One has only to look at all five major banks in Canada, each of which has some of the latest data warehousing and mining technology. Allowing for some variation according to the capabilities and performance of individuals, each bank seems mostly content to let customers manage their money without meaningful guidance. The potential is there for banks and others to target economically the individual customer, to have the customer knowledge needed to be credible and to create new value profitably.

When my wife was pregnant and bought new clothes to fit her new size, she was giving a clue to the mass merchandiser that baby furniture could be bought within months but no offers were forthcoming. Five years ago I bought a Honda, and I had the car serviced at the same dealer since new. No salesperson was in touch to see when I might want another car. In our consultancy, we have many Apple computers in varying degrees of currency, but none of the sales people at the dealers where we bought the machines are in touch to attend to our upgrade, add-on, software and service needs.

Customer knowledge and insight derives from four main attributes and capabilities of the organization:

1. An infrastructure of technology that captures, stores and processes the data needed to derive customer knowledge, and an architecture of the technology that places customer data at its strategic heart. The infrastructure and architecture should include a data warehouse, data mining tools and business processes and technologies that maintain current data on customer transactions, communications, perceptions and behaviors. Customer knowledge without data is like hiking without a compass: you might get there, but chances are you won't.

2. A culture and leadership that emphasizes customer knowledge and insight as cornerstones for long-term business profitability;

3. Explicit strategies by the company to recruit, train and retain professionals who see the customer as a core context for their work.

4. Business processes, reward and recognition that emphasize four levels of customer learning for people within the company: 1) individual learning; 2) team learning within the enterprise; 3) team learning between the company and other firms with which it does business such as suppliers and distribution channel intermediaries; and 4) team learning with customers.

3. Customer Access

Market segmentation has been further limited from progressing to individual customers by access limitations for both communications and distribution channels. Media fragmentation, the strategic use of database marketing technologies, the postal service and the Internet is also rendering this perception out of date. Marketers have long been complaining that media fragmentation is making their mass media buys costly and ineffective. Rather than longing for the "good old days," "great new days" are upon us. Media buys surely have to be more thoughtful and focused, and technology has to be employed to assemble, execute and communicate the buys. In addition, the use of database marketing engines has the potential to shift media to direct marketing to facilitate the targeting of individual customers. New press technology, such as the Indigo, can create custom four- or five-color mailing pieces that are suited to the information needs of a single customer, at mass print-run appearance and, in comparable volumes, at similar prices. You could have a can of beer with your photo on it, newsletters with information on companies in your stock portfolio and travel brochures showing locations you may wish to visit, given your historical travel patterns and demonstrated preferences. The Internet provides marketers with huge opportunities for new customer access for communications and distribution channels. On-line customer access to companies' home pages has the potential to speed customers through the awareness and even trial processes, to offer an opportunity to assemble the value they require from the available components on offer and to execute the order. General Motors thought enough of the opportunity to put over 70,000 pages on their Web site.

&c.

Marketing is dead because the old rules of identifying and satisfying customer demand no longer apply. Technology has seen to that and, in the process, created entirely new opportunities for marketers. But the opportunities are numerous and each has high levels of investment associated with capturing the potential, which can create financial risk for the company approaching the opportunities without a clear strategy in mind. This, then, is the subject of the next chapter which places Relationship Marketing in a strategic context.

CHAPTER TWO

Relationships as Strategy

Talk not of wasted affection! affection never was wasted;
If it enrich not the heart of another, its waters, returning
Back to their springs, like the rain, shall fill them full of refreshment;
That which the fountain sends forth returns again to the fountain.
Henry Wadsworth Longfellow

Marketing strategy has historically involved selecting alternative market segments to target, then allocating financial and other resources according to a marketing mix to serve each segment. The marketing mix comprises product, price, promotion and placement/distribution, the so-called 4 Ps of marketing. This traditional definition of the marketing mix is entirely appropriate when the marketer is focusing on a specific market segment. However, when that segment narrows to a single person or company, and when the objective is to create mutual and shared value with that customer over a lifetime of purchasing, the concept of the marketing mix changes fundamentally.

This chapter considers implications for strategy in recognizing relationships as the basis for allocating and aligning the resources in a company. It starts with a review of the importance of the individual customer rather than the market segment. It continues with a consideration of the changing nature of marketing primarily as a result of technological change, and the importance of this for the marketer's role, particularly the need to focus on strategic capabilities.

This chapter makes a vital point: Relationship Marketing differs from traditional marketing which focused on the product/service combination and applied the 4 Ps of marketing to manage demand and facilitate the exchange of goods for money. Now the firm must choose the customers it wishes to bond with, and work with these customers to create the value each wants. This will lead companies into a different territory — away from a focus on production, for example, and towards becoming a more complete and strategic supplier for its individual customers. And it will use different tools to do this, drawing upon four categories of capability — people, process, technology and knowledge and insight — from within the organization.

Market Segments and Individual Customers

The traditional approach to marketing includes a number of steps:

- identifying groups of customers who share similar needs but differ from other market groups;
- development through research of alternative, distinct and differentiated product concepts;
- researching product preferences;
- assessing the extent to which these customers can be accessed by communications and distribution and the costs of this access;
- calculating the cost to produce, the price/volume elasticity of demand and the profit potential available from the segment;
- engaging in trials; and
- refining what needs to be changed.

This segment-based approach has worked well for marketers since the 1960s. That is, until now. When the segment is that of an individual, when technology is widely deployed and when the business processes of the company include their customers as material contributors, the traditional marketing approach does not work. Today, three important changes have occurred that render segment-based marketing not only inappropriate, but potentially damaging for a business: more sophisticated and knowledgeable customers; dramatic changes in technology; and proliferation of competing vendors and products.

Customers' expectations are rising and competitors, often incorporating new technologies in aspects of their communications, internal and customer-facing processes and production, have been not only meeting customers' rising expectations but shaping them with yet higher standards of performance and value. And so the cycle repeats, with customers asking for more and getting it. Does the name Pavlov ring a bell?

Marketers have two choices. Either chase the next technological innovation and implement it before and better than competitors. And do this again and again, without end. Or recognize that the rules of competition have been forever changed. Sustainable growth must come from a strategic source rather than tending the implementation of new technologies until the engineers run out of ideas. Rather than being left to retroactively develop a "strategy" that really stems from tactical implementations of technology that have strategic impact, the marketer has this opportunity to shape the business:

1. Decide the customer mix and the level of resources to be committed to each customer — which customers the company will reward and in which it will invest, which it will fire, which it will manage and which it will discipline. (More of this shortly.)

2. Develop customer-specific objectives and strategies — that is, strategies that are unique to each customer.

3. Identify and implement integrated strategic capabilities — to ensure that the customer-specific objectives are successfully achieved.

In the following, we discuss the customer mix and portfolio of customers. Issues associated with setting customer specific objectives, particularly intensifying bonding, are discussed in Chapter 4. Chapter 6 reviews strategic capabilities that the company must integrate internally and with customers to advance the relationships.

At present, it is still not common for companies to have a well-formed financial view of their customer base. Companies should know the so-called "cost-to-serve" of each customer and be able to produce an integrated view of customer profitability. This would include allocating revenues, cost of goods sold and costs previously occurring below the gross margin line to each customer. The costs below the gross margin line that are rarely managed at the customer level include the costs required to attract, sell, serve and retain a customer — advertising, selling time, time for service and repair staff, product returns and other costs often unallocated by companies to their customers. It is astonishing that without this information, companies discontinue products, allocate their best sales staff, make decisions on pricing and generally manage their business. We discuss this further in the following chapter. At this stage, the message is: Have a Customer Income Statement. Begin working on a Customer Return on Investment.[5]

Not only is it important to understand which customers are profitable today, but which customers will be profitable tomorrow. This is one way to think about customer focus, as illustrated in Figure 5. This figure is not intended to demonstrate all the reasons one might want to invest in a relationship and reward a customer, at the one extreme, or terminate a relationship, at the other. There may be factors other than potential profitability of the customer that affect the decision, including, for example, whether the customer is an "orphan," diverting management time and organizational focus from the core business of the firm, whether the customer has a culture not meriting the commitment the company envisages or other factors. It is curious that a company will talk in terms of rewarding, managing, disciplining or firing its staff, yet it will not use these same terms for other stakeholders, such as customers.

It is appropriate for a company to map their customer set into a matrix such as that presented in Figure 5 and then to identify the mix of customers it chooses to serve. This could mean fundamentally reshaping the customer set to build the longer-term profitability of the company and then pursuing specific types of relationships with priority customers to achieve the Relationship Marketing objectives set for each.

Now, let's take a look at the four components of the Customer Segmentation Portfolio:

- Reward and Invest
- Manage
- Discipline
- Fire

---

[5] This requires assignment of the firm's assets at the customer level, something that would be aided if the company has been through a process of assessing "Economic Value Creation," an approach gaining currency among financial and senior management in companies such as Coca Cola, to determine Return on Investment at the business unit level.

FIGURE 5: Customer Segmentation Portfolio

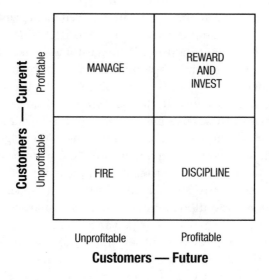

Reward and Invest

Today's ideal customers — ones that look as though they can be profitable into the future —merit reward by the company. Reward can take many forms, including investment by the company in its customers, in terms important to each. This may mean assigning the firm's best staff to serving priority accounts, giving customers access to the company's technologies, investing time with key customers, recognizing their importance in material and face-enhancing ways (such as awards dinners) and rewarding them financially (such as with points programs popular with gas and telephone companies). One company offers its best customers a secret 1-800 number through which they receive top priority service and support.

McDonald's Corporation has found that 77% of their sales are attributable to typically male customers aged eighteen to thirty-four who eat at McDonald's three to five times a week.[6] Perhaps tongue in cheek, McDonald's refers to these customers as "superheavy" users and targets customer retention initiatives to keep these customers.

---

[6] Robert C. Blattberg and John Deighton, "Managing Marketing by the Customer Equity Test," *Harvard Business Review*, July/August, 1996, p. 136.

Manage

Customers that are currently profitable but which may become less profitable or even unprofitable in the future, need management. Perhaps the reason the customer may become less profitable has to do with the outlook of their industry. If the customer makes business forms or software for Macintosh computers, a supplier may believe that the customer may become less profitable should it become more price sensitive or experience declining volumes. Like poorly performing employees, these customers' issues need to be addressed by the company, not ignored. The company owes current good customers strategic attention and an opportunity to continuously create mutual value that will enhance the business prospects for the company and the customer. In joint planning sessions, supplier and customer can explore the outlook for one another's businesses and their mutual interests, and then work to advance the strategic or other value which must be created and then shared, so that the relationship will remain profitable and merit reward in future.

Remember those old vacuum tubes in your TV and radio that would get hot enough to make toast? Before it was generally known that the outlook was bleak for these devices, tube retailers continued to view their future as closely tied to the tube industry because they profited from sales of replacement tubes and the repair of associated appliances. But the manufacturers knew that the days of the tube industry were numbered. They themselves were driving the change, engineering transistors into TV sets and radios to replace vacuum tubes. Companies such as RCA and Motorola understood before their channel intermediaries that the relationship could soon become unprofitable and would need to be managed. They would have to manage the channel relationship, seeking to move some intermediaries into the business of retailing transistorized devices, others into servicing this equipment or both. This communication would have to be handled effectively and positive financial options presented to intermediaries so that they would remain loyal to the vendor and retain the brand equity in the market when customers came in to have their old tube-based TVs and radios serviced.

Discipline

Thirty to 40% of a company's revenue base is generated by customers who, on a stand-alone basis, are not profitable.[7] Some customers are presently unprofitable, but can be *made* profitable. There are two main ways of doing this. One is to change and/or cost reduce the processes which are employed by the company to market, sell, serve, support and manage the account. Another is to charge customers in this category a fee for not conforming to the company's "rules of engagement" as a "best customer." For example, banks prefer the average consumer to use automated teller machines for their routine transactions. If banks must maintain teller services for consumers, the benefits of the technologies and processes in which they have invested will not be realized. So they are starting to charge consumers for teller services for routine transactions. These customers are being disciplined.

Fire

Not all customers merit consideration by the firm. Management would be advised to assess which among the firm's current customer base merits a continued relationship and then size and align the business in accordance with the mix of customers on which the firm has chosen to focus. A number of factors could be included in this assessment, such as:

- the profitability of customers, including the costs to serve and the costs to sell;
- the profitability of customers, by product or product line, which may suggest that certain low profit products are only being produced to serve some tactical customers;
- the historical, current and projected share of the customer's total expenditures;
- the measurement of competitive value created by the customer relationship;
- measures of customer retention; and

---

[7] *The McKinsey Quarterly*, Number 4, 1995, p. 120.

- the contribution of each customer to the firm's strategic value, in areas such as:

Innovation How has this customer helped to position the company for growth? Has it been a source for new ideas?

Process improvement Has this company provided ideas or otherwise helped facilitate improvements to the core processes of the company, such that a broader array of customers has been provided with new business value?

Cost reduction Has the customer helped the company to manage costs not only in the company's processes, but in the overall processes by which value is created for end-customers?

Acceleration of market-place adoption Has it provided an opportunity to test and refine new products? Has it helped to accelerate market-place adoption?

Enhancement of the firm's image and reputation By working with this company, has the supplier benefited from increased image and reputation, or has it received little or no benefit?

Plant loading and overhead absorption Although important in the short term, this will not be the primary reason for maintaining the customer relationship. Over the long term, all costs, even fixed ones, should be treated as variable.

Some customers are unprofitable today, will be unprofitable tomorrow and do not merit further attention by the company. Let them become someone else's problem or opportunity. Fire them. Care should be taken in any firing to manage communication with the members of the chain of relationships with which you do business. You cannot let the terminated accounts damage you in the market or in other unexpected ways. Terminated customers, like terminated employees, should leave feeling good about the relationship in which both have invested but which, for whatever reason, no longer create the value now important to you. A relationship must be mutual. A one-sided relationship is either extortion or unrequited. In either case, it is doomed.

Firing customers may actually have additional benefit for your company. It can improve your stock market valuation in an unexpected way if competitors take up your former customers and become less profitable themselves as a result. Their financial challenges may cause a flight of investor capital to your firm.

Digitization of the Marketing Mix

The marketing mix, as marketers have traditionally considered it, comprised a combination of marketing variables, with emphasis on those components marketers deemed important in securing, satisfying and retaining customers. This marketing mix bundled product, service, price, promotion and distribution options together according to the marketer's *predetermined assessment* of the value to each segment, and the most efficient and effective means of providing that value. With this approach, planning and execution was orderly. After all, the company made the key decisions regarding the research that would be conducted, the product concept and value that would be provided, the message that would be broadcast and the services that would be delivered to a segment. Customers within each segment were served as though they all wanted the same thing. Illustrating the inflexibility of mass-marketed product was Henry Ford who said, "You can have any color, as long as it's black," when customers asked the hues of a Model T.

Technology is changing this. Now, technology can combine product, service, price, promotion and distribution in infinite varieties. And it can do this in real time, or near real time, allowing customers to engage and interact with the company and all aspects of its value-creation processes. Where would a company be today if it were unable to engage individual customers should they want to order via the Internet, specify product features in person to a sales representative, receive confirmation of the order by e-mail, make changes by fax, obtain the goods on a Thursday at noon, and pay their bills by electronic data interchange?

Technology is digitizing the marketing mix. In so doing, it gives the customer virtually infinite choices. This has the effect of unbundling the 4 Ps previously carefully packaged by the marketer, and makes each component variable — for the customer to choose, not for the marketer to provide. Many companies were built in an era of mass communication, mass production and mass marketing. It is not often easy to retrofit Relationship Marketing into an enterprise that sees itself in terms of mass anything. Honda packages anti-lock brakes together with aluminum wheels. If you want one, you must buy the other. They don't need to do it this way, but they choose to. Sometimes a company needs to unlearn marketing before it can relearn alternative approaches to overcome market place barriers. Relationship Marketing is one such instance.

Technology can provide consumers with precisely what they want in terms of product, service or information, when and how they want it, at a price that represents the value they wish to receive. But if technology is only applied at the customer interface, the benefits of a digitized marketing mix cannot be achieved. This is an important point. Most companies need technology to enable the customer relationship throughout the company's value chain. While technology (and associated processes) should start with the end-customer, it should then progress backwards through the distribution channel and then all the way to the shop floor. Technology adoption should progress even further — backwards to suppliers and their suppliers. Without this progression and alignment, the promise of Relationship Marketing cannot readily be realized because the marketing mix will still comprise a finite number of packages or benefit bundles, without providing the unique value many customers seek.

It simply is not good enough for Honda to force customers to buy aluminum wheels and anti-lock brakes together in a package. Honda undoubtedly has different suppliers for wheels and braking systems, so they likely do not drive the packaging. Rather, Honda must have made a conscious management decision or perhaps something is broken in their internal processes or technologies. Clearly, this one issue does not mean that Honda does not address customer needs, but if it were symptomatic of larger Relationship Marketing issues, it may indicate an opportunity for Honda to rethink how individual customers are served. The auto industry is increasingly one in which the car companies own three things: brand equity, vehicle assembly and control of relevant business processes and associated technologies. The challenge for car companies is to build to order, have minimum inventory on hand and get the car to the customer within a very short time. They could not do this without technology in the dealership to initiate the assembly process throughout the "demand chain" — from the dealership backwards to the firm's suppliers to the assembly floor — to make the car to order and let the dealership keep track of the vehicle's progress.

Car companies continue to use mass marketing approaches and scale economies in production and mass advertising to determine their marketing mix. It was once true that it made more sense for an auto worker to put stereo speakers in every car, rather than wait to install them in only those cars where the owners ordered the stereo. Today, there are many applications where robots can be programmed to mass customize without incurring the down-time costs of labor. There is less need to package options into tiers of trim levels and option packages than there once was. This challenges the notion of using model nomenclature such as DL, GL and LS models to distinguish among the levels of trim on a car, with option packages within each trim level. Rather, the opportunity exists for customers to have, for the very first time, their very own vehicle, designed and made for each in a collaborative process, to reflect the individuality and preferences of each. Car companies should build cars with their customers to give them the opportunity to exercise choice in virtually every package offered, provide additional choices, such as in fabric selection, colors, engine sizes, wheel dimensions and tire performance ratings. They could also provide software solutions to help customers choose a vehicle based on their individual usage patterns and budget, allowing them to accept or reject decisions made by software appropriately programmed and linked to the customers' information files. When Buick asked the rhetorical question many years ago: "Can we build one for you?" they did something not done previously by car companies. They went far beyond William C. Durant's concept of offering cars in a variety of styles and colors that Ford considered impractical and engineered their processes to enable mass customization of their vehicles. For the first time, customers could choose features and paid separately for each.

Today, in another industry, Dell Computer has again applied the principle of customer involvement in product specification. Customers choose from among many options, and Dell assembles or has assembled, products as requested by the customer. This, in addition to Dell's innovation in distribution channel directness, has enabled it to become a major contender in a very competitive industry. Now Compaq has announced that it, too, plans to produce to customer order or have computers configured in their dealerships from standard components. Like most computer companies, it previously assembled products in advance, knowing as it did so, that it was almost certainly wrong with regard to the numbers it was making and the configuration of some models. Making to customer order has a side benefit: total costs can go down as fewer finished goods inventory becomes obsolete.

In the increasingly complex world of customer fragmentation, technology proliferation and process acceleration, the marketer may be faced with the daunting challenge of managing a huge number of potential product and service combinations, at different prices and volumes. But this may still be deemed preferable to managing the infinite variety possible through full application of Relationship Marketing concepts. Practically, in the near term, management may decide that the costs of full-blown technology implementation for Relationship Marketing cannot be justified economically. However, technology throws down this challenge: if you ignore opportunities to serve customers uniquely using advanced technologies, and your competitors decide to adopt this approach, what will your response be?

Relationship Marketing is a journey, not a destination. By starting with a game plan and then implementing progressively and incrementally, material progress will be made over time. Of course, today's advanced technologies will become tomorrow's ship anchors. But, by then, the costs of memory, storage, processing and bandwidth will have declined yet further. And more will be possible, at still lower costs.

New Roles for the Marketer

Relationship Marketing changes the fundamental role of marketers. In a Relationship Marketing era marketers no longer concentrate on target market selection nor manage the marketing mix. They will no longer operate in "marketing time" according to the schedule they have developed to research, plan and implement. With Relationship Marketing, the focus is on which customers the company will serve, on understanding their expectations and then putting into place capabilities within the company to deliver those expectations. Relationship Marketers will have to operate in real time. They will no longer be in charge of thrusting products into the market. They will make decisions about which customers will be served, how they will be served and how more customers (matching the profiles defined as the firm's best) will be attracted. The role of Relationship Marketers moves from managing demand and product profitability to collaborating with customers and managing customer profitability. Now Relationship Marketers have much more far-reaching roles than before, touching on virtually every aspect of the enterprise. In the process, Relationship Marketers move from strategic analysts and communicators, to operators, a fundamental change for some.

The Relationship Marketer has six distinct roles:

1. To determine which customers — the "customer mix" — will be targeted and served.

2. To develop a customer strategy for each priority customer, and to align the company's strategies with those of individual customers.

3. To manage customer profitability and to own the processes by which customer profitability is planned, delivered and improved.

4. To drive the implementation of capabilities in the company to ensure that the processes perform effectively and efficiently. To improve the favorability with which customers see all aspects of the company, including its services, value creation, people and brands. (More about these capabilities in a moment.)

5. To serve as the customer's advocate — individually and in aggregate — in the company.

6. To ensure that the company is organized around its customers — that the customer collaborates and integrates with all key processes, technologies and people in a combined effort to create value for both. Performance measurement and reward systems should reflect the importance of the relationship as an asset.

Some of these roles cross over into those historically associated with sales, human resources and corporate strategy, among others. As process owner, the Relationship Marketer becomes responsible for issues associated with what was formerly termed "account management," a sales role. As an individual responsible for measuring the relationship as an asset and rewarding people in accordance with the value they create in this asset, the Relationship Marketer links into the human resources arena, working with these professionals to frame approaches to staff management appropriate to the challenge. And as driver of strategic capabilities, the Relationship Marketer becomes corporate strategist and links with the information technology and process engineering professionals, to ensure that Relationship Marketing delivers the value customers want.

Focus on Strategic Capabilities

We have seen that marketers have the potential to use technology to create infinite variety with regard to product/market alternatives. But more than technology, marketers need a complete set of supporting strategic capabilities in the company that will let Relationship Marketing become all it can be. It now seems appropriate for marketers to be considering how to put in place the underlying components of a digitized marketing mix rather than focus on the marketing mix itself, as they did in the previous marketing era. To make a Relationship Marketing initiative profitable and successful, marketers should focus on choosing the right customers, looking for others like them, and bringing together the company's capabilities — people, process, technology and knowledge and insight — to create the value individual customers want.

When the company segments its markets to focus on the individual relationship and then develops capabilities to serve each customer, the assumption is that the relationship provides the company with enduring competitive advantage. And it should. Competitors may have comparable resources to your company, but they may be late in focusing them on the customer relationship. By moving first and fastest, a company has an opportunity to scoop the best customers, advance the relationship and create barriers for competitors.

Customer bonding could be generated and secured through personal friendships that may have developed, interenterprise technologies that may be linked, processes that may tie the companies together and supplier and customer joint initiatives — such as co-branding — to serve common customers. For example, when Chrysler advertises that certain Dodge pick-ups are powered by Cummins Diesel engines, the co-branding of the two companies makes it difficult or impossible for Chrysler to stop offering Cummins and dealing with this supplier. Some Dodge customers will expect this. A similar strategy has been followed by Intel with computer companies and by Searle's Aspartame sweetener with the producers of pop and food products. The main barrier for competitors is the knowledge and insight a company has developed about its customers. Underlying this is the data. The relationship is embedded in the data. And the company investing more in data, data management and associated business intelligence will be better positioned to succeed than the competitor that is flying blind.

Economies of Data

In the past, consultants advanced the concept of "economies of scale" and the "experience curve." This postulated that total costs decline as cumulative volume — the total number of units ever made by the company — increases. Examples from chemicals to magnetic tape showed that growth is important because it affords a company an opportunity not only to spread overheads across a larger volume base, but to reduce costs in areas apparently unrelated to volume (such as research and development) as the company and its people learn more and get better at what they do. Today, the concept of the experience curve is outdated because the advancement of knowledge reduces the life cycle of products and industries. For all the reasons mentioned in this book, there are few industries where this concept can remain tenable. The accelerating pace of change creates substitutes, new entrants and changing industry structures within a much shorter time. Economies continue to exist, but the economies are primarily in data concerning the customer relationship.

A reasonable hypothesis that follows is this: *the competitive position of a company and its relative profitability is likely tied directly to the cumulative volume of data it maintains on its customers, relative to its competitors.* (See Figure 6 below.)

FIGURE 6: Cumulative Data Curve

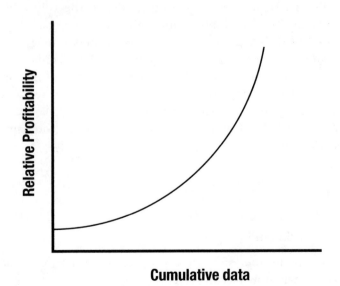

This view, currently under research, suggests that the more data companies have gathered, stored and made accessible on their customers, relative to competitors, the more profitable their business will be, again in relation to competitors. The rationale is this. If relationships are the key assets that throw off profitability for the company and if relationships are best managed through customer knowledge and insight, then the number of data points tracking the customer experience, behavior, interaction and perspective, over time, are more likely to reveal truths and more likely to provide opportunities for timely customer access and management.

Strategic Capabilities for Relationship Marketing

New capabilities are required in many companies to ensure that Relationship Marketing achieves its promise. Relationship Marketing strategy comprises the selection of priority customers and the focusing of capabilities to align with the expectations of these customers. If mutual value is to be continuously created with individual customers, the focus of the marketer is no longer on product and its mass production, communication, distribution and promotion. Rather, the marketer should pay attention to the development of capabilities that let priority customers derive the value they seek individually. This is a fundamental shift. Now the marketer echoes the voice of the customer not only into business strategy, but into, for example, those components of process design, technology adoption, personnel factors, and knowledge creation and management that impact the company's ability to create and share value with individual organizations and customers.

As illustrated in Figure 7, the main capabilities a company needs to develop are:

- People
- Process
- Technology
- Knowledge and Insight

Each of the four strategic capabilities essential to Relationship Marketing will now be considered.

FIGURE 7: Relationship Marketing Capabilities

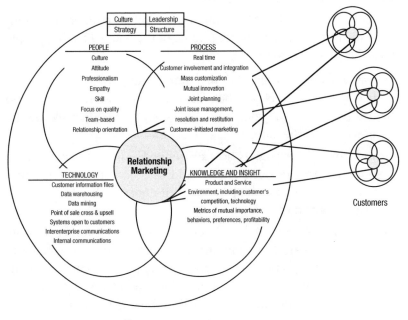

Your company

Business Is People

Relationships are all about people. People bond individually, in teams and with organizations so that organizations can bond in aggregate. People, in this Relationship Marketing era, also manage the technology and processes that deliver value with and for customers and seek customer knowledge and insight.

In traditional marketing, knowledge and decision making were centralized and communication lines were more clear-cut and personal between individuals in the company and its customers. The sales person communicated with the customer's purchasing agent, the receivables clerk with the payables person, technical people with their counterparts and so on. In this Relationship Marketing era, the people issue takes on a number of different dimensions, including the incorporation of advanced technology into daily tasks and processes that touch the customer.

People and Relationship Marketing
versus Traditional Marketing

This era of Relationship Marketing has a number of differences compared with traditional marketing. Some of the issues affecting people in the Relationship Marketing era:

- Data may be centralized or distributed and networked. Previously data resided in closely held data banks accessible to a few who had been with the company long enough or undertook specific functions in the company.

- Customer knowledge is now distributed, where it was formerly centralized in research reports and the Marketing Information System, which was not always current nor accessible to front-line personnel and others.

- More front-line personnel interface with the customer in more ways, in a manner resembling a complex web of personal and data communication. The technologies, processes and methods of interorganizational communication have changed dramatically, as has communication internal to the organization.

- Teamwork is particularly important and assumes precedence over the importance of the individual. Marketers have always been part of facilitating change in a company, largely because operations did not report to them, but had to be influenced to adopt their initiatives. Now, Relationship Marketing requires that teams be more formal than informal and that these teams also include the customer.

- People need to manage and improve the other dimensions of capability, including processes, technology and knowledge and insight. They need to operate according to defined methodologies, not just on the basis of a personal journey from which they derive interest or other benefits. Marketers have always resented having methodology thrust upon them and in most companies, sales personnel have an open aversion for methodology. (Try institutionalizing call reports in a company for the first time to understand the depth of feelings here.) With Relationship Marketing, marketers must be open to identifying and codifying the core processes involved under their mandate.

- People interact with one another in order to create real time value with customers and internally within the firm. Traditionally, people would prepare reports and provide their opinions in carefully considered responses to issues. Now people participate with others and frame solutions in a participative manner. The written word, in this time of Relationship Marketing is giving way to the spoken. Relationship Marketers must be good verbal communicators and able to interact efficiently and in real time with customers without manifesting stress.

- People focus their energies on strategic customers, not on all customers within a segment or even on priority segments. Relationship Marketers need to make choices with others in the company and with customers, and secure a broad consensus of the choices made.

- People used to seek to reduce costs internal to the company and in their customers' businesses. With Relationship Marketing, they seek to create the value each customer wants. This may still involve cost minimization, but not simple and total adherence to cutting costs.

   "Chainsaw Al" Dunlap, Scott Paper's brief-tenured CEO, improved the financial performance of Scott Paper through cost management some call ruthless and others say has left the company a hollow core.[8] He then moved to Sunbeam where he is replicating his formula for what he calls "rescuing" the company, the top two components of which include firing the company's existing senior management and cutting costs. At Scott, he may well have done better for shareholders in the long term had he made growth and a focus on customers and employees a meaningful part of the strategies he implemented.

- Relationship Marketers should be open to transferring information and building their individual, group, firm and customer capabilities rather than the traditional approach when market information was closely guarded, under the age-old dictum "knowledge is power."

---

[8] John A. Byrne and Joseph Weber, "The Shredder," *Business Week*, January 15, 1996, p. 56.

- Relationship Marketers should be developing Customer Information Systems, rather than Marketing Information Systems, with considerable detail on the customer demography, behavior, attitudes and interaction with the company.

People and Mega-Processes

Companies that have recently reengineered their processes sometimes find that the results they expected are not delivered. This is in part, a result of ineffective relationships between the people who are operating the business processes. Relationship Marketing takes the view that effective relationships between people, as between organizations, are only possible when mutual value is continuously created and shared. This requires that people who comprise the chain of relationships by which value is created for the end-customer must themselves work together to define areas of mutual interest and potential for sharing. And the company can help facilitate this by establishing recognition and reward systems that serve to unite rather than fragment the company. No longer should sales people be rewarded for shooting big game. Account development, as account retention, should be processes which are pursued by teams. If a Relationship Team working on the account of a specific customer serves to increase the value of the relationship for that customer, according to specific, pre-established metrics, then the entire team should benefit from the new value created.

Not only should any future reengineering efforts of the company pay close attention to the incorporation of relationships in the initiative, but Relationship Marketing should become the basis for the reengineering. By making relationships with specific stakeholders "mega-processes," the company can define the subprocesses which contribute to relationships, including:

- continuously creating and sharing mutual value with current customers;
- continuously developing new value to share with *new* customers;
- managing relationships with current and potential investors; and
- managing employee relationships.

The implications of redefining "mega-processes" in terms of relationships are profound. Each category of Relationship Manager — such as the czar for relationships with current customers — is to establish on which customers to focus and how to advance the relationship with the overall chain of relationships creating the value these customers want. The president has overall responsibility for the chain of relationships being aligned with business strategy and for arbitrating turf issues that may emerge. Furthermore, the president ensures that the enablers of the relationships are put in place by the company, including technology and various other capabilities needed to deliver on the relationship promise with the end-customer such as R&D and manufacturing excellence. If the focus of the firm is on relationships, all people in the firm will need to go through an orientation in the meaning of the term and how they are to incorporate Relationship Marketing *as* their jobs, not simply *in* their jobs. As noted throughout this book, Relationship Marketing is not about a facet of the company; it is the very core of the company's engagement with those who create the value for which the customer pays and will pay again. Relationship Marketing companies can be very different from today's firms if the relationship is seen to be at the center of everything the company does and if a relationship is genuinely viewed as a mutual experience in which value is developed and shared between participants profitably. This is new territory. It is likely that no firm can yet lay claim to being fully reengineered on the basis of relationships.

People and the Role of Relationship Marketing

People practicing Relationship Marketing will face an expanded and refocused role in their enterprises. See Table 1 on the following page for a few of the changes that should be expected from people in a Relationship Marketing capacity.

In the Relationship Marketing era, the expectations of marketers are quite different. Specifically, they are expected to manage according to different measures of success and use quite different variables to achieve this success. The measures for the traditional marketer were associated with financial performance and market share but, in the Relationship Marketing era, measures that matter include those that deliver profitable, long-term growth for the company. These measures are not focused internally on the product, but externally on the

TABLE 1: Marketing Personnel and Relationship Marketing

Issue	Marketing Personnel—Traditional Marketing	With Relationship Marketing
Relationship with organization	Motivators and facilitators, seeking to drive product revenue and profitability.	Team managers, integrating customer initiatives with others who manage processes that touch the customer.
Planning	Market and segment planning in a centralized, research-based, annual planning cycle.	Customer planning, data-based, collaboratively in teams, to fit with customer's planning cycle.
Rewards	Based on individuals achieving financial results and share of market expectations for the *product*.	Based on team and individual metrics for the *customer*, including peer evaluations and profitability, Balanced Scorecard measures[9] and share of the customer.
Learning	Typically mass training using standardized content.	Learning needs geared to delivering customers' require-ments of individuals. Focus could initially be on internal communi-cations, within the team and with customers, training in the processes that deliver customer value, technical skills training and change management training.
Management variables	Target market selections and the 4 Ps of marketing: product, price, promotion, placement/distribution	11 Cs of Relationship Marketing: customer; categories; capabilities; cost, profitability and value; control of the contact to cash processes; collaboration and integration; customization; communications, interaction and positioning; customer measurements; customer care; chain of relationships.

customer. Marketers work with other functional areas in teams focused on customers designated as priority accounts. Because these teams

---

[9] For a review of the Balanced Scoreboard concept, see Robert S. Kaplan and David P. Norton, *The Balanced Scorecard: Turning Strategy into Action*, Harvard Business School Press, September, 1996.

perform together, they should be rewarded together. Their rewards should be based on customer profitability, share of customer expenditures on related products and processes and revenue growth for the firm.

Customers should complete evaluations of the team's performance and key members of the decision-making unit should be interviewed by senior executives owning the overall Relationship Marketing process to ensure that the value customers expect is indeed being delivered. Individual performance can be further rewarded according to peer assessments. Thus, if the team receives five out of a possible seven points overall, the marketer leading the team should be rewarded appropriate to that level. However, if the team receives a higher than average assessment from the team members, he or she may be rewarded even more, based on the higher than average scoring within the team.

The 11 Cs of Relationship Marketing

The Relationship Marketer has a new menu of variables to manage. The 11 Cs of Relationship Marketing (see Figure 8), which replace the 4 Ps, are:

1. Customer

A key role of the Relationship Marketer is to define which customers will be served, the bonding and other objectives to be achieved and the strategies to be followed in working with chosen customers for mutual advantage. Some of the strategies include making decisions in areas suggested by the following.

2. Categories

The Relationship Marketer should define the scope of product and service offerings to be provided to the customer. A secondary decision is whether the company should produce the products or services itself or find other means to deliver it to the customer, such as by private branding or outsourcing.

3. Capabilities

The Relationship Marketer should establish which capabilities are required from the firm in order to give their customers the value they wish, and then work with others in the company to ensure these capabilities are available in sufficient scale, focus and quality.

4. Cost, profitability and value

A key role of the Relationship Marketer is to build customer profitability, primarily through creating new value with customers and then sharing this. Clearly, the company has two main options in creating value for customers: make the customer more cost-competitive or create new revenue opportunities, such as through new product development and co-marketing and sales initiatives.

5. Control of the contact to cash processes

The Relationship Marketer is to manage and control the processes associated with contacts at the account by ensuring that cash is collected. This means the Relationship Marketer needs to head the team focused on the customer and ensure that the processes perform effectively and efficiently in the mutual interest of the customer and company.

6. Collaboration and integration

The Relationship Marketer needs to take a proactive role in securing access to the key decision makers and support for joint learning, strategy sharing and other forms of strategic and operational collaboration leading to integration of some aspects of the customer's business with that of the supplier.

7. Customization

The creation of new value for the customer likely means that the company will need to customize aspects of the product and service development, production and/or delivery, and perhaps take an expanded role in the management of the product or service throughout its lifetime. For example, computer companies could provide "evergreen" programs for their customers, keeping up-to-date personal computers on the desks of the customer's staff serviced, clean, loaded with current software and fully functional rather than repeatedly making new sales of computers to the company.

8. Communications, interaction and positioning

The Relationship Marketer engages the customer with real time, interactive communications, and not with "promotion" sent indiscriminately to the customer, perhaps as a broadcast television message or a mass-mailed brochure.

The Relationship Marketer also needs to manage the positioning of the company with the customer. This includes understanding competitive activity in the account, and ensuring that the company remains well positioned in respect of current and emerging developments in the customer's business relative to competitors.

9. Customer measurements

The Relationship Marketer needs to track the firm's performance in the customer's mind. This means each decision maker and influencer of the purchase decision-making unit should provide feedback independently to the company, rating and ranking the performance of the supplier. In addition, the Relationship Marketer should track these customer measures and the progress it has made in deepening the bond with the customer.

10. Customer care

In the era of traditional marketing, customer care may have been viewed more narrowly as customer service. With customer care, the Relationship Marketer develops and manages the processes for real time information provision, training, feedback and restitution, and any other relevant services required to increase the value of the product or service in use.

11. Chain of relationships

As mentioned previously, the chain of relationships comprises the formal linkages in the company and with external stakeholders, most notably suppliers and distribution channel intermediaries, that enable the company to create the value end-customers want. This chain needs to be formally managed by the team which focuses on each customer, with the Relationship Marketer leading the charge. (More about this in Chapter 9.)

FIGURE 8: The 11 Cs of Relationship Marketing

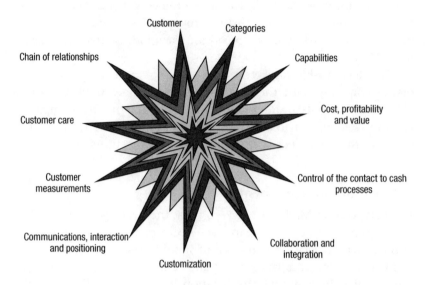

Business Is Process

Some firms have reengineered their businesses around their customers and sought to ensure that customer value is enhanced in the process. But my experience suggests this is not the typical case. More often, executives want to reduce costs and some adopt new technologies as a way of doing this. The technologies need revised processes so a consulting firm is hired to help with the associated reengineering. An additional benefit is that the company receives political justification for the lay-offs that usually result. It is very uncommon for a reengineering initiative to add new staff. Almost always, management trades labor for technology. The consultants leave just shortly ahead of the staff that have been displaced by bits and bytes.

As suggested by Figure 9, Relationship Marketing takes the view that the company should be organized around the customers it has chosen to serve, and that all technologies and processes help the company advance the customer relationship and others within the chain of relationships. According to this view, management should focus on building customers into the main processes and customers should collaborate with management in all the processes that are geared to creating value. Product concepts, for example, should be

FIGURE 9: Customer at the Center of Business Processes

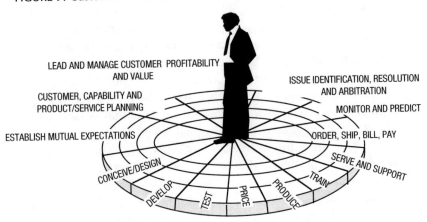

LEAD AND MANAGE CUSTOMER PROFITABILITY AND VALUE

CUSTOMER, CAPABILITY AND PRODUCT/SERVICE PLANNING

ESTABLISH MUTUAL EXPECTATIONS

CONCEIVE/DESIGN

DEVELOP

TEST

PRICE

PRODUCE

TRAIN

SERVE AND SUPPORT

ORDER, SHIP, BILL, PAY

MONITOR AND PREDICT

ISSUE IDENTIFICATION, RESOLUTION AND ARBITRATION

developed in close association with the customer, as should the product design.

The relationship itself should be viewed as a process, with subprocesses established for understanding customer expectations and assessing company performance in respect of those expectations. Companies already do this with market segments. Now they need to do this with specific customers and specific individuals within their best accounts. Processes also need to be established to structure the relationship, with the expectations clearly laid out and the mutual commitments to the relationship spelled out in a memorandum of understanding. This could include, for example, which people (by title) will be involved in the relationship, the roles they will play and the time they will commit to the relationship. Relationship objectives will be clearly laid out, as will broad strategies for delivering on the objectives, by both supplier and customer, and a calendar for joint planning and other key initiatives to build mutual profitability and create the value each seeks.

In addition, processes should be established to govern the relationship itself, to help ensure that the memorandum of understanding continues to apply and whether it needs to be changed to reflect more current conditions or direction. If performance of either company is below par, communications channels should be identified for issue resolution, and there should be more than one channel to limit the likelihood of one individual or process holding up progress of the relationship. In the event that issues cannot be resolved, a process should exist for resolution and arbitration, ideally an approach that is binding on both parties, such as using a third-party company to moderate discussion on any dispute and provide arbitration.

In the traditional "functional silo" approach, each business function operates as though it were independent of every other and rarely incorporates the customer into the process — from idea generation through commercialization and then throughout the customer's purchasing lifetime. Relationship Marketing seeks to make every process, such as those described in Figure 9, integrate with the customer, become real time, interactive and collaborative. This should also have the effect of eliminating functional silos. It should also eliminate the concept of "account management," instead shifting to "relationship management" and collaboration to create the value both customer and supplier seek. As will be noticed in Figure 9, the roles of "sell" and "market" are specifically and intentionally absent, as these roles are subsumed in the others. The marketer, in particular, as captain of relationship marketing processes, assumes the principal role of managing customer profitability and delivering value according to customer expectations.

Process Impacts in Relationship Marketing

Relationship Marketing, by putting the customer at the center of the enterprise, has a number of process impacts, including:

1. Putting data and associated guidance at the point of use by frontline personnel.

2. Shifting decision making from "hitting home runs" to "hitting singles," changing from making occasional high-level strategic decisions that could have material short-term impact, to more frequent, tactical decisions that help the company win over the long-term.

3. Gathering data on the individual customer rather than on the market or market segment. Increasing the amount of data gathered about all aspects of the customer interaction, preferences, behaviours and interactions with the company. Making customer knowledge creation and insight development a core and a continuous process of the company.

4. Operating in real time, with decisions taken on the fly, aided by technology that provides decision-making support, rather than

the more carefully analytical and labor intensive "one-off" decisions previously taken.

5. Decentralizing decision making to the point of relationship contact, where the context is more evident to the personnel. Supported by technology, they are better able to address customers' immediate concerns and offer more valuable and timely advice.

6. Integrating data about all aspects of the customer rather than having the data scattered in multiple locations.

7. Shifting from a focus on individual effort to team-based processes, including team-based management of the customer relationship.

8. Developing listening processes, including methods of communication with customers that are two-way and real time.

9. Integrating processes that touch or add value to the customer such as those associated with customer planning, capability planning, innovation, customer acquisition and customer value enhancement, including subprocesses associated with communicating, selling, servicing and supporting.

10. Extending technologies to support the processes for which they were not initially designed. For example, if a call center was originally designed to deliver outbound sales calls, it might be redesigned to also facilitate servicing of the account and more comprehensive interaction with the customer, according to the information they wish to secure or share.

Process and Relationship Enhancement or Transformation

Relationship Marketing can require that processes be radically altered or slightly changed, and that these changes occur rapidly and intensely or in a more paced fashion. The customer, in collaboration with the company, can help provide this guidance. Here is an all-too-common example: the supplier is seen by their customers to do most things well. It designs and builds a quality product, listens to the customers, communicates effectively and, in general, serves them as they wish to be served. But now a competitor is claiming to be able to do all this and more, and at a lower cost. The customer says that if the company can reduce its prices to the competitor's levels, it can retain the business. The company has a brief time to revise its pricing schedule or lose the business. It now has a number of options.

FIGURE 10: Relationship Enhancement or Transformation

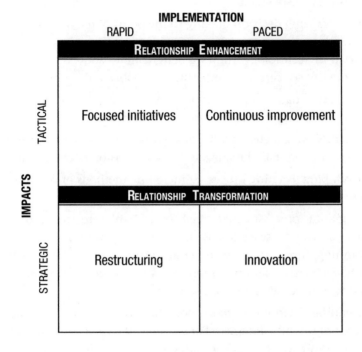

The company can reduce margin or work with the customer to manage its way to an improved situation. Perhaps costs can be reduced by asking the customer to make certain trade-offs, eliminate too-functional, over-engineered product or service or reduce or eliminate processes that create no value for them and may even be invisible to the customer. The entire process can be managed in a mechanism pre-established in the course of relationship formation and management, equivalent to arbitrating disputes for binding resolution. In this case, rapid, tactical solutions will need to be developed to retain the customer's business.

Relationship enhancement approaches require that tactical improvements in the relationship processes be adopted, either rapidly, as in the case mentioned above, or over time, continuously improving the processes to advance the relationship. Relationship transformation approaches seek to change the fundamental basis for the relationship, either by managing a customer into a position that creates more value for both over the long term, or by forcing a change in the prices or in the way the firms relate, in the shorter term. This situation was presented in Figure 5, which reviewed alternative customer strategies, including managing and disciplining customers, requiring that they alter or pay more for the processes they choose. Figure 10 describes alternative approaches to developing the relationship.

Business Is Technology

Much has been said about the power of technology in helping to add value to the customer relationship through shared information, communication and understanding. Relationship Marketing and its key components, including mass customization, is simply not possible without the enabling effects of technology to store, retrieve, process, communicate and analyze data, including customer data.

Technology Enters the Fifth Wave

Technology adoption is now in its fifth wave, an era in which the customer is integrated with the technology of the enterprise. Each wave of technology that preceded this era fundamentally changed the discipline and practice of management. Figure 11 provides an overview of the different waves that have led up to this era of customer integration. It is highly likely that this fifth wave will have the same revolutionary impact on business as have prior ones, this time with Relationship Marketing changing everything about the enterprise — the customers with which it integrates, the value it creates, the products and services it provides and the processes by which it produces, serves and manages. In essence, this book is about the changes likely to become widespread with customers becoming integrated into the very fabric of the enterprise.

The First Wave

Consider some of the changes preceding this era. The first wave automated clerical functions in companies, eliminating associated white-collar costs in the process. Manual and partially automated accounting procedures were automated through widespread adoption of mainframe computers in a centralized data processing envi-

FIGURE 11: Technology and the Five Waves

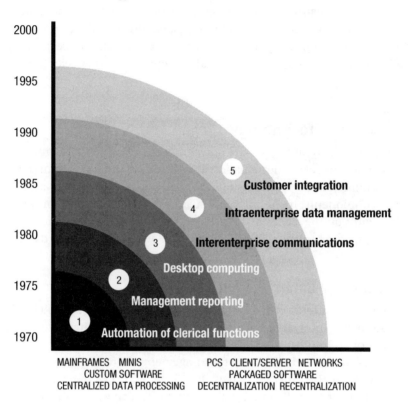

ronment. IBM established their firm in this early stage as the company that could be relied upon to install the mainframes needed to achieve the improvements in costs.

The Second Wave

The second wave was one which delivered information into the hands of management, offering reports to help them with the main functions of management — planning, leading, organizing, measuring, rewarding and controlling.

This wave was made possible by the increased performance of mainframes for the corporation and minis for many departments. Software, typically custom-coded by the internal IT shop, proliferated to facilitate the requirements of management in individual departments. With this period came an explosion in demand for smaller, more powerful department-level computers. A then little-known company proceeded to supply this demand. That company is Digital Equipment.

The Third Wave

The third wave offered desktop computing to white-collar workers, decentralizing some aspects of the IT shop and letting each worker develop and use technology to advance their individual roles. Apple captured this best when, early on, they sloganed their machines: "Apple: The Power to be Your Best." The era of desktop computing had many advantages and some drawbacks. It reduced the backlog of IT tasks and let each worker use his computer as he saw fit. But it also limited the extent to which information and data could be economically shared in an enterprise and further deepened the functional silos. In addition to allowing the best and the brightest to be even better, desktop computing led to "management by spreadsheet," the mind-robbing approach to assessing scenarios without having to think creatively about the idea in the first place. For this reason, and because technology fell into the hands of people who perhaps may have been better equipped with other tools, desktop computing often provided a new sea in which management could become self absorbed and sometimes sink.

The Fourth Wave

The fourth wave facilitated communications, internally within the company as well as between companies, first with dedicated communications lines, then over the Internet. This era of communications has created and is creating significant change in the practice of management by encouraging teamwork and collaboration. This wave of interenterprise and intraenterprise communications, massive databases and applications ties together teams of workers who may never have met one another. Clearly the management of these virtual workforces needs different approaches, organizational cultures, project management and recognition and reward. We are now witnessing the explosion of this fourth wave and entry into the fifth: the era in which customers are completely integrated into the value chain.

The Fifth Wave

This fifth wave is bringing the customer into the enterprise and blurring the lines between where the customer ends and the firm begins. The customer not only enters through the traditional technology doors (such as the telephone), but now also via the Internet and even directly to the firm's databases. Dramatic changes are occurring in the way customers can interact with the firm in areas such as product or service information, customer care, collaborative design, inventory management, warehousing and logistics and pricing. For example, Apple's Reseller Information System allows Apple resellers to establish inventory levels in Apple's warehouses, review prices and place orders, without the intervention of a person at the reseller order desk. This system has had a predictable result. There is less concern among resellers and customers that others are receiving preferential treatment and also increased satisfaction with suppliers.

In this fifth wave, technology is being adopted to create, enhance and transform relationships. Consider companies selling, for example, insurance direct to customers. Technology makes it all possible. They might use TV to create awareness and interest, inbound telemarketing to call centers to discover the individual customer's needs and provide information and solutions, send policies and bills by mail and use the banks to direct-debit the policyholder's account.

Vendor-Managed Technology

For suppliers selling through retailer intermediaries, technology can offer total integration of all or many business operations. Benetton, the noted Italian apparel company, has a sophisticated information technology backbone, that communicates from their points of sale worldwide to centralized plants. Here neutral-color garments are dyed according to demand for specific styles, sizes and colors. Benetton avoids the perennial retail problem of marking down unsold inventory because their production cycle more closely follows customer demand. As a result, Benetton has lower levels of unrequired merchandise and less need for sell-offs.

Vendor-managed technology can aid the retailer in many ways, such as with regard to:

- Product — the right assortment at the right time, in displays suitable for immediate use, bar-coded and racked, with inventory managed by the retailer.

- Price — everyday low prices, not subject to mark-ups and mark-downs that plague the industry and cause costs to spiral.
- Customer service — complete and timely support of retailers and their customers.
- Consumer promotion — retailers have access to the centralized database of the vendors, which profiles customers and demography in their market. Retailers also obtain personalized and customized promotional materials or capabilities to aid marketing initiatives.

Business Is Knowledge and Insight

Every business has succeeded to a greater or lesser extent because of the knowledge and insight it has gained and used to customer advantage. The historical focus of knowledge has been on the research underlying new products or applications. Then came a shift in knowledge focus to development and production processes. Other knowledge included market research, which helped provide balance to technology-led companies by providing the perspectives and requirements of market segments. But rarely did companies focus on gaining customer knowledge and insight and then using this to deepen and extend customer relationships. For many businesses, opportunities remain to gain additional customer knowledge and insight.

TABLE 2: Quick Customer Knowledge and Insight Quiz

Here is a brief test of your company's customer knowledge and insight. Answer yes or no for the following statements:
1. I know the names of the customers of our firm that comprise half our profitability.
2. I know the mix and profitability of my customers' customers, and the current and future requirements of their most important ones.
3. I can predict what my main customers will expect of our firm next year, in each of the major process areas, and know the impact of their requirements on our capabilities.
4. I understand the business model of my most important customers — that is, in detailed financial terms, how they make their money.
5. I know the personal preferences of my most important customers' purchase decision makers.

---

6. I understand the real strategic intent of the president of my major customers.

---

7. I understand the drivers of the board of directors and the direction they are providing to the president.

---

8. I know how the key decision makers in my major accounts view my main competitors.

---

9. I understand the strategies of my customers' competitors.

---

10. I can quantify the value our firm has created for our customers and know how this value is being shared.

If your firm produces products that are important to business-to-business customers and you cannot answer all these questions affirmatively, opportunities remain to develop customer knowledge and insight and to build deeper and more beneficial customer relationships. If you answered "yes" to fewer than eight statements, listen carefully for the footsteps of competitors because if they know more than your firm does, your company may be trampled.

Knowledge and Insight in Relationship Marketing

Knowledge and insight come, in this Relationship Marketing era, from data on customer interactions, transactions and manifested behaviours, including purchase, service and return activity. This, in turn, means that the capability of knowledge development is very closely tied into the underlying technologies that can help develop customer knowledge and, in particular, the data warehousing, data mining and predictive modeling, which allows you to forecast customer behaviours and ask "what if" questions at the customer level.

In this decade, it has become clear that competing on knowledge is one way to aid volume and margin. Companies such as Microsoft, with little to offer the world except knowledge, have shown how to create astonishing shareholder value using this valuable resource. "Chairman Bill," as Gates is sometimes called, competes aggressively for the best minds for his firm. But this seems a little ad hoc. What are these good minds to do? Where is the organizational experience and "memory," the combined understanding of what works, what doesn't and what is yet to be tried? In some companies, usually those that consider themselves entrepreneurial, this memory is resident in the leader, among others. I haven't worked at Microsoft, but I am sure people there use terms such as "Bill says..." or "Bill wants this..." when things need to be done and Bill's direction — whether real or imagined — is all that is required to ensure that the direction is "right"[10].

I have seen similar situations at work in other companies. One major communications and convergence company has a "Ted says...," another late-life cycle software firm was galvanized by a "Steve says...." As companies get larger, as the pace of change accelerates, as customer targeting fragments in this era of Relationship Marketing, no one person will have the knowledge needed to guide the company strategically or tactically.

Knowledge needs to be democratized to upgrade staff capabilities, particularly in those delayered companies where staff are now expected to perform non-traditional, far-ranging roles. Yet the science of knowledge creation is much less well understood than is the maintenance and dissemination of existing knowledge. The professional services firms, for example, have done outstanding work capturing client profiles, proposals, assignments, methodologies, industry information and other useful data. These are available for staff perusal on the network. Adept at applying specific methodologies to client issues, these same firms may sometimes lag in the processes needed to create new knowledge. Perhaps some of this is traceable to command and control organizational structures at work in some companies, which rarely achieve the real teamwork needed to build understanding.

Knowledge and Insight From *Customers*

Learning about each and every customer may be the single most powerful capability a CEO can put in place. As the chief executive of a cellular company puts it: "We can be late to market, but we cannot be the last to learn." Certainly, customers can help a company populate a data warehouse. But customer knowledge must also be created about the business environment of the customer, including the customers they serve and the competitors and regulators they face. One of the most successful telecommunications equipment companies in the world studies their customers' customers and the business challenges of their customers in a broader context than simply that

---

[10] A sort of "virtual Bill."

of supplying this one category of service. Consider the case of Amcan Castings, a supplier of engineered aluminum castings to the automobile industry. Like any other supplier, Amcan bids on contract opportunities according to a well-defined set of specifications from the auto companies. But Amcan has improved its chances of winning each contract by having more customer knowledge than its competitors. It places staff in the customers' premises and collaborates with them on product conceptualization, design and planning, blurring the line between where Amcan ends and the car company begins. Amcan has grown rapidly in this competitive industry, one contract at a time, through improved customer knowledge and mutual learning.

Knowledge and Insight With *Customers*

Knowledge most relevant comes not only from customers, but through and with them. A relationship based on learning, developing increasingly relevant and timely customer knowledge and insight is good. One based on learning *with* customers is better. Increasingly, companies are recognizing that they should work with their customers in joint knowledge-creating processes to develop deep bonding and a more informed capability to respond and shape events with the customer. To illustrate, Streamline,[11] a Boston-based virtual storefront that retails groceries, visits customers in their homes with barcode readers and takes inventory of kitchen cabinets. Now, when a customer orders pretzels from the Web site, Streamline knows what brand that customer prefers and can suggest this type and size first. If the customer chooses another, the database is updated.

The development of a learning relationship with customers provides side benefits in addition to knowledge creation. Companies marketing to other companies find that interenterprise teams that solve problems together will remain bonded, even after the problems are solved.

Companies should consider processes for securing customer involvement at multiple levels in the company and in the context of the key success factors of the firm, including strategic capabilities under development. At the highest level, this may mean customer advisory groups guiding senior executives and perhaps a customer

---

[11] Scott Leibs, "Shop, Don't Drop," *Information Week*, August 18, 1997, p. 69.

representative on the board. Operationally, it may involve customer service teams planning together and executing those plans in areas such as product development, logistics, communications, end-customer promotion and customer service. Ernst & Young, prior to its merger with KPMG, used client service teams to serve its large clients. The firm narrowed the range of customers it regarded as meriting proactive account attention and has developed multifunctional, senior-level account teams to focus on the client issues, context and strategy. Ernst & Young met at client offices to engage in account planning and invited senior client executives to attend the planning meetings, address the team and engage in mutual learning. Ernst & Young was not unique in this regard. Its competitors, particularly in the consulting arena, also have customer-focused, knowledge- and insight-building processes.

Learning about customers, particularly if technology is embraced, can provide real-time capabilities previously impossible, and let the Relationship Marketing company serve an individual consumer in an extremely powerful way. Consider this example: Your washing machine breaks down and you call the service department of the manufacturer to remedy the problem. The call-center operator says the service technician will be at your home within four hours. You wait. After six hours, you call again to find out where the person is. Your call comes into the large call center, where hundreds of employees are taking calls. Yet your call is identified and routed to the operator who told you that the technician would be there by now. The operator is best placed to handle the problem. Technology helped the company learn from your prior interaction and ensured that you could be treated uniquely and appropriately by a fully informed person.

One by-product of customer learning and Relationship Marketing more generally may well be the expansion of the scope of a company as it seeks to become more of a "one-stop-shop" for its customers. Consider the case of Lear Corp. which has recently been acquiring companies to become a global supplier of vehicle interiors. Lear has spent heavily to acquire companies such as Masland, a manufacturer of auto carpets and the seating businesses of Fiat, Ford, Saab and Volvo. Why? The future in the car business is for major parts companies to become integrators of subassemblies which will dramatically expand their range of service and geographic scope. For example, Chrysler used to have 250 engineers just to design seat covers. Now their suppliers do this.[12] Suppliers integrating with their customers will find that there is only room for a few tier one suppliers — the companies that do the actual production and project management of initiatives that involve the smaller-parts companies. Suppliers to the car business may have to go through radical change in their relationships as they decide whether they will be large and capable enough to be tier one suppliers, or if they need to forge relationships with their competitors or complementary companies that will become tier one companies, such as Lear.

ම

In this chapter, we have seen the importance of understanding the mix of customers the company serves and establishing the current and potential profitability of each. Together, these two considerations help the Relationship Marketing company develop customer objectives and strategies. Along with other considerations — the strategic value of the account for new ideas, process collaboration, the opportunity to use the account as a test-bed or to refer new customers — the Relationship Marketing company can plan to improve the profitability of its customer mix, customer by customer. Some customers will be rewarded by being designated best customers, and attract the most emphasis and best resources to reflect this recognition. Other customers will be managed to build new and mutual value. Some may even be disciplined for not complying with the processes of the company if it raises the costs of service and renders the customer unprofitable. And those customers that do not fit into the future relationships of the company may be terminated.

This chapter discussed the main capabilities that the Relationship Marketing company must manage to ensure that its customer strategies can be advanced. The main categories of capabilities that were reviewed included technology, process, people and knowledge and insight. Each of these capabilities change materially in the Relationship Marketing era. With Relationship Marketing, the customer integrates with each capability, collaborating in its development and interacting with it to achieve the promise of Relationship Marketing: the continuous creation and sharing of mutual value.

In the next chapter, we review how to bond more closely with individual customers.

---

[12] Bill Vlasic, "Get Big or Get Out," *Business Week*, September 2, 1996, p. 60.

CHAPTER THREE

Making the Case for Relationship Marketing

Act only on that maxim through which you can
at the same time will that it should become a universal law.
Immanuel Kant

This chapter seeks to help the Relationship Marketer make the case for Relationship Marketing in the enterprise, principally with non-marketing executives. It starts by asking the question "Is Relationship Marketing a good idea?" If the Relationship Marketer agrees it is, then it will be easier to convince others because they, too, will likely be asking this same fundamental question. Executives will likely also be asking other questions such as "Does Relationship Marketing fit with our strategies?" "Is Relationship Marketing part of our customers' future and the focus of business over the next decade?" "What are the barriers to Relationship Marketing?" Finally, not least important, "Will Relationship Marketing create additional shareholder value?" This chapter deals with these issues including a review of lifetime value of customers, a core component of Relationship Marketing and a contributor to shareholder value.

Relationship Marketing is not just another tool among others in the marketing tool kit. It is the key strategy by which value will be created for companies in the 1990s. It is the natural evolution of marketing strategy that has progressively shifted its view of the key drivers in the development of new business value. Hopefully, this chapter can help companies adopt Relationship Marketing and integrate it with similar emerging strategies of their customers — before their competitors do.

Is Relationship Marketing a Good Idea?

Relationship Marketing has the potential to offer companies a number of important benefits, such as developing more loyalty among customers, having an environment to foster innovative solutions, having a forgiving place to test new ideas and aligning the enterprise with customers who value what the company provides.

However, Relationship Marketing will not have equal appeal to all companies. Companies in high fixed-cost industries where there is long-term commitment of financial resources to plant, installations or capital equipment, should be very interested in building customer loyalty to provide the long-term revenue stream needed to support the investment. Industries most likely to have this orientation include: automobile, airline, cable television, car rental, electrical utilities, health care, hotel and hospitality, long-distance and local telecommunications, machinery and equipment, natural gas, primary metals, software and telecommunications equipment.

In some cases, companies applying Relationship Marketing concepts may find the approach challenging and perhaps even inappropriate to adopt in its entirety. For example:

- In some industries there may not be much value to be created mutually between the company and its customers and, even if there were, the customers may not be amenable to such value creation. Consumers buying soap, for example, may consider this a low-involvement purchase decision and one for which they are quite satisfied to have the vendor in the background, producing product.

- In some situations, although potential mutual value exists, there may be insufficient lifetime value to warrant mutual value creation. While the lifetime value of the average purchaser of automobiles may be $200,000, the average lifetime value for the purchase of specific consumer non-durables (such as food and beverages) may be a fraction of this. Clearly, Ford can afford to spend more to attract and retain appropriately profiled customers than could say, a processor of cheese, if this was the only product promoted. But when combined with a shopping basket full of consumer products they make, companies such as Procter and Gamble and H.J. Heinz can indeed apply principles similar to that of Ford.

- There are cases where the alignment of a company to serve only specific customers or customer segments may be too limiting. A famous mass merchandiser found its main customers were women of advancing age, to whom the retailer generously referred as the "blue-rinse set." The vice-president of marketing, herself young and upscale, considered abandoning the retailer's core franchise to reposition the store for upmarket young women. The plan included adoption of the principles of Relationship Marketing to engage these customers. But the president, concerned about rejecting customers without assurance that new ones would be secured, and further believing that the volume base would be too limited, killed the initiative. The vice-president of marketing left shortly afterwards.

- For companies having recently committed major sums to the design and development of products, and for those firms having also invested heavily in infrastructure or business processes, the adoption of Relationship Marketing may have the effect of rendering a portion of their investment severely depreciated or even wasted. Not that companies should be shackled by their historical investment decisions, but the reality is that the investor community will not smile on the manager who trashes recent major investment in a carefully conceived and well-communicated business strategy.

- Not all companies have the capability to apply Relationship Marketing principles with more than basic commitment. In particular, not all companies will have the financial depth, technological capabilities or Relationship Marketing sophistication to do justice to the principles. And if a company is struggling to survive, it had better pay attention to the short-term issues it faces, or there may be no long term.

In short, Relationship Marketing will make sense for some firms more than for others. The extent to which one adopts Relationship Marketing principles should depend upon careful consideration of strategic issues and economics, but one thing is certain: the trend to individualized, customized and personalized marketing is indisputable. If you don't move to serve customers as they wish to be served and your competitors do, how will this affect you and your company?

Does Relationship Marketing Fit with Our Strategies?

Marketing Strategies in the 1960s

For companies in many industries, marketing in the 1960s focused on diversification of product and market portfolios to develop a balanced business — one that could grow principally from internally generated funds. A manifestation of participation in multiple markets was the rise of the conglomerate, which often acquired companies with positions in several markets, and then sought to grow as each of the markets in which they participated grew.

Marketing Strategies in the 1970s

In the 1970s, the oil-induced recession led to the slowing and uneven growth of many markets and the basis for the conglomerate, if there was one, disappeared. Instead, companies again focused on the basics of their businesses. This time, instead of looking for small market share positions in multiple markets, they sought high market share within fewer markets or market segments. If the maxim for companies of the 1960s was "don't put all your eggs in one basket," the motto for the 1970s was to put all your eggs in a few baskets, and then to watch the eggs very carefully until they hatched.

Marketing Strategies in the 1980s

In the mid to late 1980s, market growth returned but this time, although the Reagan years brought a broadly based advance of wealth, the main manifestation was the growth of upscale market segments. Many companies innovated to capture the market demand of these upscale market segments, and some went global with their innovation, believing that there was sufficient demand in many of these areas. Witness the emergence of entirely new brands, such as Lexus and Acura, to capture opportunities in the auto industry, for example. Increasingly, the competition in this era resembled a battle between global titans, each looking to transfer market share from other competitors to their own companies, most often by focusing more intensely on targeted markets or segments. However, sometimes they concentrated quite creatively on beating the competition. When Dell and Gateway 2000 established their positions in the burgeoning US personal computer industry, they did so primarily through distribution channel innovation, selling direct to the consumer, rather than through an established dealer distribution network, as competitors did. Huggies, a Kimberly Clark brand, became the US market leader not only through product innovation — thinner, more absorbent, better fitting and leak resistant products, graphical images on diapers and refastenable tabs — but also by introducing products for different weight and genders. These strategies seemed to crowd competitors' offerings off the supermarket shelves.

Marketing Strategies in the 1990s

In the 1990s, companies have been seeking to reengineer their processes to become more efficient, but still under the business rules and business models of the last decade. Those more far-sighted are demonstrating that they cannot save their way to success, and are looking to create new business value. And Relationship Marketing is one approach to do this. Table 3 on the following page illustrates the marketing strategies from the 1960s to the present.

Is Relationship Marketing Part of Our Customers' Future?

Table 4 on page 85 outlines ten major shifts in business strategy and focus of the enterprise over the next decade, all of which are positive for Relationship Marketing.

Opportunity awaits those companies having an early recognition of the value of individual customers and appreciating the technologies that are available for economic application. The future involves bonding more tightly with the individual customer as each wishes to engage your company. And it requires that the marketer help the organization step up to the Relationship Marketing challenge to add even more value to the customer relationship — the most important of business assets.

TABLE 3: Evolution of Marketing Strategies

Era	Selected Market Drivers or Enablers	Strategic Response or Focus
1960s	Consistent expansion of most consumer and business-to-business markets.	Diversification and balance of product portfolio.
1970s	Slowing market growth, primarily from oil-induced recession. Growth of market segments uneven.	Companies focus on their core businesses and ration resources accordingly.
1980s	Expansion of upscale market segments. Growth of global competition.	Product innovation to address upscale segments. Market development to globalize regional or nationally successful products and services, and market share transfer strategies from global and segment competitors.
Early 1990s	Contraction of many upscale markets; declining product differentiation; intensification of global competition; cooperation and competition with competitors.	Simplification of products, services and processes for offerings targeted to mass markets; mass customization for multiple segments or individual consumers.
Late 1990s	Renewed expansion of upscale markets; rapid increase in stock prices and market valuation as a "rising tide lifts all ships;" challenge remains to grow revenues profitably.	Intensified focus on execution; commitment by management to growth; increased emphasis on process management and leverage of efforts through co-venture partners; recognition that three factors drive shareholder value creation: profitable revenue growth, cost management and human resources; focus on Relationship Marketing as a key approach to build revenues profitably.

What Are the Barriers to Relationship Marketing?

We have seen that Relationship Marketing is a major departure from traditional marketing and the company adopting it as a core strategy will need to change much about virtually every aspect of the enterprise. But before Relationship Marketing can be adopted, it must be defined

TABLE 4: The Outlook for Relationship Marketing

Today	Tomorrow
Look at the balance sheet for the company assets.	Look at the list of customers and the profitability of customer relationships as the enduring asset of the enterprise.
Focus business to serve market segments. Sell to all comers in the segment.	Focus on individual customers. Sell to customers according to whether you accept them as relationship partners, wish to manage them into greater profitability, discipline them for consuming resources better allocated to priority customers or fire them as customers you no longer wish to serve.
Market place success is measured by market share	Success is measured by share of lifetime value of priority customers.
Cost management and focused product/market growth strategies.	Growth through profitable alignment with existing preferred customers.
Efficiency of existing infrastructure.	Effectiveness in developing new value with desirable customers.
Mass marketing and production.	Mass personalization and customization.
Supply chain.	Chain of relationships or demand chain, with customers initiating material aspects of the value they seek.
Sell what we make.	Provide the customer with what they want, some of which we may not make.
Compete with companies that make similar goods or services.	Compete with companies that want to access the customers we have selected as our Relationship Marketing accounts.
Invest in plant and equipment to produce the goods and services the company plans to market.	Invest in customer knowledge and insight and the facilitating components of processes, people, technology and know-how to convert individual customer requirements into the value they each seek, and do so profitably.

using common terminology. At present, every function in a company will have different interpretations of this term. In fact, some may even feel that the company already pays considerable time and attention to Relationship Marketing, in part because they may not have a full grasp of the concept and its underpinnings. If all else fails to achieve common understanding, lend them this book!

Relationship Marketing changes or has the potential to change everything in the business, including culture, leadership, management and each of the capabilities — people, process, technology and knowledge and insight — that enable Relationship Marketing. If a company is to adopt Relationship Marketing in its entirety, the firm will need convincing evidence that the destination will be worth the journey. As goes an old adage: only when the platform begins to burn will people leap into the sea.

Most companies have had their fill of new initiatives that are meant to fix everything. They are tired of preppy MBAs telling them how wrong everything is and of articulate consultants selling the next flavor of the month. Management wants results, not initiatives. They will naturally be skeptical that Relationship Marketing will be this year's TQM, EVA or another TLA.[13] If change is required, it must be demonstrated that Relationship Marketing can deliver the goods. And for most senior management, the "goods" mean that Relationship Marketing must provide superior shareholder value over simply proceeding with the status quo. Shareholder value and Relationship Marketing will be reviewed next in this chapter, but first we should recognize the initial hurdles for Relationship Marketing.

The main barriers for Relationship Marketing to overcome early on are not with customers or others in the chain of relationships, but are inside the company itself. Before senior management will commit to changing a great deal about what has already made it successful, the linkage of Relationship Marketing to shareholder value creation needs to be clearly demonstrated. In addition to providing the math of Relationship Marketing to help muster support for the initiative with financial managers, Relationship Marketers can experience additional challenges, including:

- Persuading non-financial and financial management of the merits of Relationship Marketing and of all the associated investments and actions. This can be particularly challenging in companies where management may today be unpersuaded of the merits of the marketing function.
- Planning Relationship Marketing, including knowing where to

---

[13] TLA = Three Letter Acronym!

start, where to go with it and how to know when it is complete.

- Envisioning the end state of Relationship Marketing, and the investments and actions needed to achieve this condition.

- Finding best examples to benchmark and emulate in this emerging area where few companies have developed fully integrated Relationship Marketing initiatives (although many have successfully introduced key components).

- Identifying the customers on which to focus and developing the transition plan from the existing base to the desired one. This is a particularly daunting challenge.

- Knowing how to become more relevant to customers identified as meriting priority, and doing this faster than competitors.

- Understanding how to align the chain of relationships, and how each link will have to perform if organizational relationships are to be forged and deepened. (More about this chain of relationships shortly.)

- The challenge of demonstrating the feasibility of the Relationship Marketing concept by using the traditional pilot tests and demonstration of results before wide-scale roll-out. Relationship Marketing typically needs significant underlying capabilities to be in place before the customer relationship can be effectively addressed, and these investments in capability — such as changes in technology, process, people and knowledge and insight systems — can be costly. A Catch-22 phenomenon is at work here. Management that will only assign investments to the Relationship Marketing initiative once pilot results have proven effective may find that the pilot results are inconclusive or even unsatisfactory because insufficient funds were assigned to make it work.

So it is evident that Relationship Marketing can face a number of internal barriers before the company will reorient itself to accommodate the concept. This chapter continues by considering shareholder value and the financial calculations some companies use to assess the benefits of Relationship Marketing.

Will Relationship Marketing Create Additional Shareholder Value?

Today, many senior executives are focused on creating shareholder value for their companies. They screen new initiatives in large measure based on strategic alignment and shareholder value creation. If Relationship Marketing is to be seen as an area worth management time and investment attention, the link to shareholder value will need to be demonstrated. Without seeking to do in these few pages what financial professionals study for much of their lives, it is important for the marketer be in a position to articulate the linkage and potential for Relationship Marketing to create new business value for the company. The following discussion is intentionally technical because the Relationship Marketer will need to engage financial managers on their terms.

The Value-Driver Model

Let us briefly consider some of the main approaches used by financial professionals to assess and project company value. The three main ways in which this is done are: the Value-Driver Model, the Discounted Cash-Flow Model and the Free Cash-Flow Model.[14] We discuss the Value-Driver Model, but the others should yield identical valuation. The Value-Driver Model is based on the total market value of the company rather than accounting-based approaches such as earnings per share and price earnings ratios, which are no longer viewed as current approaches to financial analysis of the value of a company.[15] This model involves six main factors:

1. the after-tax operating profits of the company;

2. the tax benefit of debt financing;

3. the amount of net new capital available for investment in a given year;

---

[14] For a thoughtful and detailed treatment of this subject see the excellent books: G. Bennett Stewart III, *The Quest for Value*, HarperCollins, 1991; Tom Copeland, Tim Koller and Jack Murrin, *Valuation: Measuring and Managing the Value of Companies*, John Wiley and Sons, 1990.

[15] This stems partly from the work of Professors Miller, University of Chicago, and Franco Modigliani, MIT. For a more detailed consideration see: G. Bennett Stewart III, *The Quest for Value*, and most financial texts in use at B-Schools.

4. the after-tax rate of return on invested capital;

5. the cost of capital of the company; and

6. the time period during which investors expect management to secure competitive advantage and make profitable investments before competition or other factors limit their options and opportunities.

New Value from Current Customers

Central to most companies increasing shareholder value is the need to increase profitability principally from current business operations. Doing so will maximize the value of the current assets your company has deployed. Current customers buy the products of your current operations and infrastructure. Improving the performance of these assets requires customer involvement in all relevant initiatives. For example, should you choose to add or shed assets, what will be the impact on your customer? If you decide to operate a second or third shift to gain more productivity out of the assets, or to run the machinery, equipment, distribution or other aspects of the business faster, what will the impact be on business processes and customer requirements? In short, Relationship Marketing has the potential to develop significant new value for the company by matching the requirements of current customers with the productive capability of current assets. The new value from current customers will come from three main areas:

1. Cost reduction — from improved logistics and more efficient processes such as eliminating duplication in processes which occur in both the supplier and the customer (e.g., quality control in production and quality assurance of incoming supplies and components).

2. Reduced time to market — by having the customer closely involved in all phases of the new product or service development process.

3. Lessened business risk — from longer-term contracts and fewer product failures, for example. Financial managers may be particularly intrigued at the prospect of matching, as banks do, by balancing short- and long-term liabilities and assets. For the most part, companies have invested long term in capital assets and

information technology, with no assurance that the customers for which the outputs are intended will support the investment with their patronage. With Relationship Marketing, there is a greater prospect that cash flows from the company's main customers will be matched with the expected lifetime of the assets needed to generate these flows.

The Value of Growth Opportunities

Shareholder value also depends on the value of growth opportunities available to the company. Relationship Marketing's focus on the company's most desirable customers has the potential to accelerate growth for the company. For example, higher success rates for new product and service opportunities are possible by working with important customers in continuously improving existing product, and together conceiving and charting directions for new products and services. In addition, customers bonded to your organization through Relationship Marketing can help you to improve the processes you need to test, refine and produce the products so that the prospect of market acceptance is improved in subsequent roll-out.

In more specific terms, if Relationship Marketing is to create additional shareholder value, the long-term after-tax rate of return on invested capital should exceed present rates of return. Accordingly, the metrics of the initiative, both investment and return, need to be established and communicated and related to the company's current levels of performance. It may be useful for the marketer to involve a member of the financial staff, as both work through the financials of Relationship Marketing in order to demonstrate the workability of the entire initiative.

One approach to securing interest from finance could be to identify the level of investment required in technology such as hardware, software, networks, communications and soft costs (including installation and human factor costs), and then to calculate the required return on this investment using the current after-tax rates of return on invested capital. The question then becomes: "If I can demonstrate that Relationship Marketing will achieve after-tax profits in excess of current returns and will improve long-term growth opportunities for the company consistent with our mission, can I count on your support?"

Calculating the Financial Benefits of Relationship Marketing

Virtually everyone agrees that it is more expensive to acquire new customers than to service the existing firms or individuals with which companies do business.[16] Yet every Wednesday, the newspaper is crowded with price promotions from supermarkets looking for the business of price-sensitive shoppers. Ukrop's, a twenty-three store chain mentioned earlier, has done the reverse. It has rejected the cherry-picker in favor of marketing to its database of "Value Customer" cardholders. In so doing, it basically eliminated advertising in favor of seeking a higher share of individual spending among those customers that already shop at Ukrop's. The Ford Motor Company is doing the same thing, when it encourages prospective customers to use a Ford Visa card to accumulate a credit towards the purchase of a new Ford car. Why are Ford and others prepared to pay thousands of dollars for the opportunity to sell the customer a new car?

Money Making Strategies

It has to do with three things: knowing that the mass market can be economically served at the segment-of-one level, understanding the current value of each of these customers (and potential customers of that type) and knowing the value of each customer to the company over the customer's purchasing lifetime. One car company believes its average customer is worth $200,000 over his/her lifetime. That is why firms such as Ford are prepared to pay relatively more to acquire the customer in the first place and keep their loyalty through such programs as that employing Visa, referenced above.

Another car company sent van customers in its database a coupon for several hundred dollars off the purchase of a new vehicle. The phenomenal response far exceeded even their optimistic budget. Anticipating a response of a few thousand customers, they have been astonished to find that tens of thousands of coupons have been redeemed. For an investment of less than $20 million, the firm achieved sales of over $700 million. They proved to themselves that

---

[16] It can cost five times as much to acquire a new customer compared with the costs of servicing an existing customer — Forum Consulting, Boston, MA, and Customer Service Institute, Silver Spring, MD.

loyal customers are their greatest asset and that an ongoing relationship with them is an effective way to ensure that the economic cycle from production to consumption continues again and again.

Britain's Land Rover took a novel approach to attract buyers. Rather than employing mass media to communicate with a media-saturated mass audience, this company identified just 11,000 people as potential buyers. For about $50 each, it sent gifts that were a bit off beat such as shells, flowers and leaves. It paid off — 85% of the recipients visited a showroom to see the new $60,000 Range Rover, compared to just 1-2% who visit dealers with mass media advertising.[17]

Calculating the Lifetime Value of a Customer

The lifetime value of a potential customer is simply a projection of the customer's expenditures minus the company's costs of producing the product (well known) and serving and supporting each customer (not as well known in most companies). A brief example follows, then we review more general concepts.

The example and figures that follow are presented for illustrative purposes only and are not intended to fully or necessarily accurately describe the deliberations of a car company. Over a forty-year purchasing lifetime, a typical customer who buys a car for, say, $20,000 (in constant dollars) every three years will buy thirteen cars, spending $260,000, assuming this customer buys a similar car each time. If the dealer margin for each car is projected to be 12% (or $31,200) on average over this time, the car company will derive $228,800 in revenues from this customer. In addition, parts revenues may be estimated at a further 20% of car company sales (or $45,760), bringing total revenues to $274,560. (Service revenues accrue to the dealer.) From these revenues, the car company must net all the costs of attracting, retaining and providing for the customer's requirements.

[17] "Down the Data Mine We Go," *The Economist*, August 23, 1997, p. 48.

TABLE 5: Example of Customer Lifetime Value — Hypothetical Car Company

Revenues (Cars and parts)	$282,600
Less direct costs:	
Cost of vehicles produced (13 @ $12,000)	$156,000
Less cost of parts produced (45% of $45,760)	$20,592
Cost of warranty work reimbursed to dealer (13 @ $1,000)	$13,000
Less costs of financing customer	Nil
Less relationship costs:	
Time to manage customer feedback and restitution — low involvement customer	$5,000
Depreciation of customer's portion of communication capabilities (e.g., call center, Internet site)	$5,000
Depreciation of customer's share to put in place relevant capabilities, such as a customer database and dealer access and training in the use of the database	$5,000
Cost of communicating with the customer directly and through the dealer	$5,000
Less other costs directly attributable to the customer relationship	$10,000
Net lifetime value of relationship (in constant dollars)	**$90,008**

Questions to Ask

There are a number of possible questions that arise from these calculations:

- If each customer matching this customer's profile is worth approximately $90,000 to a car company, how do we make sure we get all of this for ourselves?

- How much are we prepared to spend to attract a customer such as this at the outset even though it may take some time before the investment in the customer relationship breaks even?

- If this customer delivers $90,000 over his lifetime, how do we maintain the customer for life? What initiatives are required from us to keep the customer? For example, can we provide the customer with a "cars for life" program, which provides them with a new Ford, say, every three years, and provides substantial incentives for committing their lifetime of purchases to Ford?

- How should the car company reward a lifetime customer as opposed to a customer not as tightly bonded with the firm? Do best customers want financial incentives or other forms of recognition? What other recognition could we give them? For example, would they value an opportunity to preview new models before they are available to the general public? Would they like to collaborate in new vehicle exterior and interior design or service improvement concepts? Would they like to join with other best customers at the Indianapolis 500, say, in a company-sponsored event?

Customers that are bonded more tightly to a company should be treated quite differently than those who are less loyal. This is discussed in the next section of this chapter.

Issues to Be Considered

A number of issues need to be considered in calculating the lifetime value of a customer, including:

- The need for an integrated information profile on each end-customer. Many companies have information about the purchases of the retail or distribution channel intermediaries, but have insufficient data on their end-customers.

- An ability to mine the data to understand customer behaviors uniquely, to track this over time, predict future behaviors and develop strategies to intercede with each customer to sell when each is most ready to buy. What has been the annual purchase volume of this customer from *all* companies in your industry each year? What have been the purchases of this customer with *your* company?

- An ability to project expenditures and replacement rates of each customer, based upon the demonstrated behavior of each individual or business.

- A reasonable assessment of the customer's purchasing lifetime. This could include consideration of issues such as the lifetime of the company itself, the longevity of the company's purchase processes or other factors.

- An understanding of the profitability of the customer, for all the products and services they buy from your firm. How much did this company contribute financially to your organization last year?

- In industries where prices and costs could be subject to significant change, the firm will also need to be able to project prices and costs forward over the effective lifetime of the customer. Most industries are not subject to such definitive planning so it may be better to consider projections in constant dollars, based on the current year, with some judgmental overlay as to margin trends, industry competitiveness, dealer industry structure, competitive position and other factors.

- If working in inflated dollars, the firm will need to apply an average weighted cost of capital, or the hurdle rates of return employed for capital purchases, to discount the profitability of the financial flows to the present.

Information Technology Support

This is the lifetime value of the customer. Making this calculation for a single company is challenging and repeating this for many customers can be overwhelming, without the support of the Information Technology (IT) department, as appropriate. For example, it is likely that IT can advise the average lifetime that accounts have been active with your firm and their total profitability. At this stage, account profitability may exclude all the costs of service, warehousing, returns, special orders, repairs, installation, training and other costs that may be unique to each customer. It may also be appropriate to work with IT to identify the key determinants of lifetime value, such as the absolute size of the account, the account's growth rate, ownership, culture and the market positioning of its products in order to determine which accounts have the highest projected lifetime values.

Where an understanding of individual customers cannot yet be feasibly obtained, the company can still address its customer base as though it knows a great deal about each individual. This requires that the firm run statistical packages on the data set of customer purchases, looking for meaningful characteristics by which customers can be segmented, based on their *demonstrated behaviors* such as purchasing patterns. This is in contrast with the more traditional approaches to market segmentation such as demography (age, income, education, etc.), or psychographics (lifestyles and attitudes).

Behavioral segmentation, based on actual purchase behavior, can enable a clearer view of the customer categories.[18] For example, customers can be categorized into classes according to the three dimensions often applied, based on an assessment of the recency of the last purchase, the frequency with which customers buy and the amount they spend, the so-called RFM measures. However, this approach lacks information such as the costs of the product or service and other costs associated with making the sale and serving customers (direct costs, such as the costs of supporting the customers on-line, repairs, restocking, etc.). The lifetime value of customers would then be calculated according to the average annual value of customers in the category within which each falls, the projected lifetime of the customers as purchasers and the projected changes in their purchasing volume over time.

Approaches

If employing statistics to work on a database of customers, the Relationship Marketer could adopt the following approaches:

- Define what a "customer" means. Is this someone who has bought from your firm this year, this month or ever? Is this someone who buys a lot from the company, or will any amount do? Is this someone who buys willingly from the company, or because they have limited options? Is this someone who buys often? Think in terms of a continuum of relationship intensity which serves to bond your company with your customers. At the one end of the continuum, you have the non-customer, and at the other end is the patron who loves you for what you are. In a sense, the bonding continuum can be compared with the evolution of a marriage, from the "I hardly know you" stage, to the "I have some interest," to "crush," "casual dating," "serious dating," "newly-weds," and then "long-term marriage." Defining

---

[18] I prefer the term customer categories to describe segments based on behaviors rather than market segments because segments can be determined based on objectively measurable factors before any purchases take place, such as the age and education of the buyers, while customer categorization based on behaviors may have to await actual purchase behavior, before customers can be grouped in a process of analyzing the data after the purchase.

the customer in terms of a bonding continuum of progressively escalating relationship intensity is described in the next section.

- Group each category of customers into clusters according to the criteria by which you have defined a customer.

- However you have classified your customers, assess the sales volume they represent to your firm and, ideally, the profits or contribution each cluster provides.

- Assess the average number of months (or years, if your clientele are very loyal) each cluster has been doing business with your firm and weight the total sales of each cluster by the number of months.

- Add the weighted totals for the clusters and divide by the total number of people in all the clusters.

- Multiply this number by the average monthly sales to arrive at the lifetime sales to be derived from the customer base. To arrive at lifetime value, you should conduct the above calculation using contribution to overhead figures instead of sales numbers, which is a more difficult challenge for many firms as they typically do not have these numbers.

⸺

This brief discussion introduced the reader to the calculation of lifetime value of a customer. Opportunities remain in most firms to introduce similar ideas and use them as a basis for understanding, investment in strategic capabilities and the framing and implementation of customer-level strategies. Ford may know how to retain a customer, but without the necessary investment in the technologies that engage each customer and which allow customer knowledge and insight to be derived, Ford will not be able to fully benefit from the customer strategy. By conducting a granular analysis of the value of each customer, Ford can implement customer-appropriate strategies and tactics to advance the relationship, helping customers into the right car at the right time. Many companies lack the awareness, technology and other capabilities to bond more intensely with each customer at present yet doing so can offer enormous opportunity. We discuss customer bonding in the next chapter.

CHAPTER FOUR

Customer Bonding

Out where the handclasp's a little stronger,
Out where the smile dwells a little longer,
That's where the West begins.
Arthur Chapman

This chapter considers the ways in which companies and customers bond. It starts by noting that customers differ in their importance to the company and that this importance is typically a function of the nature and extent of bonding. The way a company chooses to bond with its customers can affect a great deal about its strategies and capabilities — which ones they put in place and how they align them with customers. The chapter concludes with a review of alternative approaches to bonding.

A Customer Is Not a Customer

The word customer is used even for the most loyal purchaser — the individual or organization in whose mind your company has no competition. Surely these and other categories merit different terminology — and different treatment to reflect the differences in value each represents. The Inuit have many words for snow, geared to reflecting different features of this most important dimension of their environment. As important as snow may be to the Inuit, the importance of the customer to the enterprise is at least as great. Curiously, businesses have but a single word for customer, no matter if she is a disgruntled shopper, someone who buys often and pays more for premium goods and service or is a cherry-picker, buying infrequently or only low-priced product or items on sale.

In the following section, purchasers are grouped according to their demonstrated behaviors into six categories, each differentiated from the next by both the increasing share of business and "share of mind" derived from each. Share of business refers to your proportion of the customer's total expenditures on goods and services for which you might be eligible. Share of mind means the extent to which your company enjoys favorable repeat purchase intentions and a perception that momentum favors your firm in your industry. Customers' purchasing and other behaviors link to the share of mind your firm enjoys. Although share of business and share of mind are challenging to measure at the customer level, the firm should undertake such a measurement, at the very least, with its best customers to help understand the current state of bonding. By understanding the current situation, the Relationship Marketer can set objectives to improve the intensity and extent of this bonding, ideally in a process of collaboration with the customer. The word customer is reserved for the buyers as a whole and is the total audience from which the company and its competitors derive their business. All the subsequently mentioned categories are subsets of the term customer, as described in Figure 12 on page 102. Each category of buyer is discussed below, according to the nature of the bonding of the customer with the company. Bonding is discussed from the lowest to progressively higher levels.

Categories of Customer Bonding

Prospects

Prospects are those customers drawn from the general population whose profiles match that of your desired audience. If you consider the recency, frequency and expenditure value of current customers with your firm and the costs of serving them, you can identify the kinds of customers that appear, on the face of it, to offer interesting potential as a relevant fit with the focus, capabilities and products and services of your firm.

Testers

Testers are prospects who have become aware of your company and its offer and have begun to explore the extent to which you are relevant to them, perhaps with initial trial purchases. Based on their satisfaction with this experience, they will wish to gauge the potential to establish a more significant flow of business to your company.

Shoppers

Shoppers are testers who are satisfied with their initial experience and have begun to do business with your firm, but not as a matter of course. They likely continue to do business with their current supplier, but are interested enough in your offer that they consider your firm an appropriate second source or alternative in the event that their main vendor fails to satisfy them in some dimension.

Accounts

Satisfied with the period during which your company has been catering to their needs, the shoppers standardize key aspects of their procurement and purchasing processes to include your firm as a major supplier for their needs. As a result, these types of customers become what is termed as accounts. By this stage, you have earned the accounts' business, but not yet their full trust. As a result, they retain alternative sources to the business they direct to you. Accounts can still switch to your competitors or slide back in the bonding continuum to shoppers or even stop buying from your firm entirely. And they do not feel a need to give reasons for the change. You remain in a state of being constantly under evaluation and trial. Even small, missteps can create the dissatisfaction that can erode the trust relationship.

Patrons

Patrons are longer-term accounts whose trust you now have, and who have adopted your processes and values as their own. They will seek to integrate your company not only in their procurement/purchasing processes, but also in other key strategic components of the business. For the business-to-business sector, this could include design and development, for example. In so doing, the business-to-business customers do more than give your firm a progressively higher share of their business. The high share of mind you enjoy leads to a higher share of their future business. As your future and theirs become interlinked, your mutual commitment will grow and lead to the next step in the continuum. In the consumer market, patrons will consider buying from your firm as a matter of course, with little or no consideration of competitors, expecting that this time the result will be the same happy outcome it has previously been.

Advocates

With advocates, your company enjoys patrons who are so committed to your firm that only a major violation of trust would erode this goodwill. You have virtually their entire attention in this product or

FIGURE 12: The Bonding Staircase — Customers' Relationship Intensity and the Purchase Process

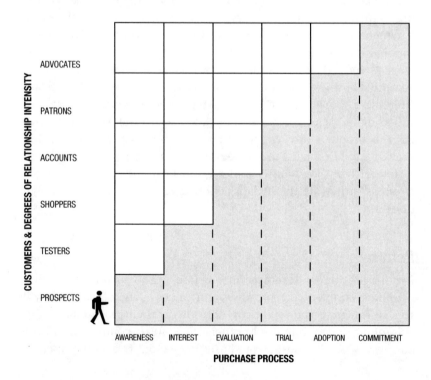

service category. An advocate will stand up for your firm and tell others of your wonders. They will make business referrals. They will be "good complainers," inviting you to get better without being negative in their guidance. The Saturn division of General Motors has succeeded in bonding with customers at this level. Saturn hosted an event to invite owners to come to the factory where their cars were built. Thousands enjoyed a rain-soaked weekend in a muddy Kentucky field, without complaint. When a Saturn owner's t-shirt invites people to ask her about her happy ownership experience, Saturn can claim customer bonding that transcends the relationship most people have with many other car firms.

Bonding Staircase Issues

Three issues are suggested by Figure 12:

1. Progress along the relationship continuum can occur in either direction. Trust, like antipathy, is cumulative, but it is more difficult to build and easier to erode. Thus it is harder to progress up the hierarchy of customers than it is to fall down or off the staircase. The main reason most retrogression occurs is as a result of ineffective communication processes and style between the organization and its customers. An appropriately sensitive company, with scripted responses and processes that effectively manage key areas of potential discord, will more likely preserve gains on the bonding continuum and even accelerate progress. Unhappy customers whose complaints are recognized and remedied, for example, tend to be happier than others at the same level of bonding, and they communicate their happiness, shifting them towards the advocate.

2. Advancement along the continuum must be won one step at a time. As in any courtship, it is unlikely that the heart of the intended can be earned forever in a single encounter. (If they were, it would be one amazing encounter!) While heroic efforts help, it is more important to know in which level each customer is in your relationship continuum and to have objectives for customers at each level of bonding. Then processes can be defined and plans built to achieve the objectives. This is discussed in more detail in the following chapter.

3. The purchase process and the end-state of the customer category are closely linked. Prospects who have limited awareness of the firm and its relevance are unlikely to become shoppers until awareness increases. Thus, elevating levels of company or product-service awareness may be an important issue for shifting customers from prospects to shoppers, but may play no role in moving the customer from patron to advocate. Figure 12 describes the linkages between the intensity of customers' relationships with the firm and the purchase process through which they proceed as they increase their share of business and share of mind with the firm.

The Shape of the Customer Profile

In the bonding staircase presented in Figure 12, consider the number of customers your company has at each level and the lifetime value[19] you derive at every level of the staircase, and in aggregate. The shape of this profile will not only be descriptive of your relationship base, but will also be prescriptive regarding relevant actions. Consider situations in which a company has many prospects with a potentially high lifetime value from this group, but progressively fewer customers and less lifetime value at each higher level in the continuum. At the other end of the spectrum, consider a firm with many, intensely bonded customers and high levels of lifetime value, but few prospects. In Figure 13, these cases are presented as A and C respectively, with B being a firm with similar numbers of customers and lifetime value at each level.

The descriptive assessment made by charting the relationship intensity with the customer base can now proceed to considering how to advance bonding according to the shape of the profile. In Case A, the company should focus resources on creating accounts, patrons and advocates. In Case B, the firm may have a more balanced portfolio and, in a more even allocation of resources, could concentrate on progressing customers along the continuum. In Case C, the firm either needs to attract and convert prospects or, in an industry where they already deal with most customers, they have achieved a desirable balance, and should focus more on customer retention and new value creation for mutual advantage.

---

[19] If lifetime value calculations cannot be performed with the currently available information, use revenue or a contribution assessment without the relationship component.

FIGURE 13: Lifetime Value for Each Customer Bonding Level

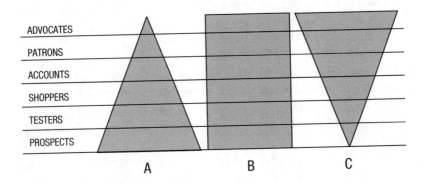

ADVOCATES
PATRONS
ACCOUNTS
SHOPPERS
TESTERS
PROSPECTS

A   B   C

Levels of Customer Bonding

One approach to maximizing the value of current customers is to encourage the migration of current customers up the value staircase, from relatively low lifetime value contributors to those who create higher value. This requires that companies assess the key dimensions by which they bond with their customers and seek to enhance the main drivers of bonding. The firm seeking to enhance customer bonding should ask two main questions: "What alternative approaches might be adopted to bond with customers?" and "Of these, which type of bonding do we want to intensify?" Doing so successfully, can not only lead to positive reasons for the customer to wish to remain bonded with the supplier, it can raise the real and perceived risks and costs of switching to alternative vendors.

There are seven main levels or ways a company can bond with its customers:

1. Structural Bonding
2. Brand Equity Bonding
3. Attitudinal Bonding
4. Personal Bonding
5. Information and Control Bonding
6. Value Bonding
7. Zero Option Bonding

We discuss each next.

1. Structural Bonding

In structural bonding, the customer and the company are operationally and structurally linked or integrated, often employing technology to facilitate the interaction. For example, the customer that is able to query the inventory in a supplier's warehouse or purchase online is more likely to be bonded to the company than the customer easily able to switch suppliers. Often familiarity with the technology and/or its user interface can present a barrier to switching.

Structural bonding may be intensified when the company has aligned its technologies, people and business processes with customers, and even integrated them with the customer in a manner that raises switching costs, time, knowledge or risk. When American Hospital Systems put a computer on the desk of a purchasing agent in every health care institution in America and the purchasers became knowledgeable about the AHS system, the likelihood of them buying from anyone else became remote. In fact, Baxter Corporation bought AHS to help ensure the successful sale of its products to health-care institutions using the AHS front-line system.

Structural bonding needs strategic alignment to bring about and accelerate the integration of organizational capabilities. Companies that plan together, make money together.

Proactive and joint customer-supplier innovation has the potential to further deepen structural bonding. Amcan, a castings company supplying the auto industry mentioned earlier, independently advances ideas for auto companies to consider, which helps increase their win ratio for these ideas and other opportunities. For example, the firm recently showed a car company how to take weight out of their product by combining a number of forged engine parts into a single light-weight casting. The car company adopted their suggestions so Amcan is now in a position to supply many thousands of such castings over the model life of the vehicle.

2. Brand Equity Bonding

Brand equity bonding includes the value a customer derives by relating to the product directly, both the brand's functional attributes and the emotional or other non-functional attributes captured in the brand. For example, some customers may relate to an auto brand such as Mercedes Benz because of the fine performance, fit and finish of the car. Others may derive emotional benefits such as a feeling of enhanced prestige, power or self-esteem by owning such a vehicle. Mercedes will have paid attention to enhancing the value of the brand in the minds of their customers by focusing on both these dimensions.

A number of companies enjoy enormous brand equity. Apple Computer's users, for example, embrace their Macs as though a conspiracy exists to separate them from their virtual brain. Bonded so tightly are Mac users to Apple that even hackers used to stealing software feel it their moral duty to pay for the new Apple operating systems. Using a Mac is much more than using an electronic appliance. For the Mac devotee, Apple is about supremacy of the individual. It is about being different in a world of conformity. Apple is religion.

Harley Davidson, for some of the same as well as different reasons, enjoys the benefits of customers bonding at both levels of function and emotion. Buyers think Harleys are well-made machines, but they are quite happy to tinker with their bikes should they need maintenance. Harley owners are no longer just from bike gangs, the result of a long-term marketing commitment by Harley to broaden the appeal. Harley owners are in love with the brand and the free-spirited individual experience of ownership, all of which Harley fosters with t-shirts, leather jackets and HOGs — Harley Owner Groups.

But perhaps the most extreme example of a narrow customer profile bonding with the brand is the experience of Porsche. The German sports car company has found that customers who buy a Porsche have always owned one — in their minds, at least. Even first time buyers have always imagined themselves in a Porsche.

3. Attitudinal Bonding

Attitudinal bonding occurs when customers bond with the company because of its professionalism, skills, customer focus, values, culture and responsiveness. Customers of banks and other services often bond at this level. One of the reasons they do is that their company's culture may focus more on the customer than some of their competitors. Contrast the cultures of Wal-Mart and Kmart and you could have one explanation for the faster growth of the former.

4. Personal Bonding

Personal bonding is where customers like to work with specific people and will do so regardless of the company with which they work.

Consumers prefer certain hairdressers, travel agents, consultants or accountants. Businesses bond with some reps regardless of the companies they represent, paying more attention to the individual who is at the front-line in creating business value than the organization behind the individual.

Personal bonding occurs at multiple levels in the organization, from the most senior executives and the board interacting with their counterparts in a customer's organization, to the payables and receivables personnel and processes working together. Personal bonding can represent a major barrier to switching because people buy from people they like, all else being equal, and from people in a company that has been endorsed by senior executives. A "politically sanctioned" supplier is likely to do better than one that operates at more junior levels in the company, again, all else being equal.

5. Information and Control Bonding

Information and control bonding is where customers benefit from the reporting and other information systems that can help them with operational and financial management. For example, companies such as UPS and Fedex have invested heavily in elaborate "track and trace systems" for their parcels. Customers can learn where a parcel is at any time, which helps reduce the customers' perceived risk of the parcel going astray. American Express provides detailed reporting tailored to the needs of customers for expense tracking and other purposes such as taxation.

6. Value Bonding

Value bonding occurs when customers repeatedly derive the value they seek from their suppliers, and have every reason to believe that they will continue to receive this value over an extended time horizon. Customer loyalty programs, such as those that provide consumers with points or rebates, fall into this category because they offer additional financial and in-kind incentives to continue buying from the supplier.

Value bonding can occur as a result of the supplier being obsessed with quality and/or being guided by pricing according to the value the customer wants to obtain. Value bonding can also occur according to the focus of the vendor on mass customization, which has the potential to create unique value for individual customers not available elsewhere. For example, incorporating technology for mass customization of consumer financial services, a financial institution has the potential to engage you at the counter or automated teller machine and add value to your transactions, perhaps recommending alternatives better suited to your requirements. Extra cash in a savings account, why not put that in a term instrument? Peaks in your cash balances for just a few days at a time? Would you like information to secure higher yields from this short-term money?

7. Zero Option Bonding

Zero option bonding refers to the situation in which companies may have little choice but to bond. Their choices may be limited by the regulatory environment, such as for mail and electricity.[20] And their choices will obviously be limited or non-existent for services reserved for the Federal, State or local governments, such as social services, taxation and defense, for that matter!

The zero option can also apply where suppliers have made a financial investment in their customers, making the supplier preferred under all but the most extreme situations of poor performance or insufficient product line. This is certainly one way for companies heavily dependent on a few customers to secure their future. In the hotly contested Canadian photographic retail film industry, where Fuji and Kodak are locked in intense competition, Fuji acquired one of the largest volume retail camera and film chains, potentially helping that firm to maintain its strength in this important channel.

In some industries, customers may wish to change suppliers but may not do so because of the high costs or perceived risks of switching. Structural bonding may have increased these costs and risks, but the costs of switching can be materially increased if customers really have no choice but to remain with the supplier. For example, specialized on-line transaction processing software used in industries such hotels, retail, libraries and financial services, once successfully installed and accepted by the users, are usually not rapidly replaced

---

20 Obviously technology is creating some options for mail and deregulation of the electricity industry can offer choice to customers, but these industries have lagged regulatory change elsewhere, such as in telephony, financial services, airlines and transportation.

with competitors' systems. The costs and risks of conversion are very high, so customers often wait until the reasons for switching far outweigh what will likely be a challenging conversion. Recognizing this, some software companies are building their businesses rapidly and profitably by acquiring firms with large customer bases and then earning out their investment quickly by cutting costs associated with marketing, support and new software releases, rather than investing for growth and in customer relationships. They do this to transfer value from customers, employees and suppliers to shareholders.

Companies practicing this type of bonding still follow some of the principles of Relationship Marketing to keep the customer as long as possible to extend and increase their return on the initial investment. These acquirers also pay attention to relationships with software companies with large customer bases, hopefully leading to the acquisition of these companies in future. While detractors of this type of business practice maintain it is not sustainable, there are examples of firms that are rewarding shareholders mightily by pursuing this strategy. They will be able to do so as long as they can acquire customers faster than the old ones migrate to competitors.

FIGURE 14: Seven Levels of Customer Bonding

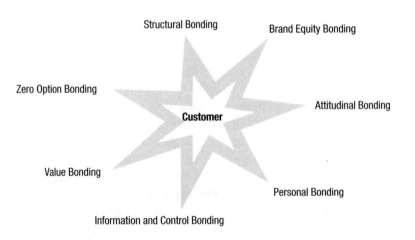

ော

In general, the challenge for the marketer and for management is to establish which of these types of relationships are to be advanced, and with which customers. Each customer will usually help the supplier identify how best to focus its relationship development. If the company decides to pursue more than one type with each customer, as may be possible and even desirable, the firm should prioritize and sequence the order in which it will advance each type of relationship to avoid complexity in an already complicated situation.

Bonding between an organization and a consumer or end-user can be different than bonding between two organizations. Consumers typically do not have rigorous policies and procedures, nor do they make explicit the processes by which they buy. Bonding becomes very much a state of mind rather than the more formal formation and maintenance of a relationship which organizations deploy with other businesses.

Next, we will discuss the differences between consumer and business Relationship Marketing.

CHAPTER FIVE

Consumer Versus Business Relationships

I hear it in the deep heart's core.
William Butler Yeats

The term "Relationship Marketing" is widely used within a company and in the media, but Relationship Marketing differs markedly according to the business issues the company faces, its mix of customers, its chosen strategies and even, as will be discussed in this chapter, according to the industry the company is in. In particular, Relationship Marketing is different if the firm markets business-to-business. Where end-user demand is concentrated among fewer customers than is the case for consumer markets, these business customers assume particular importance to a supplier.

As customers, consumers like you and I differ fundamentally from businesses, so relationships formed with consumers differ from those with businesses, too. Consumer markets comprise individual buyers each of whom must be won and kept, but the firm may survive and prosper even if it does not succeed in winning every customer it would like. For example, while a newspaper may be eager to develop and maintain a relationship with each of its readers, it would probably survive even if some of them stopped reading. However, the company that provides the newspaper with newsprint depends heavily on the business of each of their customers, particularly the larger papers. In some cases, the defection of a single major customer could damage the company beyond repair.

Had this book been written just a few years ago, it would have been clear that any relationship formed between businesses would remain quite different than a relationship with consumers. But now technology has the potential to make a consumer appear to an organization as though each were a business customer — just a much smaller one than many companies have typically served directly.

This chapter explores selected differences between relationships formed and maintained with consumers and businesses and the implications for the marketer building these relationships. For businesses, the reader may think of and substitute other concentrations of market demand, including governments (federal, state, local), institutions (schools, hospitals or prisons), industrial manufacturers and service providers (financial institutions, advertising agencies and accounting firms).

Consumer Versus Business-to-Business Market Places

Consumer market places differ from business-to-business in many dimensions, including:

- Goods and Services
- Market Structure
- Distribution Channels
- Decision-Making Criteria
- Decision-Making Process
- Buyer-Seller Relationship
- Reciprocity
- Mutual Value Creation
- One-Way Relationships
- Brand Equity

Each of these issues is discussed next.

Goods and Services

Consumer goods and services may be classified according to their use as convenience, shopping and specialty. Convenience goods or services are typically priced at levels many consumers consider to be low and for which consumers are willing to expend limited effort in the acquisition process. A newspaper is a good example of such a product. Specialty goods are those for which consumers pay a great deal and for which they are prepared to expend considerable time and effort to make the right selection decision. A house, car and the services of a highly regarded criminal lawyer fall into this category. Shopping goods fall somewhere in between convenience and specialty. The consumer pays enough to warrant some expenditure of time and effort in the selection decision, and is prepared to travel a modest distance to make the purchase. Most clothing and financial services can be described in this way. The value a consumer derives from each type of good or service differs. Convenience goods have short consumption time horizons — the value sought is typically rapidly realized. A newspaper is read, a chocolate bar is consumed, the cat has its fill of canned cat food.

Specialty goods have much longer horizons over which the consumer derives her utility. When the consumer makes such a purchase, she initiates a psychological contract with the purchaser that says, in effect, "I will give you my money now and will consume this product or service over a fairly long time. By giving you this money, I am also providing you with my good faith and trust. If your product or service fails to meet my expectations over the consumption horizon I feel is reasonable for this good, you will be in default of my trust. And you will pay a price for that. Perhaps you will incur higher costs satisfying me, by listening to me, fixing the problems, providing me with replacement or loaner units and otherwise bearing the costs of poor quality. And I may tell my friends about the experience. And I may never give you my trust again, even if you do things much, much better."

The value the Relationship Marketer of convenience goods seeks to create together with the consumer may be quite different than the value developed for specialty goods. Taking the case of a newspaper, a Relationship Marketer may provide the consumer with the ability to assemble the news they want rather than the news the paper chooses to provide. Technology could be a key component of mass-customizing news at an affordable cost. For a specialty good, the Relationship Marketer will need to have a complex series of initiatives that create the more enduring value the consumer seeks. For example, the Buick division of GM must have people, processes, customer knowledge and technologies that converse with and involve the customer before, when and after they buy, and throughout their ownership experience. This complexity is similar to the relationships required by some businesses and their suppliers than it is for other business-to-consumer products and services.

Business-to-business products and services may be categorized as follows:

- Process infrastructure and installations that enable the business processes of the company, such as computers, networks and production equipment.

- Accessory equipment which are ancillary to the main business of the company, such as fire extinguishers, intrusion alarms and exit signs.

- Component parts and subassemblies which are integrated into the higher value offering, such as spark plugs used in a car engine and automotive interior subassemblies incorporated in the vehicle.

- Process materials that cannot be identified as parts and are inputs to the production process. Products such as plastics and resins extruded in the fabrication of plastic toys and water pipes are examples.

- Raw materials that are constituent components transformed in the process of production, such as ingredients for pharmaceuticals and chemicals.

- Consumables, such as the maintenance, repair and overhaul supplies used in production operations to ensure the continued operation of the plant, and packaging.

- Services supplied to businesses, including environmental management and accounting services.

These product and service categories typically have different buyers within a company and will be bought for different reasons, in varying amounts and frequency. The relationship expectations of each of the product categories would also be expected to vary according to factors such as the strategic importance of the product or service category, the substitutability of the vendors and the level of expenditures that are made. However, there are few products or services that cannot be made more strategic and those firms competing on product or service functionality and price, while selling to the purchasing managers, may well be missing important opportunities to bond, find new business and become more relevant to their customers. With relevance, comes more business and higher margins. Consider the company providing lawn maintenance services. Are they selling closely cropped, well-manicured lawns for an annual maintenance fee, or are they enhancing the personality of the firm in its physical environment. If the latter, perhaps they could also be maintaining other components of the exterior of the building, providing landscaping, painting, sign maintenance, window cleaning, snow removal, parking-lot maintenance and other services. As their offer becomes more complex, so too does the need for effective relationship management.

Market Structure

Business-to-business markets tend to have more concentrated end-user demand than do consumer markets. Consider the case of detergents. When sold into industrial markets, specialized detergents may be required in the edible oils industry, for example, where the oil which goes to make up margarine can make the floor of processing plants very slippery. Detergents to clean away the muck must have special characteristics to cut through the grease. These characteristics will differ markedly from the detergents needed for other manufacturing applications. The users of edible oils can be readily identified, and each will be an important potential customer for the purpose specific detergent. Consumers, on the other hand, are numerous, and the business of one specific customer will not make or break the supplier. This is not to say that each customer is unimportant, just that the business of specific industrial or commercial accounts can be more important to a supplier dependent on such demand.

Business-to-business markets can also be more concentrated geographically than consumer markets. Vendors of printed circuit boards are likely to find many major customers for their products within driving distance of Houston, Boston and Palo Alto, for example, and suppliers to the financial services industry will need focus in New York and San Francisco. Looking for customers for consumer electronics and financial services? They are everywhere, perhaps in greater abundance in some areas than others, but with more fragmented demand than for businesses.

Concentration of end-user demand offers more opportunity to identify and research business-to-business customers in depth. Their needs and those of their customers can be explored. The strategies of their competitors can be examined. And a supplier can afford to make the investment to develop the relationship, because the anticipated pay-off from such an investment can be very significant.

Technology can help vendors understand their customers in consumer markets, but the technology will need more sophistication and modeling than in business-to-business markets to have the same yield. Companies cannot invest as much time and money to understand each consumer in a fragmented market as they do for more concentrated industrial, commercial, institutional or government market places.

Distribution Channels

Business-to-business market places typically have had shorter distribution channels than consumer markets. Often, business-to-business companies serve major or national accounts directly, smaller ones through distribution channel intermediaries, and medium-sized firms through some combination or one or the other. Companies marketing to consumers often go through multiple layers. In the case of consumer electronics and computers, it is not uncommon for manufacturers to access the consumer market directly to high volume retailers and chain stores and through distributors to smaller retailers.

It has not been common for consumers to buy directly from their suppliers — until now. With the advent of the Internet, and electronic commerce more generally, technology has the potential to remove levels in the distribution channel and offer consumers the chance to buy directly from their suppliers.

Distribution channel intermediaries will not go away any time soon, but their growth may be more limited if they are not finding ways to use technology to bond with customers and use the vendors' solutions to help them do so. Michelin distributors use the tire manufacturer's dial-up network to obtain information about inventory and answer their questions about tires, such as what tire is needed for a specific car. This helps the installers provide faster and better service to their customers, while Michelin benefits from the efficiency with which orders are handled and the way they are perceived by their dealers.[21]

Decision-Making Criteria

There are four types of buying situations according to whether the purchase is made for the first time, a straight rebuy — when the product or service is routinely bought again, a modified rebuy — when there is some change to the purchase requirement, or a new task situation — when the product or service is being bought for a different application. For all of these situations, businesses often buy, or say they buy, for reasons that are rational and based in the economics of the offer and strategic rationale, such as improving the customer's market positioning.

Consumers buy and buy again for many reasons, including criteria which are not derived from rational economic arguments. Both businesses and consumers want to manage risk, but in the case of businesses, the financial health of the business — near and long term — and the career of the buyer are important considerations. For years, IBM benefited from the phrase which had wide currency in the business community, that "no one ever got fired for buying IBM." Xerox, too, may have benefited from purchase behavior that viewed Xerox as a natural selection for photocopying requirements in large businesses.

Even though business managers may talk in terms of rational-economic and strategic considerations, there are emotional and less rational issues at work in some purchase situations. Consider the customer of a vertical market software company that operates as though it could care less about the individual customer, constantly cutting resources from software support and new product development, for example. Why would customers continue to deal with them? For some, the software is strategic to the business and cannot be rapidly dispensed with. In addition, users have become familiar with the look and feel of the user interface and its functionality. And technical people have developed the knowledge they need to keep the

---

[21] Nick Wreden, "Good Deal for Michelin Dealers," *Information Week*, October 20, 1997, p. 99.

system up. So, even in the face of better suppliers, the customer comes back for the new release and for software support and maintenance.

More generally, business-to-business purchase criteria may be categorized as follows:

- Help the company conceive and adopt products, services and processes that will add value to internal and external customers of the company, lowering costs, improving quality and otherwise helping the company to improve its customer performance and competitive position.

- Produce products of consistently high quality and be in a position to demonstrate assurance of that quality, such as statistical process control and adoption of, and conformance with, ISO 9000 standards.

- Ensure that products conform with the customer's expectations and specifications.

- Provide the products to customers when, how and in the volume required, appropriately tagged, stacked, racked and packaged.

- Consistent with the product specifications and ancillary requirements for service and support, for example, ensure that the initial, lifetime and value-in-use prices are the lowest among competing vendors.

- Support the products with services, helping to improve the value of the products in use, such as by providing training, vendor installation and maintenance, diagnosis guided by technology and customer support.

- Be easy to do business with.

- Keep internal customers happy.

- Demonstrate professionalism, caring, responsiveness and attention, helping the company to manage difficult or unexpected situations.

On the other hand, decision-making criteria for consumers may vary according to many factors, including issues associated with the product category as a whole, the consumer's values and the consumers' perceptions that a given brand may be readily substituted for another. Figure 15 views the risks of consumer decision making in respect of product and brand dimensions.

FIGURE 15: Consumer Decision-Making Perceptions: Product Versus Brand

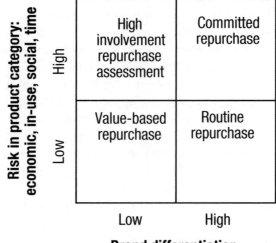

Every time a consumer buys a good, he is exposed to many types of risk. Understanding these risks helps explain some of the attitudes that drive consumer behaviors, with examples of the way some consumers sometimes see each risk category at an articulated or less conscious level:

- financial exposure: "I might waste my money";
- social risk — belonging (fit in): "my friends might ridicule me";
- social risk — elevated standing within reference group (stand out): "my friends may not see this to be much better than what they use, and so my own standing in the group may not be enhanced";
- risk in use: "the product may not perform as I expected";
- self-worth risk: "I am a person who does things right and everything I buy reflects this view of myself and this product may not be up to my personal standard of perfection"; and
- time risk: "I may waste time assembling this and returning it if I cannot get it to work."

When consumers view different goods, they may see some brands to be substitutes and others to stand alone. In the extreme, brands can be seen to be unique. Some gangs, for example, define their membership in part according to the sneakers they wear. Wearing Nike in an Adidas neighborhood could substantially elevate one's risk!

Seen from this perspective, consumers will be most committed to repurchasing differentiated brands where they consider the product categories as high risk. Consumers would be prepared to expend significant time and effort to facilitate such a purchase, going to unusual lengths to camp out for an opportunity to buy a Cabbage Patch doll, for example. Why? Because the opportunity to simultaneously fit in and stand out within reference groups by making this highly differentiated purchase is enormous. A Cabbage Patch doll is not about quietly giving little Jane the thrill of a lifetime. It is all about telling friends that you gave little Jane the thrill of a lifetime, and that, by going to unusual lengths to make the purchase — such as lining up for hours before the store opens and then stampeding for the display without being trampled underfoot — you are a more committed parent than are they. Hmm.

Consumers who have found that purchases have not exposed them to risk on prior purchase occasions of a brand they consider differentiated, and whose perceptions have been reinforced, are likely to seek out a product and routinely repurchase it. But they could be prone to substitution. No Crest on the shelf? I'll take Colgate. One will probably protect my teeth as well as the other.

Low-risk decisions for brands that are seen as substitutes leads to purchases based on criteria such as price and convenience. No Brand A skim milk on the shelf? I'll take Brand B. They are both skimmed and who would know the difference?

High-risk purchase decisions within a product category where brands are not essentially differentiated can have consumers seeking information from dealers and advertising, weighing prior purchase decisions, evaluating the views of peers and generally taking stock of the category as a whole. Golf clubs are seen by many men as a high-risk purchase. Go out with a poor choice, and every bad shot will be the problem of the clubs. And this risk is only compounded if someone in the foursome chuckles at the brand selection you made. Among the available brands, though, there is fleeting differentiation. Fads wax and wane. How does one make a decision on a brand that will not be subject to such risk? Information.

Decision-Making Process

Businesses decision making comprises many different decision makers for most product categories, each playing different roles in a process that can be quite complex and may differ substantially from firm to firm. The decision-making unit often comprises one or more of:

- an initiator who recommends that a purchase be made;
- influencers, who motivate the purchase decision, guide the process and have input on key decision dimensions, such as the criteria for the decision and the specific selection;
- a sponsor, who takes up the view of the initiator and backs the recommendation;
- an approver, usually a person in higher authority than the other decision makers, who validates the purchase recommendation; and
- a purchaser, who actually makes the purchase.

To demonstrate the complexity of business-to-business purchase decision-making processes, consider a company that makes margarine, such as Fleischmann's, in different shapes and sizes. Margarine is deposited in single servings within a small molded tray, after which foil is cut to fit (called registration), placed on the top of the plastic and heat sealed. In our case, they have experienced problems in the packaging of margarine in these small-portion sizes. The foil that is placed over the plastic cannot be accurately cut, so there is much variation in the placement of their logo, brand and product information from tub to tub. The result is considerable product loss in scrap and rework. The current equipment supplier has indicated that there is nothing they can do to correct the situation.

An equipment company wanting to supply margarine manufacturing machinery identifies the issue and assures the plant manager that their machine can significantly reduce waste. The plant manager investigates the new machine and has his plant engineer render an opinion. After having a pilot run with the company's own foil, they see that registration is accurate and all other aspects of the margarine production are satisfactory. Both then agree the supplier has a good machine that would offer improved foil registration and less waste, but the saving cannot offset the capital equipment cost, even after selling the existing equipment, within the financial guidelines for payback, as stipulated by the company. They need marketing's concurrence and support to position the equipment not only as needed for production improvement but also for market gains because portion packs help "seed" the market with sample sizes and encourage competitive brand switching to the higher volume products. The improved packaging would build the brand position.

With marketing's agreement and the tacit say-so of the VP, manufacturing and VP, sales, the plant manager initiates the purchase decision and has his staff help with the business case. Plant purchasing considers available equipment alternatives and engages in discussion with the incumbent supplier. The plant engineer compares performance and price, among other criteria, the plant superintendent validates operational feasibility and the plant accountant develops the necessary metrics. Corporate engineering and VP, manufacturing formally confirm the plant level assessment and marketing lends their support to the decision. The accounting manager in corporate finance reviews the business case and financials for compliance with capital asset procurement processes, budget availability and strategic fit, and the VP, finance signs off. Just before the purchase order is issued by purchasing, the plant superintendent has an idea, prompted by the suggestion of the incumbent equipment supplier, who is getting nervous about losing this account. What if the existing foil did not require registration, but was designed to be cut in a more or less random manner. This idea is advanced to the plant manager who thinks it worthy of discussion with marketing. Marketing insists on accurate registration which can only be done with the new machine. After this protracted process, the purchase order is executed.

Contrast this with the purchase decision of a typical consumer. There are four main views that would govern how a consumer would make the purchase decision. On one hand, the consumer could be seen to operate according to a Stimulus-Response model, the theory of instrumental conditioning followed by the behaviorists. According to this model of buying, advertising serves as a stimulus for trial purchases, then the initial purchase is reinforced through satisfaction, and repeat buying results, leading to customer loyalty. On another hand, cognitive researchers believe that consumers go through problem solving when they make their purchase decision, comparing brand attributes in the context of their needs and selection criteria, which leads to favorable attitudes, which in turn drive

FIGURE 16: Consumer Purchase Decision-Making Processes

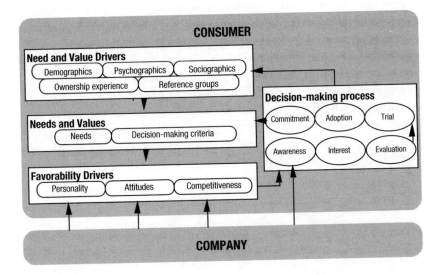

purchase behavior. Cognitive researchers view customer loyalty as a state of mind, with high levels of favorable attitudes being determinants of loyalty, while behaviorists view loyalty in terms of repeat purchase.

A third view comes from social-psychological theorists who believe that making appeals to the group affects individual purchase behavior, and so they look to role models to become opinion leaders for the broader group. They want their customers to want to fit in simultaneously with their peers, stand out from them and know that opinion leaders can help facilitate this. When Nike started signing sports stars to major endorsement contracts, they must have had this view of their audience's involvement with these role models.

Finally, involvement theory suggests that, for product categories which are relatively unimportant to the buyer, consumers can be influenced by using low involvement media, such as TV, with limited information transfer and high levels of repetition. High involvement purchases, as already discussed, require high levels of information transfer, and may thus use high involvement media, such as print.

So how do consumers buy? The model suggested by Figure 16 illustrates one integrated view of the consumer purchase process.

Consumer Needs and Values

According to this model, consumer needs and values are influenced by several factors such as demography, socio-economic and related background elements, psychographics of the consumer, lifestyle considerations, prior experience with the product and company and word-of-mouth influence from peer and reference groups. The consumer needs and values, also called determinants of choice, affect the manner in which the strategic decision set is framed and the perception of alternative offerings in the set. The company may act to improve the favorability with which the customer views the company's brand, such as by having a company and brand:

- personality that accords with the customer's preferred image of the organization and its offerings, in areas such as trust, professionalism, skill, sophistication, technology adoption, flexibility and honesty;

- attitudes that speak to the customer in a manner that the customer sees as friendly, progressive and appreciative of their personal and individual interests; and

- competitiveness that demonstrates superiority over alternative offerings and options.

Of course, achieving high levels of favorability will typically require more than simply communicating effectively, although it will require this, too. It will also require aligning people, process, knowledge and technology to achieve bonding in specific dimensions (value bonding, psychological bonding and infrastructure bonding), as previously discussed. With high levels of awareness and consumer favorability, interest in the company and brand may be expected to build the attitudes necessary to drive desired behaviors.

Consider potential for Relationship Marketing in the case of a sneaker purchase. The baby boom is nearing the end of their peak exercise years. Some individuals in this cohort are stretching out their exercise years, while others have given up on the demanding stuff and are more willing to opt for more sedate activity. Simultaneously, boomers are entering their peak earning years and have the disposable income to shower, a little paradoxically, on the most sophisticated shoes. The needs for shoes may therefore be, for some consumers, helping the athlete maintain a self-image as such, regardless of the extent of actual physical exertion. The determinants of choice may include factors such as leading-edge technology, a perception of heightened ability when using the product, footwear weight and peer group acceptance. The company may seek to build favorability by building a personality umbrella within which the relationship will be nurtured.

The personality may be positioned as high-tech, high-performance, perfectionist, dependable and trustworthy, for example. The firm may emphasize attitudes that engage the customer openly, seeking to build the knowledge base to serve customers as they want to be served, in a considerate manner, respectful of their individual preferences, value-in-use and feet shape and balance. This may lead the company to develop a capability to mass customize footwear to the unique dimensions customers need, perhaps developing an electronic pad onto which the customer steps, allowing personal measurements to be passed to the factory for unique production. In the process of this service provision, and associated training of front-line and other personnel, the company has the potential to demonstrate product advantage and competitive superiority, and reinforce this message with personalized and customized communications to the prospect and committed buyers, learning more about the customers over time as their needs evolve, with each repeat purchase. There could be a price premium to be had by the vendor for working so hard to satisfy unique customer requirements and to cover associated hard and soft costs. Against such competition, would Nike and Adidas really have a chance?

Buyer-Seller Relationship

In business-to-business market places, close personal relationships are commonly formed, more so than for consumer market places. Try playing golf with all your consumers — either your golf score would approach that of Tiger Woods before you scratched the surface of your customer base or someone would complain about your expense account! In business-to-business markets, customers expect to be recognized for their importance and for their suppliers to take steps to bond with them and their organizations. If this means playing golf with the customer, then the supplier should be able to play golf. Interpersonal bonding, comprising a matching of people and process, enabled by the knowledge suppliers have of their customers and the technology to put this knowledge to work, are important components of this bonding.

Consumers, on the other hand, can be more fickle and in some markets may be prone to switching behavior not evident in many businesses. In many instances, consumers form their decisions without direct intervention from the supplier. If they see Colgate and Crest as similar toothpastes, believing that both reduce cavities, then they may be inclined to switch among the two brands according to the pricing of each. If a consumer decides to buy Colgate instead of Crest this time, no salesperson is there to intervene. Consumer purchasing behaviors are simply less personal than business-to-business purchasing, for all but the most significant purchases such as those for consumer durables, such as cars and houses. When you last bought a shirt or a suit, did the salesperson know your size, color and style preferences? If they did, they were either a small scale tailor or a company that has put technology to work.

But, even though technology has the power to put more personal flavor into contact with consumers, the business-to-business environment will remain more personal than the consumer equivalent. The lifetime value of a business-to-business relationship simply exceeds that of most consumers and merits considerable attention by the business-to-business marketer. The opportunity for the consumer marketer is to use technology, process, people and knowledge to focus on the unique needs of individual customers, taking a leaf out of the business-to-business company's business model, and employing similar ideas in the case of consumer markets.

Reciprocity

In business-to-business markets, it is common for firms to extend their business relationships to become customers of one another. For example, our consultancy uses the products and services of our clients, whether they supply computers, computer carrying cases, photocopiers, courier services, or Internet access. Our clients have given their trust to us and we return this honor.

It is not common for such a view to prevail in consumer markets. The supermarket takes my money for the groceries I buy. I do not expect them to volunteer to baby-sit my kids in exchange. Not surprisingly, they have yet to offer to do so.

Mutual Value Creation

Beyond reciprocity, is the matter of continuous mutual value creation. In business-to-business markets, suppliers and customers have the potential to work together to create new products, processes, value chains or even entire businesses and new enterprises, and then to share in the new business value. This may mean opening themselves up in ways that were previously almost heretical, such as by providing suppliers with access to their customers or by sharing proprietary knowledge. Those companies that keep themselves closed will invariably achieve less shareholder value than those that unlock their control and look for new value to create and share. Microsoft and NBC created MSNBC to capture new business value from infotainment from the same consumers both target in their traditional businesses. AT&T also has alliances with many companies across the spectrum of converging digital technologies.

At the same time that Microsoft's share prices have headed skywards, Corel, which bought WordPerfect from Novell in an attempt to challenge Microsoft in the suite market place, has yet to fully appreciate that their software bundles do not need to comprise just the product they develop, and that they do not need to control the total value chain to win against the ferocious competitor Microsoft. Still in the computer industry, Compaq learned that price protection and the cost of inventory in the distribution channel is adding greatly to the cost of their product and the declining margins of their dealers. So they now have moved from a build-to-forecast model whereby computer product is produced and supplied to the channel for onwards sale, to a build-to-order model, where the product is pulled through a demand chain. By eliminating inefficient capital in the value chain, such as surplus, aging and obsolete inventory, this new approach shares benefits for both the channel intermediary and Compaq.

While new value can be created and shared between businesses and consumers, the value creation is often based on different characteristics, and may more often employ technology to facilitate personalization and customization in communication and in the product/service bundle. Levis "Personal Pair" jeans are custom fitted pants to accommodate the growing girth of baby boomers. Levis employs technology to produce jeans in lot sizes of one, to get customer information to the point of production and then the jeans to the consumer.

Unlike businesses, the consumer participates at key milestones in the value creation rather than continuously, which is often common in business-to-business relationships, and according to the dimensions of Relationship Marketing on which the vendor has chosen to compete. Levis does not offer fabric or style selection. They do not offer to match custom pants with custom jackets. They do not attempt to outfit the consumer's wardrobe with other Levis apparel, customized and personalized. They just want to fit the customer more comfortably into Levis jeans — at least for now.

One-Way Relationships

For some products, most notably those for which the product category is of limited interest to the purchaser such as can occur in high-frequency repeat purchase/low-involvement decisions in consumer markets, the buyer may prefer little in the way of dialog, mutual value creation or other engagement with the vendor. In my case, I do not want to interact with Procter and Gamble about my toothpaste or with Kimberly Clark about my toilet paper. And, thankfully, they do not seem much interested in engaging me in this discussion. The products from these vendors are fine as they are and I plan to continue using them. I will re-evaluate the purchase decision if they do not keep meeting my needs, provide fairly priced product or let competitors get ahead. I do not consider my individual interests and needs to be different from others in my segment, nor do I feel that I personally need customization of any aspect of the product. I want no after-sales service from these vendors, except for the occasional replacement or refund for substandard product. Sandpaper in my roll of Scotties? I will need assistance and they should be prepared to help. Otherwise, I will be perfectly happy with a one-way relationship: from the vendor to me. This was illustrated in Figure 15, where the brand is differentiated but the product category represents a low risk to the purchaser.

This situation could apply equally to consumables and low-involvement capital goods for industrial or other business-to-business applications. Most companies, though, even for routine repurchases, have a higher interest in the relationship than would be the case for comparable categories of consumer products. Consider the case of dishwashing detergents used in a major restaurant and contrast that with the dishwashing detergents consumers buy. While detergents may be seen by the restaurateur to be similar from company to company, the services wrapped around the product may be quite differentiated. The skill and knowledge of support personnel, the company's processes in service and training, and the data maintained by the firm on their customers, dishwashing equipment, cleaning processes and detergent usage can result in better sanitation, safety and economy. This can thereby improve the business of the restaurateur. If Lever sent around a technician to evaluate my cleaning processes at home, I would wonder about their business judgment!

Brand Equity

The value of the brand to the customer over and above the core functionality needed for market place participation may be termed the brand equity. This additional value is the goodwill consumers are willing to pay to obtain a specific brand over another product or service, the same in all respects except for the brand name. In both consumer and business-to-business markets, the brand itself has considerable power to influence the purchase decision. If customers are engaged by the brand alone, this represents the main vehicle by which the company forms a relationship with its customers.

Brand equity can be seen in terms of two categories of attributes, those that describe the functions the product performs and emotional or other non-functional attributes captured in the brand.[22]

Most companies focus most on building a better mousetrap. They often pay insufficient attention to the emotional appeal of their products. Chrysler makes great mini-vans and makes a persuasive rational case for buying their product. Sales of Ford's Windstar were expected to suffer when Chrysler introduced its newly redesigned product. Actually, Ford's sales went up as they built the emotional value of the brand, saying in effect that families would be safer in the Ford, a claim they supported with government crash tests results. Goodyear makes a rational appeal for customer purchase by communicating that they make great tires. Watch any car race and you will see the Goodyear brand on display and the tires in use. Michelin builds emotional value in their brand by putting children in the middle of their tires. Do you want to race your car or keep your kids safe?

---

[22] Additional perspectives on brand equity can be gained from David Aaker's books, *Managing Brand Equity* (1991) and *Building Strong Brands* (1996), The Free Press.

In most companies, the opportunity remains for marketers to bond additionally with their customers on an emotional level.

Brand equity can also indirectly solidify business relationships. When Intel branded "Intel Inside" with end-customers, they created value for manufacturers of personal computers and also made it more difficult for these companies to buy from competitors such as Cyrix or AMD.

Brand equity has the potential to be, for both business and consumer markets, the equivalent of the encyclopedia salesperson's foot in the door. It provides a more receptive opening to the mind of the customer and a basis for achieving a higher share of the customer's business. If the Moore business forms company stands for just "business forms" in the minds of their customers, they obviously will have considerably more difficulty penetrating accounts and becoming a more broadly based supplier than if their firm was positioned more broadly, such as "providers of information solutions."

Insufficient brand equity can also impede the development of additional opportunity. When Singer wanted to offer more than sewing machines through its several thousand outlets world wide, they chose to purchase companies in the consumer electronics arena, such as Marantz and Sansui, rather than extend the consumer brand of Singer to this category. Perhaps they felt that most consumers would see Singer to embody sewing machines and their service, rather than a more broadly based brand. Sony has no such difficulty. Most consumers likely see Sony as working hard to "build leading edge, quality electronics for me." The Sony brand has been an umbrella for the firm to broaden its product line in the fast-paced consumer electronics, services and software/content arenas.

Brand equity can increase the firm's revenues sometimes even in areas unrelated to the firm's main business. This is being appreciated in emerging or deregulated industries, such as electricity, where the notion that electricity is a commodity is being challenged. Enron, an electricity wholesaler that does not own generating assets, is investing heavily to brand itself as a supplier of energy. Enron will likely find that their investment pays off as markets become more open and new customers — industrial, commercial and residential — consider Enron more favorably. Once relationships are first forged, the opportunity could exist for Enron to provide natural gas, communications, security services and cable television services.

In addition to sustaining and expanding a business, high levels of brand equity contribute significantly to its durability. How else would you explain why people make trips to Graceland as though they are visiting Mecca? Years after his death, reports of Elvis sightings are almost as frequent as the sound of cash registers ringing in the purchases of Elvis-related products. And the cash registers ring a lot — amounting to more than $500 million in sales each year. The US Postal Service, given to using pictures of dead presidents and bridges on their stamps, built further equity in the Elvis brand by placing his likeness on a stamp. By interacting with his image, sound and sanctioned products, by visiting his shrine and by eating in his restaurants, consumers have an opportunity to continue their affinity with Elvis and to deepen the bond. Through the canny management of Priscilla Presley and others, the Elvis Presley brand has never been stronger. Paradoxically, he may be more alive today than when he was alive.

ᘒᘒ

In this chapter, we have seen that consumers differ markedly from business customers, in virtually every aspect of their needs, decision making, the value they place in a relationship and the value they bring to it. The Relationship Marketer will develop an entirely different relationship, using different processes, technologies, people and knowledge and insight, with consumers than with business customers. In Relationship Marketing, not only should the individual customer be engineered into the business processes, strategies and approaches of the company, but the firm should be cognizant of the type of relationship it is seeking to develop and how it can plan to make this relationship even better in the future.

This chapter contrasted types of relationships between consumers and business-to-business customers. The next chapter discusses how to plan to improve relationships.

CHAPTER SIX

Planning for Better Relationships

We never know how high we are
Till we are called to rise
And then, if we are true to plan
Our statures touch the skies.
Emily Dickinson

If mass marketing employed a shotgun approach to marketing, target/niche marketing, a rifle and direct marketing, a laser, then Relationship Marketing is like Krazy Glue™. If you can bond with your customers such that both you and they feel good about being glued together, and are now prepared to work as one for mutual advantage, you have achieved the vision. In this chapter, we review approaches to plan an improvement in Relationship Marketing, hopefully enabling you to become more intensely bonded. In subsequent chapters, we consider key issues in implementing the plan, including technology, customizing and building a chain of relationships.

Many companies talk of relationships quite separately from the other aspects of their business and have no formal plan for advancing the customer relationship and deepening bonding. Relationships are not informal states of mind. Nor are relationships simply having customers like the supplier, although this is obviously desirable. Being "nice" and helping the customer, in itself, does not constitute a relationship. Rather, relationships can be, and should be, explicitly planned. And if the company begins to understand the full importance of the customer relationship through this planning process, it will start to place the relationship at the center of the business and link its various strategies and capabilities to improving relationships with all stakeholders.

As we have seen from earlier chapters, Relationship Marketing can have broad implications for a company and cannot simply be layered onto marketing, with business otherwise proceeding as before. Relationship management has organizational-wide implications and will need the concurrence and support of senior management and department heads in most areas of the company. Simply put, to market to a segment of one will require fundamental change in many areas, including the way the company sees its business, organizes to serve and communicate with its customers and aligns with both customers and suppliers.

A company wishing to assess and plan to improve relationships with its customers could employ an eight-phase Relationship Marketing process:

- Phase 0: Plan for a Plan
- Phase 1: Customer Assessment
- Phase 2: Benchmarking
- Phase 3: Company Assessment
- Phase 4: Statement of Opportunity
- Phase 5: Future State
- Phase 6: Business Case
- Phase 7: Change Management and Implementation

Each of these phases is described briefly and graphically in Figure 17. Detail of specific subcomponents follows.

Phase 0: Plan for a Plan

Phase 0 occurs before the actual process begins. It is essentially a pre-planning stage, providing management with justification for the expenditure of time and effort, and outlining the various components necessary to ensure the initiative delivers to management's expectations. This phase comprises the preparation for the assignment and includes:

FIGURE 17: Planning Relationship Marketing

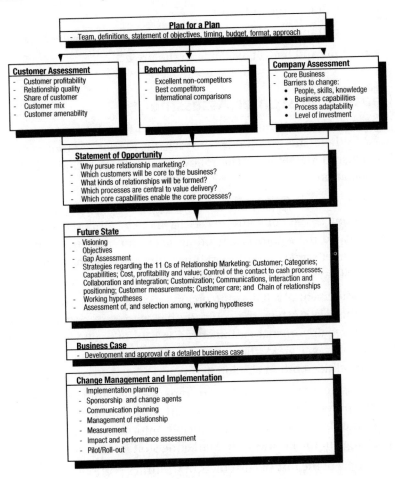

- formation of the team to work on the project, as well as definition of the project mandate and individual roles and responsibilities;
- confirmation of the definitions to be employed by all project members concerning terms such as Relationship Marketing;
- statement of the business issue to be resolved by the initiative, and how the team working on the project will know it has achieved its mandate;
- statement of the rationale for undertaking this planning initiative;
- the approach by which resolution will be attained;

- the format for reporting;
- who will lead the initiative;
- who will sponsor the project with corporate management; and
- the time and budget available to the project.

Phase 1: Customer Assessment

Phase 1 comprises a number of steps geared to answering the question: "Where are we now, with regard to our customers and Relationship Marketing?" The following should be included in this consideration:

- Customer profitability, reviewing with which companies and customers the company makes its money. All costs should be allocated to customers, including sales and marketing, finance, customer service and support, inventory carrying and other costs not always attributed to specific customers.

- Measurement of relationship quality, considering the current state of the relationships the company has with each customer. This may require original customer research to fully understand how the customer views the company, its services, people and other capabilities, both in absolute terms and relative to competitors.

- Assessment of the share of a customer's expenditures the company enjoys, and consideration of how much this will grow in the future, based on currently available information, and with no change in the Relationship Marketing strategy in place currently.

- Review of the mix of customers in the firm's portfolio. Assess and categorize them as "Reward and Invest," "Manage," "Discipline" and "Fire," as discussed in Chapter 2.

- Assessment of the context for a relationship within the customer's organization and the willingness of customers to participate in a deepened relationship and support such an initiative.

Phase 2: Benchmarking

Phase 2 is conducted to ensure that competitive considerations are included, and also to provide the plan with a review of pitfalls and opportunities that may not have been otherwise considered.

The firm could consider exploring leading practices in Relationship Marketing as undertaken by competitors, domestically and internationally, particularly in respect of their strategies and tactics concerning the 11 Cs of Relationship Marketing: Customer; Categories; Capabilities; Cost, profitability and value; Control of the contact to cash processes; Collaboration and integration; Customization; Communications, interaction and positioning; Customer measurements; Customer care; and Chain of relationships. When benchmarking competitors, consider exploring the current and emerging skills the competitors are developing in support of their 11 Cs. Pay particular attention to their focus on customers your firm designates as its best.

A number of books have appeared in recent years on the subject of competitive intelligence and benchmarking. The reader is referred to these[23] for a more detailed consideration of benchmarking practice and competitive intelligence as a driver of business strategy.

One way to assess the competitor's Relationship Marketing prowess is to become a customer of the competitor. This will allow you to observe selected key processes first hand, even though you will likely not be seen by the competitor as a core customer. (However, depending on your industry, you may be. Some companies simultaneously compete, cooperate and purchase from one another, such as in the aerospace and defense businesses.)

Xerox used to buy Kodak photocopiers for detailed analysis. When a machine failed, Xerox called in the Kodak repairman and put a stop watch on the individual to establish time to diagnose the problem, locate spare parts (and how often he/she must defer repairs because spare parts are not at hand), install the parts and presumably, make note of things such as repair quality and durability[24].

To assess production processes and to render a judgment on flexibility, you may wish to buy your competitors' products and tear them apart to see what they are providing to their customers. Engineers in Detroit and Tokyo have long done this to examine the cost structure, assembly techniques, contents and quality of competitors' products. General Motors, for example, has had a "Vehicle Assessment Center" to dismantle and lay out the contents of up to

---

[23] For example, see Ian Gordon, *Beat the Competition, How to use competitive intelligence to develop winning business strategies*, Basil Blackwell Publishers, Oxford, UK, 1989.

[24] G. Jacobson and J. Hillkirk, *Xerox, American Samurai*, Macmillan, 1986, pp. 230-231.

fifteen new cars a year for 19,000 engineers, designers and managers to examine.

You may also wish to examine the Relationship Marketing capabilities and processes of companies in similar industries, perhaps internationally. This can give you some of the information needed to develop leading-edge Relationship Marketing, without regard to current industry practice. For example, a company producing fireplace inserts and gas and wood-burning stoves is comparing Relationship Marketing in their business with that of a leading "white goods" company which manufactures household appliances such as stoves, fridges and washing-machines. Both these firms produce consumer durables and many aspects of the purchase and consumption processes are also similar. This may provide the fireplace company with useful perspectives on forming customer relationships and retaining customers.

If you want to engineer customer response systems for Relationship Marketing, you might want to take a look at L.L. Bean. Do you want your consumer-care processes to give individual customers the value they seek? Disney is outstanding here. Do you want world-class relationships with your distribution channel intermediaries? Procter and Gamble has much to teach. See what they have done with Wal-Mart. And so on.

Not only can companies benchmark Relationship Marketing practices in their competitors and leading-edge non-competitors, but those competitors that have experienced business reversal could be reviewed to establish the role of backward Relationship Marketing approaches that may have caused this. For example, some companies in the computer industry have paid a high price for allowing inter- and intrachannel competition. Both of these factors have contributed to margin pressure on the distribution channel intermediary, such as a reseller of computers. This situation has been compounded by also allowing too many resellers of their computers within a given distribution channel and geographic region. In extreme cases, computer and photocopy companies have competed with their own resellers, sometimes bypassing them with direct sales initiatives. No wonder, then, that these relationships with channel intermediaries soured and the suppliers experienced declining sales. There are likely similar war stories in your industry and some companies have persistently experienced market share declines even though their products may have been just as good. These may be worth reviewing.

In addition to comparing the value of your company in the minds of customers relative to competitors, it is appropriate to ask questions such as:

- How have competitors been able to achieve this position?
- What can we learn from them?
- What are their strategies concerning Relationship Marketing and more generally?
- Can we target their customers or distribution channel intermediaries for transfer to our business?

Phase 3: Company Assessment

In Phase 3, the company needs to take a close look at itself to determine what kinds of relationships it is most suited to, and even whether Relationship Marketing, as discussed in this book, is appropriate. For example, some companies may simply say they are in the business of producing high-volume goods at the lowest possible price, and that Relationship Marketing will distract the company from its single-minded focus to be the low-cost producer in its industry. But even for companies such as these, Relationship Marketing may still have an important role, such as with distribution channel intermediaries. For example, HON Industries, headquartered in Muscatine, Iowa, is a major producer of office furniture and offers a full line, including low-priced products often seen in smaller businesses. HON is focused on production efficiencies and price competition based on cost advantage for these and other products. HON's customers buy from the major box stores, such as Staples and Business Depot, so HON markets their filing cabinets, desks and other office products through these categories of outlets. Even though HON is focused on cost management, it needs sophisticated Relationship Marketing strategies for its distribution channel intermediaries in order to create the value they want.

In this phase, the objective is to "know thyself" and understand the implications of this assessment for Relationship Marketing. The following are some key issues in this review:

- Understanding of the core business in which the company is engaged. Is it reasonable to ask the company to focus on the needs of individual customers and work with each? Does the company see as its current and future business model a focus on mass production and mass service?

- Consideration of the barriers limiting the company's ability to make Relationship Marketing a success, such as:

  – The culture of the firm, which may not include the attributes necessary to take Relationship Marketing out of this book and into reality. For example, if the culture does not emphasize self-respect, respect for others and a commitment to mutual and active listening, then work needs to be done on reforming the culture first before proceeding with the Relationship Marketing initiative. For most companies, some cultural shift is needed. One company implemented a "Listening Company" program to help people recognize the importance of listening, really listening, to the other party and being open to their views.

  – The strategies of the firm and the firm's leadership. No meaningful relationships will be formed if, for example, the president and others are incapable of forming relationship themselves.

  – The people now in the company, including the skills and knowledge they have.

  – The capabilities of the business, including the technologies and processes of the company and their adaptability.

  – The level of investment that the company has made in existing technologies and processes, and the extent to which this investment represents a restriction on options.

  – The state of relationships throughout the chain of relationships that must perform well in the service of the end-customer.

Phase 4: Statement of Opportunity

Phase 4 comprises a summary review of the preceding assessments, geared to answer key questions, including those identified in Figure 17:

- Why pursue Relationship Marketing? What is the business issue that Relationship Marketing resolves?
- What are the main Relationship Marketing options that exist to address the business issue as stated?
- What kinds of relationships will be formed?
- What processes are central to value delivery?

- What core capabilities enable the core processes?
- If our firm is typical, given the above options, how much must we invest and how much more will we make as a result of addressing these components?
- What are the main risks associated with this initiative and how can they be managed?

In addition, a number of issues from the customer assessment, benchmarking and company assessment should be reviewed now to bring clarity to some fundamental questions, such as where the company presently makes its money and which among its various customers it sees as being core to its earnings stream and its future. If there is opportunity associated with building a different base of core customers, such a statement and analysis could appear here.

Core Customers, Processes and Capabilities

Core customers obviously are served by processes, which themselves have important and peripheral components. What then are the core processes by which value must be created for core customers? This consideration should appear here, and should be fact-based, building on a customer value assessment, employing a methodology similar to that reviewed later in this chapter.

Core processes are enabled by key and less vital capabilities. The link between capabilities and processes is presented in Figure 18.

FIGURE 18: Core Processes and Capabilities

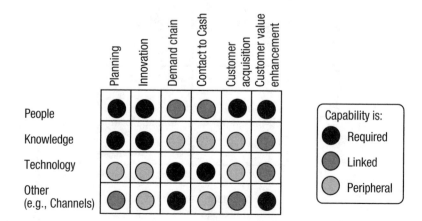

By using a chart such as Figure 18, it should become clearer which capabilities are the most important in ensuring the success of Relationship Marketing processes. Then these capabilities can be explored in more detail in the next phase, Phase 5: Future State.

Positioning for Relationship Marketing

At this stage, reflecting on the assessment of the current situation already conducted, you may wish to confirm that your organization is indeed appropriately positioned for Relationship Marketing. Refer to Figure 19. If you are in a market where individual customers have similar lifetime profitability to your company (lifetime revenue potential net of cost to access, engage, serve and support), your processes likely do not need to be flexible unless your company sees this as an opportunity for improving operations and/or reducing costs. It is more likely that your firm should position itself for Relationship Marketing where customers' behaviors result in fundamentally different requirements from your company, where these requirements deliver different levels of lifetime profitability, where customer preference results in product/service bundles that are more or less unique and where communications, production and logistics processes can be organized in a flexible manner to deliver the value customers require.

FIGURE 19: Relationship Marketing in Relation to Other Strategies

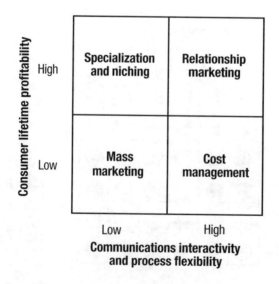

Consider that less than 1% of the population accounts for most of the cars rented in America today. The value of customers to a car rental company is therefore disproportionately skewed to a few high-value customers. These renters may have very different preferences. Some may want cars that have not been smoked in. Others may want a large vehicle. Some may want to be recognized for their importance with significant price discounts, being able to go to the front of the line or any number of things. In short, the car-rental business must have flexible processes to cater to individual preferences. If they are able to use data to predict buyer behavior, such as asking a frequent renter if they want to have a car guaranteed at that location every second Tuesday of the month, they may be able to secure even more business.

In some industries, the lifetime profitability from individual customers is not high enough to warrant an all-out Relationship Marketing effort. In the food retailing industry, for example, supermarket chains secure a very modest return on sales, usually less than 2%. Here, the lifetime revenue potential of an individual customer and the costs of bonding to each may be uneconomic for both the retailer and the consumer products company that produces a single brand or just a few products. In these situations, it may still pay the company to cater to market segments and local or regional market preferences with micro-marketing initiatives, or focus on frequency marketing by providing inducements for the customer to shop at the store again or to repurchase the brand, rather than adopting Relationship Marketing as a strategy.

Does the Customer Merit Relationship Marketing Attention?

The following main issues should be examined to determine if the customer merits Relationship Marketing attention:

Lifetime Profitability of Customer

- lifetime revenues of customer;
- lifetime costs, including measures of cost-to-serve, as previously discussed;
- share of customer spending — past, present, future, with future share of the customer's business predicted based on trends, and the firm's position with regard to the customer's strategic initiatives;

- customer history and business retention; and
- contribution to strategic value in areas such as innovation, process improvement, cost reduction, acceleration of adoption of new products in the market — whether by referral, reputation or other factors, and the extent to which the business is required based on current fixed cost absorption.[25]

Cost of Making Processes Flexible

- customer knowledge and insight;
- customer access, interaction and engagement process;
- production;
- inbound and outbound logistics processes, including warehousing and distribution; and
- order, shipping, billing and financing processes.

Preconditions for Relationship Marketing

A number of preconditions must exist for Relationship Marketing to make sense to the company:

- Each customer must want a solution that is unique, customized or personalized and see that she has derived additional value from the company catering to this need.
- The company must be able to derive a value premium for providing this requirement, either in reduced costs, a higher price or both.
- The company's capabilities: people, process, technology and knowledge and insight must be able to be flexible and adaptable enough to accommodate the individual preferences of customers. If they are not, the company must be prepared to make necessary changes to its capabilities.
- By providing the customer with an individualized solution, the bond between company and customer must deepen and the cus-

---

[25] Care should be taken that plant loading and overhead absorption do not become the basis for customer retention and focus. In the long term, all costs are variable. A thoughtful plan should treat them this way.

tomer must want to repeat this experience or engage the company in another opportunity to create value together.

- Individual customers must be economically accessible for the company to interact and communicate with them, which is particularly important for fragmented consumer markets.

- Individual customers must be economically accessible for the company to provide the physical goods. While groceries can be bought on-line, the process to date has not yet been economic for most firms providing these customized shopping services because it is still quite costly to fulfill, transport and deliver individual orders.

Phase 5: Future State

Phase 5 is conducted to answer the question: "What might be?" with regard to the realistic possibilities of Relationship Marketing. This phase comprises a series of assessments and activities to allow the company to envision the future of this initiative, set measurable objectives for its attainment and then gauge customer amenability to the vision and objectives, as stated. The analysis should be done thoroughly so that even the skeptics in the company (and there will be some) view this as a vision, not a hallucination!

The Future State assessment should incorporate core customers early in the evaluation, so that their perspectives ensure that your review is well founded, grounded and actionable. This collaboration would also demonstrate that both you and your customers (or selected or representative customers) are beginning to live the vision. There could be other benefits. Customers could validate the current state assessment and commit their information, human and knowledge resources and capabilities to the initiative, making it more likely to succeed. When Wal-Mart and Procter and Gamble collaborated to build their relationships, early participation by senior executives from both companies helped ensure success.

The Future State visioning exercise should be externally oriented (i.e., seeing all aspects of your company from the point of view of the market place), seek to arrive at a unique answer and frame the destination and position of excellence for the enterprise. The Future State Relationship Marketing vision should be the purpose to which employees will be proud to commit, which will advance the core customers up the relationship staircase to a progressively higher point of bonding. This may offer advantage in the market because it may be difficult or impossible for the competitors to emulate. How easy would your company find it to become bonded to core customers which your competitors have actively, methodically and rigorously courted?

The vision should be the big-picture end-state the firm is trying to achieve through Relationship Marketing. An example of a vision statement is "Our company will market to segments of one. We will recognize the differences individual customers have by addressing their needs uniquely, serving them personally and collaborating with them to provide the value they want. Our organization, technology and processes will ensure that we deliver on this promise."

To become actionable, the Relationship Marketing vision will need goals, describing the desired capabilities of the organization and the position the company should occupy in the minds and wallets of core customers. Then realistic and attainable objectives can be established as the accomplishments that must be achieved within the specified period in support of the goals, as noted.

Having described the current situation in phases 1-4, and the desired end-state in the above section, you could now review the gap between where you are and where you would like the company to be.

Identify the Gaps

Identifying the gaps could be done in terms of the key dimensions referenced above, including:

- Core customers are those customers that your firm designates as its best and protected customer, that will provide your firm with current and long-term profit, as well as providing for qualitative factors, such as making a contribution to strategic value. There are many dimensions of strategic value beyond profit in the near or even the long-term. These could include value from customers:

  – Helping your firm to innovate.

  – Providing a test environment for any required pilot assessments of product or market acceptability prior to roll-out to a broader audience.

– Guiding the improvement of business processes or information technology.

– Helping to reduce costs for the entire value chain comprising their firm, your own and others.

– Providing market intelligence.

– Collaborating with real time support in design and development.

– Additional strategic value may be derived from customers that are the biggest complainers, as long as their complaints are well-founded and constructive. In some companies, the biggest complainers are seen as the ones to ditch, because their complaints make life more difficult and serving them as they wish to be served may disrupt processes and reduce profitability. In some cases, it may be a wise decision to cut the complainers. In others, these customers may make the company better.

- The bonding differential is the gap between where you are presently on the bonding continuum with your immediate customers and where your vision calls for you to be. In addition, employing the concept of a Chain of Relationships (as discussed in Chapter 9) should your customers be distanced from your firm by one or more layers of a distribution channel, you may wish to consider the bonding gap between your immediate customers and the end-customer, with a view to closing this gap.

- Core processes are those that drive the creation of value for core customers.

- The principal capabilities required to deliver Relationship Marketing benefits to customers: people, technology, knowledge and insight and process.

Strategies to Close the Gap and Capture the Vision

Now go to work on the strategies to help capture the vision and close the gap relative to the current state. Some of the main strategic areas you may wish to consider are those initiatives which drive the capabilities, of people, process, knowledge and insight and technology. Among these, the following are likely to merit particular focus, because these play a particularly important role in the success of Relationship Marketing:

Customer Information Files and Intelligence Systems

These are used to improve organizational memory and understanding of customers and their direction. Important for business-to-business marketers, the databases must enable the company to be ready and well-positioned to sell to the customer when he/she is ready to buy. For consumer products or services marketers, the challenge is to use the database to predict buying behavior and provide the unique value individual customers want, at the right time. This, in turn, typically requires that capabilities be further evolved in the areas of database marketing, database mining and warehousing, predictive modeling and comarketing.

Real Time Interactivity of Relevant Communication and Business Processes

This is used to facilitate collaboration on key initiatives, such as customer-initiated product specification and purchasing. Other areas in which collaboration between the company and its customers might occur are: business and strategic planning, product and service innovation, enhancing the value of current customers, customer acquisition, management of the supply chain, and process improvements to manage time in key processes and become more responsive and flexible.

Mass Customization and Personalization

This ensures that all the marketing flows of the company are engineered to create the unique value expected by individual consumers. Marketing flows include the flow of goods through distribution channels to the end-customer, as well as flows historically associated with the pre-sales, during sale and post-sale components of marketing:

- Pre-sales: such as individualized communications, advertising and promotion to the end-customer (consumer "pull") and initiatives with the intermediary to provide unique product and wrap the services around the product that customers want.
- During the sale: including such as on-the-spot unexpected offers, financing, just-in-time training and computer-assisted customer management, for upselling, add-on selling, selling substitutes or cross-selling.

- After the sale: including warranty and service support, customer recognition, reverse-distribution channels — for any product that needs to be returned and activities geared to building value as individual customers would expect next.

People, Culture and Knowledge

This is used to help the company build customer knowledge; develop insight about its customers; their needs and the evolution of those requirements; and become progressively better at proactively serving customers, ideally in real time.

The customer also derives value from the learning relationship by benefiting from the results of the collaborative effort that builds progressive learning into the relationship. Manifestations of this learning could include the quality and timeliness of data in the company's data warehouse and in the contribution it makes to teamwork on relevant business processes. When Matsushita Electric Industrial Company was producing a bakery system, the company's internal team's first prototype failed. To address the problem, a key member of the project team was apprenticed to the Osaka International Hotel to learn how this reputedly best bread maker kneaded their bread. From this learning emerged a new prototype with special features. It produced wonderful bread.[26]

Using Information Technology (IT) and Business Processes

These are used to support and even transform Relationship Marketing. Companies embarking on a Relationship Marketing initiative might find that their current policies and procedures have become outmoded and that new approaches need to be adopted to support Relationship Marketing. For example, some companies require that their customers supply a purchase order number before they will proceed with the order. With Relationship Marketing, this process could be questioned. The supplier may simply confirm the order using a delivery means the customer specifies, such as mail, e-mail or fax.

---

26 Example drawn from Ikujiro Nonaka and Hirotaka Takeuchi, *The Knowledge Creating Company*, Oxford University Press, 1995, p. 109.

IT and revised business processes may themselves become the basis for a transformed customer relationship. When IT is used to change the rules, it may even *become* the business. For example, one of Canada's largest banks, the Bank of Montreal, has stolen a march on its competitors by introducing a virtual bank concept called "mbanx," which allows customers to do business with the bank from any host terminal in any location. According to this definition, banks no longer have walls, but are information repositories and facilitators of data transactions. Customers who wish to do business with the bank using computer terminals, telephones, automated teller machines or (even!) people, can do so. In this example, the bank institutionalized business processes and IT to facilitate an ambitious approach to serve individual customers as they wish to be served.

Check Your Assumptions

The gap analysis described above showed what needs to change in your firm to provide customers with unique and shared value. The development of strategies deepened the focus on strategic capabilities and approaches to communicate with, and give individual customers the value they seek. Now you are in a position to provide more focus and check out your assumptions with core customers. This might be termed the development of working hypotheses. A working hypothesis extends the sentence: "To engage the customer collaboratively and provide each with the value they seek, I'll bet we need to ...." For example, a firm noted for marketing standardized products to customers that are increasingly seeking to differentiate themselves in their own market with customized solutions, could frame a working hypothesis as: "I'll bet we need to create flexible manufacturing and logistics collaboratively with our core customers, and then to link our IT systems such that we produce components to enable them to customize solutions for their customers." More detail could be provided about specific options to achieve this destination, as seen from the viewpoints of the key stakeholders within the core customer.

In short, the working hypothesis is intended to make the broad vision and strategies concrete and to provide a straw man for discussion on this subject matter with customers, leading to a better solution than may have been otherwise possible. By confirming the working hypothesis with customers, you have an opportunity to validate the strategy and check its underlying assumptions. This could lead to refinements, validation of the current path or rejection of the initiative. Had some retailers and gas companies adopted this approach before embarking on some ill-fated or much-regretted loyalty programs, they may have found that their underlying assumptions regarding the level of retained business and margin levels may not have been sufficient to launch the initiative. And a program once introduced with much fanfare to customers is very difficult indeed to discontinue or even to materially downgrade.

Relationship Marketing has a number of implicit assumptions that also need to be confirmed. These include:

- Differential value can be created for customers in your industry. That is, customers are not alike, and their needs and preferences reflect this. Moreover, they are prepared to pay commensurate with their differences.

- Customers with higher differential value can be distinguished from the others;

- Customer profitability varies according to not only the differential value of customers, but also the cost to serve these customers.

- The costs of serving individual customers is now, or can be made, economic.

- Improved economics can flow from more flexible processes, such as those used for customer communication and product customization.

- Introduction of flexible processes will not bring the business to its knees.

- "Points of touch," where the company and the customer connect for communications or transactions, can be tracked, measured, managed and used as a basis for predicting behaviors, leading to proactive management of high differential value customers.

- Information technology can indeed enable flexible processes while providing organizational memory, facilitating learning about customers and cost-effectively supporting the key business processes.

However, these are but assumptions. As such, they need to be validated if the business case is to withstand scrutiny.

Involve Your Customers in the Vision

Now that you have a Relationship Marketing vision, goals and objectives, strategies and a working hypothesis or hypotheses, core customers should be approached to review their willingness to support the changes you are considering making. If customers were not previously collaborating in the framing of the vision and the other elements of the Future State, they should be intimately involved now. In this way, they can help to refine the Future State, strategies and the straw man hypotheses so that much of the risk associated with customer rejection of major initiatives, including IT or process changes, can by reduced.

When forging relationships with businesses, it is likely that the amenability of the customer to the desired Future State will differ according to the roles of the different protagonists within the enterprise. The customer's president may buy into the Relationship Marketing vision. The VP, IT may agree with your perceptions in general terms concerning the role of IT in creating the business value her company seeks, but disagree with architecture or other issues associated with information sharing. The VP, operations may see value to business process changes foreseen by the working hypotheses, but may resist tying his operations directly to yours, because of a restriction on options that might result. The VP, sales may feel that the suggested changes have the potential to fundamentally change the role of sales, and, in many cases, the envisaged changes will do just that. The VP, marketing could see a different core end-customer than the one you intended. And so on. Securing a definitive and collaborative answer to the straw man hypotheses you have advanced with core customers may not be easy, but simply advancing the initiative and providing potential solutions could lead to more intense bonding than at present.

When agreement is attained, it may result in your company having clarified the focus, roles and other strategic issues in the companies of your core customers. This may be a time-consuming and challenging process, but it is also vital. Sufficient time should be allowed in your Phase 0: Plan for a Plan to let this series of activities be performed well and to set the stage for an interactive approach to the development of more detailed strategies.

Integrating the customer into the vision can also be done with consumers. Technology usually plays an important role in mass customization and the creation of unique value for consumers in

Relationship Marketing. Where it does, particularly at the user interface, the consumer should be closely involved in helping to refine the alternative approaches. When Harley Davidson was developing a multimedia configuration and design tool for consumers to customize bikes to their personal tastes in the dealership, the firm involved "rubbies" — rich urban bikers, customers Harley covets — in helping to frame the solution.

It is common that so-called "front-ends" — the graphic user interfaces with the customer —are routinely mocked-up by software companies to assess approaches to refine the acceptance and use of their programs. And the prototype approach is also employed in areas other than software. A Big 3 car company's interior trim division mocks up alternative vehicle interiors and invites customers to experience each interior and provide their perspectives. Obviously each individual customer cannot be paraded through the interior or interact with the software. But, if this is done with a sufficient number of designated "best customers," then the firm can be more certain that the product or service will be approved by the customers who matter most.

Overcoming Barriers to Change

Having been through Phase 5, you will be in a position to understand many of the barriers to change in your core customers. This will help you to plan for, and address, these issues in the next phase. But the biggest barriers to change may reside within your own enterprise. Establishing a fully fledged Relationship Marketing vision has the potential to turn your company upside down. Your company was likely engineered to provide discrete products and services, to defined market segments, in a more-or-less standardized manner. Perhaps the challenge of increased market fragmentation was addressed by pumping even more products and services through the various processes of the company's design, development, production, distribution, sales and customer service system, with variety further compounding the complexity of the company and leading to calls for simplification. And with marketing now occurring to ever smaller and smaller segments, using yet more media, complexity grew and existing systems became further challenged. Companies may wish they could reduce the complexity, and some may yearn for bygone days when "one size fit all." Others may appreciate the need for Relationship Marketing and see how all the emerging developments in their companies make Relationship Marketing a logical path to pursue.

A number of questions remain unanswered for some roles in this new era. This elevates the risk of adopting Relationship Marketing in its entirety. For example, what is the role of a sales force where most interaction is electronic and some aspects of the sales process invisible? What is the role of marketers when market segments are just one customer, where products are no longer standardized, when customers help engineer the value they want, initiate the purchase decision and decide on the value elements for which they will pay? How does operations change when production runs are of one item? What skills should human resources seek and develop amidst all this change? And then there is finance and accounting, still measuring what used to be and the tangibles of the business when real value in this digital era is often intangible, to be found not in inventory, work in process and accounts receivable, but in the minds of people, the memory of computers, networks with customers and suppliers and the processes that make it all happen. What are these people to make of the proposed change to Relationship Marketing? You guessed it. Some will suggest you start small, perhaps with a pilot project. Some will suggest you start not at all. Both situations are similar. There is no intermediate step for a process that leads to bonding with core customers. If Relationship Marketing is Krazy Glue™, either you are glued to them or you are not.

The impact of this initiative could be disruptive. But it can also be rewarding. IBM's resurgence is greatly due to its rediscovering Relationship Marketing and applying many of these concepts as they did before — but now with renewed vigor. Strong leaders, like IBM's Louis Gerstner, make Relationship Marketing happen. They sweep away the barriers in the minds of their staff. In an environment of weak or ambivalent leadership, there are significant barriers to overcome. In this case, find and/or educate the strong sponsor and let the initiative be theirs — be it an IT, marketing, sales, operations or other initiative.

Phase 6: Business Case

Phase 6 is the presentation that asks management for authorization to proceed, make the investment, commit the resources and facilitate the initiative more generally. The reader may well have developed business cases for other initiatives in the company, so this one should simply follow the prescribed methodology or formula that has proven successful. This time, though, there is likely to be particularly lively debate because the initiative is so fundamental to the company and its strategies, and because it could touch almost everyone who works there.

The business case should address issues such as the size and nature of the business opportunity, the approach to accomplishing it, the timing of cash flows for investment and return and high-level implementation considerations. Describe the opportunity in words and graphics, if possible, and provide supporting rationale. In this discussion, you should lay out what it is you are trying to resolve and how you believe this resolution can be accomplished. Components of this discussion have already been covered in Chapter 3. Some of the rationale presented for Relationship Marketing in Chapter 3 may be incorporated in early internal communications and introductory components of the business case.

The business case should demonstrate the value yet to be captured for your firm by Relationship Marketing. It should be clear about how you plan to focus your resources more narrowly to cooperate and align with specific customers more intensely, and what the benefits will be from so doing. This discussion might include consideration of profits to be derived from opportunities such as those described in Figure 20, including profits from:

- revenues from new referrals by current customers;
- increasing your share of customer (abbreviated as SOC in Figure 20 on page 158) for the products or services you now supply;
- developing new opportunities for products or services for which your firm can become a trusted supplier (whether you make the products or not); and
- incremental margin that could come from reduced operating costs or even a price premium and from reduced acquisition costs of customers for whom referrals were made.

Risks to Attainment

Risks to attainment of the vision should be identified and either addressed in the presentation or contingency plans should be noted. There are many potential risks and each key one should be recognized and considered. A few areas of risk that may emerge in your firm follow as examples.

FIGURE 20: Costs and Benefits from Relationship Marketing (Hypothetical)

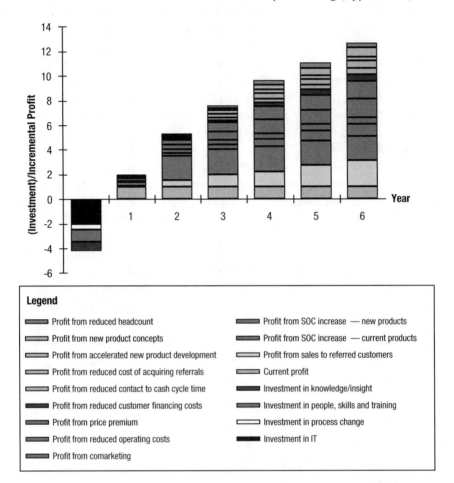

Legend

- Profit from reduced headcount
- Profit from new product concepts
- Profit from accelerated new product development
- Profit from reduced cost of acquiring referrals
- Profit from reduced contact to cash cycle time
- Profit from reduced customer financing costs
- Profit from price premium
- Profit from reduced operating costs
- Profit from comarketing
- Profit from SOC increase — new products
- Profit from SOC increase — current products
- Profit from sales to referred customers
- Current profit
- Investment in knowledge/insight
- Investment in people, skills and training
- Investment in process change
- Investment in IT

What would happen if competitors duplicate your initiative?

What if they, too, target your core customers for bonding in a similar way? What will be your response? One approach is to accelerate implementation so that competitors' actions will either be too little or too late.

What would happen if customers reject the initiative?

Effective customer research, involvement and collaboration can help limit the potential for this risk at the outset, particularly among core customers. And for non-core customers, be prepared to consider the possibility that they may consider themselves better served elsewhere, particularly if you have a Relationship Marketing mix engineered for core customers, with products and services priced on the basis of the cost-to-serve. Such a pricing arrangement would take into account all costs associated with managing the account including the costs now assigned, such as cost of goods sold, as well as costs that may not yet be assigned to a customer such as pre-sales communication and promotion, direct and indirect selling costs, post-sale service and support (e.g., inbound call handling and repairs). Pricing on this basis could recognize the higher costs of serving non-core customers, raising prices to this group and making them effectively unwelcome as customers of your business.

What if IT implementation is not on time or within budget?

It happens. Planning for this contingency could be hard, particularly if you are not responsible for IT, but, in many companies, the rule of thumb is to double the time lines that the IT executive gives. (And he/she is likely doubling what he/she has been told!)

What if the organization's culture rejects the initiative?

The culture will probably not be used to selected key concepts in Relationship Marketing or their implications. For example, customer-initiated purchasing may shift responsibility for the order from outbound to inbound sales, with the call center now inducting the order into your processes. The role of salespeople could be changed. Their compensation plans might need revision. How are they now to be compensated and recognized? The answer is quite differently than they are now. Sales people need to be organized and rewarded according to the tasks required by the customers. If the focus is on current core accounts and account retention and penetration, then sales people need to be aligned to this. If customers want more strategic value, sales people need to be able to provide the high-level thinking needed to add the value customers expect. Many good sales people were trained to open new accounts, then hand them over to others to develop. They then move on to hunt for more game. They are hunters. And Relationship Marketing needs farmers.

Phase 7: Change Management and Implementation

In Phase 7, you should be planning the implementation of the entire initiative. This will require extraordinarily strong project management skills, for three main reasons. One is sheer scope. If Relationship Marketing impacts the entire company, then the project manager will have considerable ground to cover. Secondly, Relationship Marketing may face some barriers to adoption, particularly from those whose activities may change significantly. Thirdly, many companies do not have much depth in project management and a far-flung initiative could stretch what skills they do have. If this sounds a little like your firm, you may wish to consider outsourcing project management and implementation.

The overall project should be broken down into subcomponents, such as IT, people, knowledge and process. Sponsors should be sought for the overall process and for each of the subcomponents. The sponsor should appoint a change agent, who has responsibility for the planning of the implementation and management of their area of responsibility. The detailed planning for each area should confirm the scope of the exercise and describe the tasks, responsibilities, timing and costs associated with implementation.

Implementation will benefit from thoughtful communication of the initiative within the company and to its customers and suppliers. Communication within the firm could be met with Dilbert-like apathy or hostility, as a flavor of the minute project, to be replaced by something of equal endurance shortly. Any such prevailing attitudes will need to be dispelled quickly by the president. Have him or her issue a "White Paper" describing the initiative and putting his/her authority and reputation into making this work. If the president wants it done, it will happen. If they are unwilling to commit, communicate and communicate again until they are indeed willing. But do not proceed without the president's formal blessing. This project will affect much of the company and only the president has the authority to commit the company.

There is a saying that change does not occur until the pain of staying where you are is greater than the pain of change itself. Change-management specialists talk in terms of the burning platform and the need to jump before being consumed by fire. So where is the burning platform in Relationship Marketing? If this is simply a good idea, then it will compete with many other good ideas in the company, and perhaps be relegated to the backburner until a more persuasive case can be made. You need to identify the reason your management and staff should come with you on this journey and then articulate this effectively. Possible reasons could be competitive necessity or a survival imperative. Markets have been segmented into smaller and smaller niches. Now technology enables economic segmentation into the ultimate niche — that of the individual consumer or company. New value can be created by the firm to serve individual customers. That value can include utilities of the type not previously available to individual buyers in your industry, such as place, time and knowledge utility (such as having the product available where and when required, without even having the customer initiate each purchase). But if competitors get there first, and they are probably working on this now, where will we be? If the customers we would prefer to be core to our business become core to the business of our competitors, how much more difficult and expensive will it be for us to intercept the processes, IT, people, knowledge and other enablers that the competitor has put in place?

I keep Table 6 as a reminder to myself and to clients:

TABLE 6: Relationship Marketing is in Your Future

On the one hand:
> If you go out and get customers and can't keep them, you won't stay in business;
> If you keep customers but can't sell more to them, you won't stay in business;
> If you keep customers, sell more to them but don't participate strategically, your share of their future will decline and you won't stay in business.

On the other hand:
> Much of what you need to know about Relationship Marketing you have already learned from your spouse!

The Governance Process of Change Management

The management and governance of the business relationships you may be putting in place will need to be formally established. This initiative could and probably should blur the lines between where your company ends and theirs begins. Once you have achieved at least partial integration, there is no easy going back. You will become much more interdependent — like being joined with Krazy Glue™. How will disputes be resolved? It will no longer be a question of the customer taking the majority of their business elsewhere. They will now depend on you. So, what will happen if you seek exorbitant price increases? What if you cut some product lines or reduce service to some geographic areas? An effective governance relationship will mean that your firm may have to relinquish some control over aspects of the four Ps of the business strategy — product, price, promotion and placement/distribution to ensure that full alignment is attained with core customers. On the other hand, customers may make demands that cannot be economically met. Who will say that their preference cannot be recommended?

The governance of Relationship Marketing between core customers and the company should best be accomplished using a charter and a board of governors, for the resolution of strategic issues. Working groups struck between your firm and individual core customers should be in a position to manage day-to-day issues and others narrowly applicable.

The charter spells out the rights of customer and supplier. The board of governors comprises senior representatives from both your firm and core customers, perhaps with members elected by all core customers to the board. A third party might be involved to chair the meetings, manage the agenda and help ensure resolution and progression. I have not seen many firms manage the governance process well. Most companies are earlier in their strategic development and have not yet fully appreciated that Relationship Marketing goes so far beyond platitudes to affect fundamental issues in the business, such as the degrees of freedom discussed above.

While governance of the relationship, as suggested, applies particularly to companies engaged in marketing to other enterprises or organizations, firms engaged in marketing to individual consumers also need to consider how the relationship will be governed. Many consumers will work through the technology the company puts in place to create the value they want. As they will not be facing the companies managers directly, the question needs to be asked: "Who will be the advocate for each consumer within the company?" In traditional marketing, the theoretical role of the marketer was that of advocate. With Relationship Marketing in consumer companies, the relationship would benefit from a user group of each of the three main categories of customers with which it will do business; those the company views as being its best, to be rewarded and to merit investment in the relationship; those it sees as needing management to maintain a profitable relationship; and those engaged in a relationship with the company that needs to be changed in some way, such as the approaches used by the customer to access the company, prices charged or other factors. The user groups should meet quarterly to formally structure and advance the relationship. Membership in the group should be temporary. The initiatives pursued by the groups should receive broader review by other customers in each category. Relevant technology could be employed to communicate with each to discuss issues and options.

Measure How You Are Doing

Measurement of the progress of the initiative should be part of the project planning and implementation process. In addition, a number of key metrics could be put in place to ensure that the company is deriving strategic value from what will likely be a heavy investment. Selected strategic measurements are described in Table 7.

TABLE 7: Key Measurements for Relationship Marketing

- Revenues and costs (all costs — pre-sale, during sale, post-sale, cost of goods, carrying costs on receivables and inventories etc.) by customer. Analysis of trends, including those of cost to serve.

- Acquisition costs of new customers.

- Retention rates of current customers.

- Revenues and profitability for current customers versus revenues and profitability from new customers.

- Revenues by purchasing unit within the company.

- Share of customer for products and services now made.

- Share of customer based on their expenditures defined more broadly, such as including those products and services your firm could supply, even though it may not make them.

- Competitors' shares of core customers' business.

- The value that core customers derive from your firm (using a process such as that described below). This is one component of an assessment of progression along the bonding continuum.

- Progression along the bonding continuum, using a combination of value (noted above) and other factors, such as share of customer and share of future, appropriately weighted. Your firm should define what each level of bonding means to you and how its attainment will be measured.

- Share of future comprising the share of customer business you expect to derive, based on current positioning in terms of the customers' strategic initiatives or demand trends. If your firm is involved in the major strategies of your customer, you could be well positioned to increase your share of future. If not, competitors are more favorably positioned in the account, and action to improve the relationship will become necessary.

- Frequency and cost of communications needed to advance customers along the purchase cycle, by type of media (Internet, telephone, mail, mass media).

- Share of revenues represented by core versus non-core customers.

- Number of issues arising at the board of governors, and time to resolution.

- Relationship management measurements established in accordance with the benefits customers seek from your firm. For example, if responsiveness is a key value and one of its components include time from placement of the order to receipt, this time should be measured.

Once implemented, provision should be made for assessing the impact of the overall endeavor on your business, including an assessment of the extent to which the original goals and objectives have been attained.

If the implementation was designed on a pilot-program basis, the plan should naturally incorporate go/no go assessments and planning for roll-out to a broader audience or to other geographic regions. It will likely not be easy to pilot test more than a few components of this initiative because, as mentioned, IT and enabling processes, once adopted, will change the company's ability to operate the way it used to. The company will thus likely need to do it all — or not at all.

∞

To summarize, there are eight main phases to be undertaken to help make the Relationship Marketing initiative successful:

- Phase 0: Plan for a Plan
- Phase 1: Customer Assessment
- Phase 2: Benchmarking
- Phase 3: Company Assessment
- Phase 4: Statement of Opportunity
- Phase 5: Future State
- Phase 6: Business Case
- Phase 7: Change Management and Implementation

Framing Relationship Marketing strategy, formalizing and institutionalizing processes and adopting advanced technologies will prove formidable challenges for companies that have not yet been through such an approach, as will securing real buy-in from the people affected. But the initial and most important challenge will be to bring the senior management team along for the ride.

Technology, thoughtfully and strategically adopted, has the power to help the company bond very tightly with its customers and other stakeholders. This is discussed in the following chapter.

CHAPTER SEVEN

Technology for Relationship Marketing

Before I built a wall I'd ask to know
What I was walling in or walling out.
Robert Frost

In Chapter 2, we reviewed the 11 Cs of Relationship Marketing: Customer; Categories; Capabilities; Cost, profitability and value; Control of the contact to cash processes; Collaboration and integration; Customization; Communications, interaction and positioning; Customer measurements; Customer care; and the Chain of relationships. In this chapter, we focus discussion on the subject of technology because this, more than any other change in the marketing environment, will enable the 11 Cs of Relationship Marketing. Above all else, technology's power can put "custom" back into the word customer. But technology, inappropriately applied, can also serve to put the customer on the outside of the firm's walls.

Companies are investing very heavily in technologies associated with computing and communications within their enterprises, and between themselves and their customers, distribution channel intermediaries and suppliers. Data warehouses are proliferating. Enterprise computing is reaching companies of all sizes and making processes more uniform. Few companies, however, are relating their investments in technology to the strategic value they are seeking to create for their customers. This chapter places technology in the context of Relationship Marketing and reviews some specific technology developments in this light. This chapter also provides the Relationship Marketer with information with which to engage IT professionals to help advocate the perspective and requirements of the customer in any technology strategy.

Technology Changes Everything

The declining price and improved performance of digital technologies and their main building blocks — memory, storage, bandwidth, silicon, software and processing — is providing new benefits for consumers and a new framework for marketing to them. Now consumers can be communicated with and served in real time and the same question need never be asked twice of a customer. The potential exists for the company to have an information architecture that gives a complete, current and intelligent profile of the customer to the customer interface, whether call-center, Web site or sales automation. Used appropriately, technology can help the company learn from every customer interaction and deepen the relationship by advancing ideas and solutions likely to suit the customer, and ask questions so that next time the customer can be served even better. In this digital era, the 11 Cs of Relationship Marketing can come together simultaneously to create the value customers want, as described by Figure 21. Technology drives the mega-processes needed to provide value for customers. It is key to the 11Cs of Relationship Marketing noted in Figure 21 and as discussed in Chapter 2 and below.

1. Customer

Technology provides the computing and communications capabilities that helps the Relationship Marketer decide on which customers to focus and facilitates the interactions needed, both within the enterprise and with its customers and suppliers, to deliver customer value. Without technology, marketers would still be thinking in terms of serving the mass market or market segments. They would still be thinking in terms of broadcast, one-way communications. They would still be thinking in terms of long production runs of standardized products, one size fitting all. With technology, the specific customers the

FIGURE 21: Technology Key to Relationship Marketing Processes

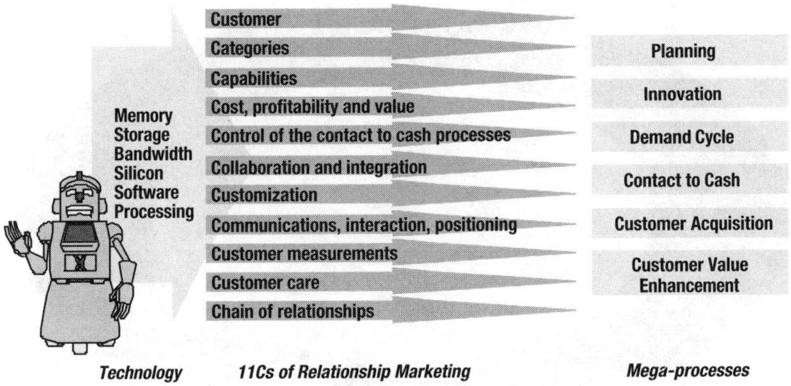

Technology	11Cs of Relationship Marketing	Mega-processes

company wishes to do business with can be identified and further evaluated for their amenability and suitability for a long-term relationship. If the data warehouse is built appropriately, the marketer should be able to "slice and dice" the data in an infinite number of ways, in a way that people not trained in technology can find easy to use. (See the section on data warehousing that follows shortly.)

2. Categories

Technology can also help the company make two other key strategic decisions: what categories and types of goods and services should we provide to our customers and should we, ourselves, produce the goods and services customers want?

When making the decision regarding scope of service, it is useful to understand the full range of value the customer perceives they derive, directly from the company's products and more indirectly. Figure 22 illustrates the tangible and intangible components of value often associated with physical goods. The intangible components may lend themselves more to real time customization and personalization than the tangibles, and can be assembled with the tangibles by someone other than the manufacturer. Thus, some of the decisions the manufacturer must make are which benefits will be provided and by which company in the chain of relationships. For example, if a company makes home furniture, should it offer financing to its retailers for them to package financing terms to customers?

FIGURE 22: Tangibles and Intangibles

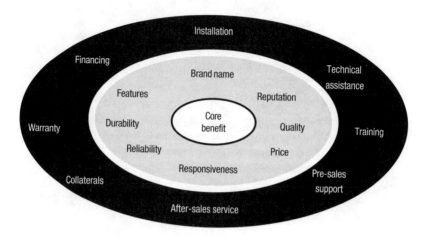

Consider the case of a customer buying furniture. Here the physical good comprises "hard" features and benefits, such as the style, fabric and construction. It may also comprise softer, less tangible features customers want in addition to the physical good. Canada's leading furniture store chain, Leon's, advertises their store and their financing terms, but rarely if ever makes mention of the specific brands they carry. Their financing is a layer of soft benefits important to consumers, added, in real time, to the value the consumers want from furniture. The consumer may also value a number of other intangibles, such as how long it takes to get the furniture, financing terms and repayment schedules, perhaps consultative advice from the salesperson, the benefit of a convenient location, returns policies, warranties, delivery by the store to the consumer, set-up and other benefits. Leon's wraps information, knowledge and other intangibles around the product to satisfy the end-customer. And, by not dwelling on the manufacturer's brand, Leon's has created its own brand equity in the minds of its customers.

3. Capabilities

Technology has vital roles to play in the advancement of a company's capabilities. Technology implementations themselves comprise the heart of the Relationship Marketing company's capabilities by providing, for example, computing, data warehousing, content —

say a Web site or Interactive Voice Response (IVR) front end to the customer and communications linkages within the enterprise and with customers.

Let's follow a typical consumer through a purchase decision in which technology plays an important role. Consumers go through a five-step purchase process: awareness, interest, evaluation, trial, adoption. This means a consumer for a new purchase — say for a new consumer electronics product — must first become aware of the ability of the product or service to satisfy the need, then develop interest in the category and specific solution, before seeking information to evaluate the solution more completely. Then follows trial which, if satisfactory, leads to continued purchase — the adoption phase. This situation is presented in Table 8, which contrasts the traditional roles of consumer marketing with Relationship Marketing, where technology is incorporated as a key component of strategy.

TABLE 8: Examples of Technology in Relationship Marketing

Purchase Process	Traditional Marketing	Relationship Marketing
Awareness	Use broadcast media targeted to the market segment to develop brand awareness or achieve other advertising objectives, such as securing repeat purchase.	Develop a database of end-customers, from prior purchases on store cards, loyalty cards, warranty cards, mass research or other approaches such as calls to the call center. Develop a profile for each consumer that includes the media to which they are most receptive, the technologies they have available to them (e.g., Internet access) and other relevant household and demographic information. Use targeted media to develop awareness of an interactive communications process by which the company can be contacted, for example, by providing a 1-800 number, a Web site address or information on in-store kiosks.
Interest	Secure interest by demonstrating brand superiority or ability to satisfy a need.	Secure interest in engaging the company's technology by providing benefits for doing so in the firm's communications. When the consumer accesses the technology, the database is updated.

Purchase Process	Traditional Marketing	Relationship Marketing
Evaluation	The consumer obtains information informally, or the company provides the information consumers typically want, to help them make an informed decision.	Provide opportunities for the consumer to learn a great deal about the features and benefits of the company's customized or personalized products and services, how they contrast with competitor's, their value in use and how to obtain them — now, interactively, with the company's technology. Track the process by which the consumer makes a purchase decision and have technology help them along the way. For example, the call center operator should have a detailed database of frequently asked questions, as well as the specific user's profile, the kinds of questions he/she might ask and the responses to give.
Trial	The consumer initiates a trial purchase.	The company provides a real time opportunity for the customer to initiate trial, such as by providing a free sample or by having the customer take a tour of a car from the comfort of their home, in 3-D over the Internet, as BMW has done. After a risk-free trial has been provided, the company provides an opportunity for the consumer to make the purchase.
Adoption	The consumer either has their purchase decision validated by the benefits in use, in which case they will likely rebuy, or they do not, in which case trust will be hard to recover.	The consumer buys the product or service and technology follows up with the consumer to establish if there is anything at all with which the consumer is unhappy. The database is updated. The consumer is encouraged to retain an open dialog with the company with incentives to revisit the same access point they used at the outset. The company closes the communications loop with the consumer. Using predictive modeling on each consumer, it seeks to be proactive by suggesting specific solutions or making offers it knows the consumer will be interested in.

For the company to present a single face to the customer, all technologies need to be integrated and any vestiges of functional silos not eliminated in previous reengineering or other initiatives, need to be swept away.

As a capability, technology clearly supports many of the other processes in the company, and enables the Relationship Marketer to develop the 11 Cs on which he/she wishes to focus.

4. Cost, Profitability and Value

Technology can help the company manage the costs of securing, serving and retaining customers by allowing marketers to understand, in real time, the revenues and costs associated with each customer. This can obviously help the Relationship Marketer to control and focus the relationship.

Technology can also intercede and help manage the costs and value of the relationship, drawing upon previously developed "business rules." Business rules incorporate decisions management makes to guide the administration of its business and interaction with customers. For example, administration responsible for the management of local libraries may decide that any books that are more than three days later than has been the historical return practice of borrowers should result in a phone call being placed to remind the borrower the books are overdue. The call is placed by an automated dialer with a recorded message. When the borrower returns the books, late charges can be applied automatically after the books have been logged. Frequent borrowers might be allowed a longer period of time than infrequent borrowers, and different messages might be employed. Companies such as Ameritech Library Services, DRA and Geac currently offer libraries some aspects of these features in their software, and could extend their offering to learn from the behaviors of individual borrowers, before helping librarians to engage their patrons interactively. "I see that you like books by Author X. Did you know we have his new one on our shelves?"

5. Control of the Contact to Cash Processes

Whatever the role of technology, it must perform a control function to ensure that value is indeed being created for customers and for the company, and that bills are sent and payment received on time. Most companies have invested heavily in information systems that have served well for company-driven marketing, from the firm to the market. Now, with the boundaries of the enterprise blurring, with customers framing the value they each want and initiating the purchase decision, dimensions of control are becoming simultaneously more tactical and more strategic.

Tactical controls seek to ensure that the process performs as designed. Strategic controls ensure that new relevant measures are tracked. Cases in point: in the courier industry, real-time track and trace systems are common means of watching the progress of the package through the system. This is an essential, highly tactical and non-financial means of making sure the package absolutely, positively gets to the destination as promised. Some courier firms have invested heavily here. UPS provides on-line tracking for all domestic "time-definite" services[27] through its cellular tracking system. Its vehicle data transmission systems allows customers in the US, Canada and Germany to have deliveries verified minutes after completion.

Strategic controls include those necessary for tracking not just product profitability, but customer profitability, by product, with all costs (such as account management, servicing, support, communication and others) assigned to the customer and product. This assessment can help with the management of the customer mix. At present, many companies manage just their product mix and make decisions to discontinue individual, slow-selling or unprofitable products without regard to the relationships that are often affected. An analysis of the type suggested here allows profitability to be managed for both products and customers, and any cross impacts to be understood before action is taken.

Strategic controls are being put increasingly in place that go beyond financial measures, such as those using balanced score-card concepts. This approach requires that objectives, measures, targets and initiatives be established and tracked for measures that impact customers, business processes and learning and growth, as well as financially.[28] The principal measures for customers include customer

---

[27] UPS, SEC 10K filing, 1996 — excludes UPS SonicAir Service.

[28] For more information, see Robert S. Kaplan and David P. Norton, "Using the Balanced Scorecard as a Strategic Management System," *Harvard Business Review*, January-February, 1996.

retention, customer acquisition, customer satisfaction and customer profitability. Employee learning and growth measurements could include employee retention, employee skills, employee satisfaction and employee productivity. Business process measures are typically specific to the processes being measured. In each of these cases, technology has a role to play in providing the data needed by the Relationship Marketer in real time, or near real time, to enable additional investigation or action. If there is a customer retention problem or a share of customer problem, for example, technology can be operating in the background, unseen to the Relationship Marketer, gathering and evaluating data, and providing the Relationship Marketer with exception reports. One company uses the colors of the street lights to provide early warning of emerging strategic or tactical problems. Green means all is well for a specific issue. Yellow means conditions are changing and should be monitored. Red means that immediate attention is required. Software such as Crystal Reports and Forest and Trees make these executive information systems easier to design and implement. Software companies, such as Ottawa-based Cognos, have developed business intelligence systems that can be customized for Relationship Marketing purposes.

6. Collaboration and Integration

When the customer is invited into the processes that create value for her, she is more likely to increase the level at which she is bonded to the company and its products. The processes which create the value she seeks could be in any or all processes. Thus the customer could work with the vendor to collaborate in areas such as product and service conceptualization, design, development, production to order, value bundling, distribution and service/support. Doing so would help to take time out of the business processes and make them interactive and/or near real time in nature.

Technology can help customers collaborate with their suppliers to continuously create new and mutual value. The new value can take many forms. Quality and speed can be enhanced through, for example, joint authoring and desktop videoconferencing that let companies and individuals share information collaboratively and in real time. Customer response can be improved by deploying applications such as Lotus Notes, IVR and EDI (Electronic Data Interchange), all of which provide long-term benefits as customers become used to the technologies and as a data history is developed, for subsequent analysis.

EDI, in particular, has had significant impact on order-taking, shipping and invoicing processes, causing improved turnaround of orders, cash flow and structural bonding. EDI is often pushed by large retailers, government and manufacturers that have the bargaining power to require that this be adopted so that they and their customers can streamline their processes. Lacking resources, EDI can pose challenges for smaller companies to implement initially. Once they have done so, though, they derive benefits similar to larger companies. This includes an opportunity to leverage the investment, experience and knowledge gained by employing EDI with a partner other than the original one.

Businesses may also find the Internet an important vehicle for communicating with other businesses, but EDI can be more robust and secure. EDI has been around longer for sensitive commercial applications and the standards are better established. The Internet and EDI appear to be converging, with more and more transactions occurring over the Internet as security improves.

7. Customization

Customization should not to be confused with personalization. Customization allows the company or the customer or both to develop a product, service or communications that reflects the value the customer wants. For example, customers of Federal Express (Fedex) can interface with the company on-line and in-person on the phone. Many customers prefer calling to have their packages picked up by leaving a message in a personalized voice-mailbox accessible only with the company's code.

Personalization is the process that enables communication, product and service to bear the name of the customer, adding value to the customer as they position themselves with others. Some personalization has more value than others. When I receive direct mail which includes my name, it is quickly apparent that the mail has been personalized and is not personal. I am not deluded into returning my sweepstakes offer because my name is among three potential winners of $1 million. Some personalized products may be of interest to customers, though, such as monogrammed shirts, logo-emblazoned watches, golf balls, caps, t-shirts and letterhead. When personalization involves the customer through collaboration, interactivity or both, it can become a more powerful dimension of the 11 Cs. For example, on-line customers of America Online can specify the name for an electronic mailbox, which can then be used for other purposes. I have set up a mailbox to communicate with you. Write me, if you wish, about anything in this book or any related experience you have had. I can be reached at rel82ian@aol.com

When personalization is combined with customization, people start reaching for their wallets. Lutron Electronics Company, Coopersburg, Pennsylvania, became the leading producer of lighting controls in the US in the face of stiff competitive pressure from a major competitor focused on product standardization and developing scale economies.[29] Rather than standardize, Lutron went the other way and was so successful that the major competitor, denied the volumes it sought, quit the business. Lutron raised prices and provided highly tailored, customized solutions that increased its market share. For example, its electronic lighting systems, used in conference rooms, ballrooms and hotel lobbies, are unique to each customer. Lutron believes that part of their success is attributable to having engineers undertake tasks that were traditionally the role of marketing, including responsibility for understanding the customer.

In the consumer context, personalization and customization have even more opportunity to benefit from technology and process advances. While businesses such as Lutron can identify their customers by name and serve each uniquely, the same opportunity now exists for the consumer marketer. Say Mrs. Smith bought maternity wear at XSolento Department Stores in March and more, in a larger size, in May. It is a reasonable bet that she may soon be needing baby furniture. What if XSolento dropped her a personalized note including literature offering promotional items and personalized service, with some of the products and services reflecting, but not necessarily noting, her particular circumstance. So, for example, it could mention that personalized service is available by appointment with an interior designer to furnish any room in the house, including say family rooms and baby nurseries, and that this service is free to a "best" customer, such as Mrs. Smith, whether they buy as a result of this appointment or not. Perhaps a discount on the sale could apply

---

[29] Joel S. Spira, "Mass customization through training at Lutron Electronics," *Planning Review*, v21n4, Jul/Aug, 1993, pp. 23-24.

if the appointment is made within two weeks. The ingredients helping to drive this purchase — personalized communication, customization of communication and service, and increased value by employing this offer — was magnified in this case by time limitation. Customization is central to value creation in Relationship Marketing and will be discussed shortly in a separate section.

If the customer can be integrated into the customization and personalization processes, through collaboration in real time, an intense relationship can begin. IMG — Interactive Media Group — operates interactive voice-mailbox/chat lines across the country and internationally. They use interactive voice response technology — IVR, produced by Dialogics — to link callers, first in a time shift mode, then in near real time, then, with the agreement of each caller, in real time. In this way, callers can meet one another on the telephone. For a small percentage of the population, but a significant number, IMG has secured customers who use the system frequently and at length, finding it preferable to the bar scene or other approaches to meet people with similar interests and orientation.

One implication of concurrent collaboration to create customized value is that the customer drives demand and the supplier responds to the requirement to satisfy the demand. The supplier sells the customer less and serves him/her more. The notion of producing a one-size-fits-all standardized product no longer fits with marketplace trends. Now, the customer initiates the purchase and drives a series of events that lead to the product and service combination being delivered as ordered.

This suggests that the concept of the supply chain — long used by logistics and other professionals — is outdated. The supply chain considered logistics and associated processes from the perspective of supply. The customer is involved to the extent that necessary information is required to ensure that the supply system would deliver to their expectations, most of the time. Then the supplier procures input materials and subassemblies, produces the products, distributes them and provides services in association with the product, as the customer requires.

With a transaction either initiated by the customer or worked on collaboratively, it is more appropriate to think in terms of all supply being driven by demand, and with the customer being involved throughout the process. This may be termed the demand cycle, which never ends. As shown in Figure 23, customer data and knowledge of

FIGURE 23: Demand Cycle

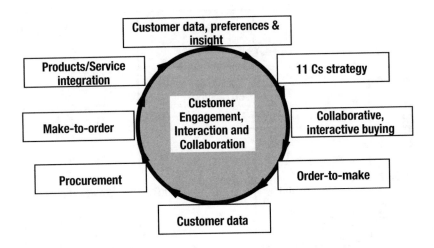

customer product, service and media preferences leads to insight and the opportunity to define a strategy of the 11 Cs of Relationship Marketing, to engage the customer proactively and interactively in a purchasing process. This leads to an order-to-make, to additional customer data being developed and a database being updated, and to procurement for the make-to-order product. After the product is made, the company wraps individualized service around the product and places it with the customer in the time, place and manner the customer expects. The services, like the product itself, need not be made by the company, but the company should take total responsibility, whether they make each component of the product or service or not, to prevent customer confusion and reduce perceived customer risk. And so the process continues, without end.

8. Communications, Interaction and Positioning

Mass marketing required mass-promotional vehicles such as TV, radio, newspapers and outdoor media. In a fragmented market, the promotional channels are much narrower and more highly targeted, including specialized magazines, advertising on everything from park benches to ski chair lifts and unaddressed admail (junk mail) to specific parts of a city, such as wealthy suburbs. That is, broadcasting (what might be termed "one-to-many" communication), first

FIGURE 24: Communications Become Interactive

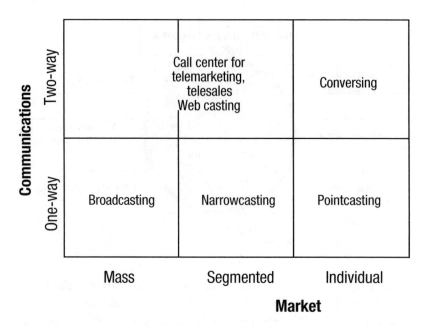

became "narrowcasting" (communicating with a segment of customers), and has now become "pointcasting" (addressing a single customer). When pointcasting is interactive and real time, it may be termed conversing, just as a conversation between people. Conversing occurs at the initiation of either the customer or the company and can involve technology such as call centers, the Internet or interactive voice response and others. A stockbroker, for example, while speaking with a key client, may simultaneously fax a research report and debate the relative merits of an investment with the client, using the document now in the client's hands to advance the discussion. Other forms of interactive communication have emerged, including interactive telephone-based communication, using the call center for so-called telemarketing or telesales, and communication over the Internet that offers an opportunity to engage the supplier, called "Web casting." These alternatives are described in Figure 24.

Technology can help the company converse with individuals at a cost that reflects the value of the communications, and can discriminate among the purposes of different communication, assigning the appropriate media to fulfill each task. For example, if the purpose of the communication is to add no customized value to the customer, then mass or target media can be used. If interaction is required, the company may choose to deploy Web casting or call centers for outbound calling. If the intention is to deliver considerable, customized information, then it is more appropriate to use people — either distribution channel intermediaries or the company's own sales force. More commonly, a combination of these is required, so it is appropriate for the company to allocate the lowest cost technology or approach to achieve each communications objective.

The Internet will be a vital vehicle in customer communications for the next several decades. Vendors have yet to fully appreciate that the Internet is not about putting all their traditional, one-way communication vehicles into cyberspace. It is about engaging the customer in a two-way interaction, providing hitherto unavailable benefits associated with the reception, processing, management, aggregation, linkage, archival and delivery of multimedia information and making it ubiquitous. This could be of considerable advantage to companies selling to individual consumers because the process of communication, purchase information seeking, engagement and after-care can be orchestrated and systematized while costs can be reduced.

Technology provides the knowledge and insight to let the firm contact the customer at the right time — when they are ready to buy — and use the media each customer prefers to make this communication. In this age of continuous mutual value creation, technology also lets customers begin the communication, or respond to messages each message receives. Using "intelligent agents" — software that can search for information — or other approaches, customers can even specify the information to be sent, and then the agents either go out onto the Web to find the information whenever they have been programmed to do this, or the vendor, with so-called "push technology" sends information as specified to each customer. These are fast-evolving approaches and will change again within a few years, as the technology changes and the applications develop. Whatever approach is used, technology should provide a method for customer-initiated response, whether via the Web, fax, voice response, letter or human contact. Technology should be used to action, analyze and store data for subsequent insight. Technology should provide the knitting among alternative communications channels, whichever the customer has chosen to use, and keep the information current in the customer's file.

FIGURE 25: Integrating Technology at the Customer Interface[30]

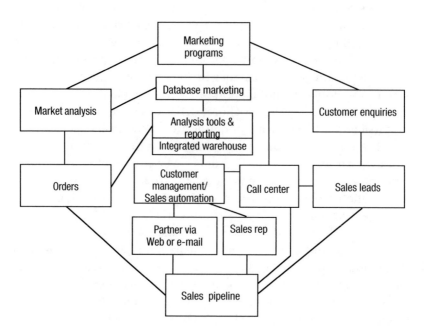

Figure 25 describes the approach adopted by Digital Equipment Corporation to accomplish the complex task of integrating technology for communications and interactivity at the customer interface and within the company in support of the customer.[31] This diagram reflects information flows, the internal organizations that manage the information and the systems supporting the organization and information.

In addition to the management of communications as described, technology can play important roles in positioning with each customer. In traditional marketing, marketers may partition their markets, developing different products and messages for different audiences or distribution channels. For many years, several manufacturers of white goods, such as ranges and dishwashers, have made slightly differently branded products for retail chains. This lets each chain position the product differently in the market place — on price, service, quality or other factors. For example, for functionally

[30] Source: Eric Hjerpe, Director of Sales and Marketing Information, Digital Equipment Corporation, September, 1997.
[31] Ibid.

identical products, each retailer can claim that theirs is the lowest price for the item! With Relationship Marketing, customer partitioning can be practically adopted and technology can make this feasible while maintaining consistency. Many of the major management consultancies maintain client service teams comprising professionals skilled in different functional areas to serve the client. They train their professionals in selling techniques, which includes the establishment of a relationship grid, comprising a list of the key decision makers in the account and the level of bonding each professional has with each executive. Objectives are set for each relationship and the contact and message is carefully managed on each call. Data warehouses of the firm's methodologies are drawn on to apply to each client situation. Software such as ACT! is used for contact management and Lotus Notes to track client response.

9. Customer Measurements

Technology can assist the company to understand current and emerging customer issues, while there is still time to address the problems without damaging the relationship. For example, measurements can be maintained on timeliness of delivery, waiting time before customer calls are answered, and time to address customer complaints, including the time at each step of the complaint resolution processes. All this can be done in the background, using technology to manage the information and provide the management reports. Technology can also be used to track measurements such as customer profitability, share of customer expenditures and the customer's state of mind, with research data logged into databases and trends carefully monitored. Once compensation is linked to customer measurements such as these, including customer satisfaction and favorability, this area will assume unprecedented importance and attention.

Smaller companies are also finding that technology can help a great deal with customer measurements to aid in bonding. Capitol Concierge[32] in Washington, DC, provides concierge desks in eighty-five buildings housing thousands of companies, including lawyers, lobbyists and office managers. By asking key questions, Capitol

---

32 Susan Greco, "The Road to One-To-One Marketing," *Inc. Magazine*, October, 1995.

developed detailed customer profiles, became more familiar with each of their clients and were able to provide more consistent and individual customer attention. For example, they tracked through which door the customer enters the building, how clients prefer to receive service information and the names of client's clients, in addition to data associated with the traditional concierge and other services — through partners, such as florists, courier services and travel agents. Their software integrates with their accounting function, letting them match orders from customers with bills from partners, and their marketing database enables them to predict individual customer requirements, based on historical use.

10. Customer Care

Technology has a major role to play in providing customers with the care they want. The Internet can be particularly cost effective in shifting cost structures from human operators for inquiries where the customer needs basic, standard format or repetitive information. Need to locate a dealer for a fireplace insert or automobile? Head to the Web. Enter your Zip or postal code and presto — the local dealer's name is provided. Want to figure out how much your car repayment will be? Enter the total amount to be borrowed, interest rate and loan term to obtain your answer from a payment calculator on the Web. Not just for consumers, Compaq provides their Value-Added-Resellers (VARs) with an opportunity to use the Web to investigate the company's inventory and place orders. The dealer needs a "key" with which to enter, excluding casual site visitors.

Computer Telephony Integration (CTI) is another emerging area of technology which has the potential to vastly improve customer interaction and care. Consider the following situation. Mr. Big, a high-roller investor, phones his broker to make an investment decision. At the time of the call, the broker is talking to Mr. Small, a minor customer. While Mr. Big is waiting for his call to be taken by the broker, Mr. Bigger calls the same broker. CTI has the potential to manage call sequencing in such a way that the key customers are ordered according to the importance placed on the relationship and that the receiver is prompted about who is waiting in line, giving an opportunity to bid Mr. Small adieu, or place him in a virtual waiting room, where he could review various products or initiate trades. When the call is taken, a customer file pops up on the computer screen with such information as the customer's trading history, balance on account, preferences and profile. Where implemented, customer care is taking major strides forward (especially if you are Messrs. Big or Bigger!).

In a number of vertical markets, technology is being applied to facilitate and add value to customer relationships. Check into a major hotel chain and see the power of their reservation systems at work. They are becoming increasingly sophisticated, with guest history records and customer profiles, enabling a much more personal and useful dialog to be engaged.

11. Chain of Relationships

A chain of relationships comprises the series of linkages between the end-customer and all the stakeholders which contribute to the value the end-customer receives. These stakeholders include suppliers, distribution channel intermediaries, employees, customers and others, such as investors and the board of directors. They are all to be forged into a strong chain that will add ever-increasing value to the end-customer relationship. The relationship the company forms with end-customers will be only as strong as the weakest link in this chain. All are needed to maintain and deepen the relationship with the end-customer. The chain of relationships is discussed in detail in Chapter 9.

Technology has an important role in the structural bonding among all the components of the chain of relationships. For years, companies have used independent and often proprietary solutions — those that they developed themselves — to achieve this bonding. They put the software and/or hardware on their customers' premises to give them the power to initiate paperless ordering. They used HRIS (Human Resource Information Systems) to manage the careers and skills of their staff, among other benefits. They used EDI to transact business with their suppliers and major customers. Software companies, particularly those with enterprise software for large companies such as Manugistics and i2, developed integrated solutions with application to the requirements of multiple stakeholders. Some included functionality for "supply-chain management." Now one of the most common enterprise software applications found in business — SAP (in SAP R/3 V.4) — offers electronic commerce and attention to "supply-chain management" processes. This software addresses collaboration between suppliers, distributors and retailers. For example, it lets companies receive product orders over the Internet, automatically generate a delivery order at the warehouse and update both the merchant's and supplier's inventory data for the product ordered.[33]

Technology is reshaping relationships between companies in an industry. For example, in the retail industry — Quick Response (QR) — and in the grocery industry — Efficient Customer Response (ECR) — take customer-driven demand and quickly feed the data upwards, through the chain of relationships, to help ensure that all suppliers in the chain give the customers the value they wanted, while doing this efficiently and rapidly. Information can then be fed back to the customer, such as when the product was built, shipped and so on.

The Changing Roles for Technology

Four major changes have elevated the role of technology as a strategic capability. These include:

1. The Internet
2. Computer Telephony Integration
3. Data Warehouses
4. Mass Customization

The first three issues are dealt with in this chapter. Mass customization processes are considered in Chapter 8.

1. The Internet

The Internet provides an opportunity to engage interactively the customer using processes that are standardized, but which afford customers the opportunity to assemble the value they want in a customized product. Many vendors have been quick to take notice of the potential of the Internet, making investments before the demand was proven, based largely on their vision and commitment to the associated opportunities. The Internet probably has over 50 million users over the age of sixteen in the USA and Canada.[34] Of the 98.2

---

[33] Tom Stein and Clinton Wilder, "SAP Expands Scope," *Information Week*, August 11, 1997, p. 14.

[34] CommerceNet/Nielsen Media research, 25 March, 1996. Other sources dispute the size of the Internet population, which has been variously assessed in 1996 as between 9 million users (Morgan Stanley) and the figure quoted here from Nielsen.

million households in America, 14.7 million use the Internet[35] and 23% of the US population sixteen and over have access to the Internet.[36] Whatever the numbers, it is clear that the Internet is no longer geek territory. And the outlook is for far more growth. By the year 2000, the total number of Internet users could be 163 million in the US.[37] Consumers are beginning to make heavier use of the Internet for shopping, financial services, on-line banking and information, consistent with the heavy user profile of a well-heeled professional. Indicative of the potential growth in on-line shopping: one out of five Internet users has shopped on-line,[38] with slightly more men likely to do this than women. On-line purchasing was about $500 million in 1996, and could grow to $6.6 billion by 2000.[39]

Businesses have been helping to fuel the growth by setting up opportunities to engage the customer on-line. In January 1996, there were 100,000 commercial Web sites and 9.5 million host computers.[40] By January 1997, this had grown to 650,000 commercial Web sites and 12.9 million host computers, an astonishing change in just one year.

The Internet offers two main types of virtual experiences for customers, using so-called "pull" and "push" technologies. Pull technology is employed when customers visit a Web site and make a product or information selection decision during the course of the stay, not unlike traditional shopping. Push technology is like a standing order some customers set up with their retailers. For example, historically, a fashion-conscious customer may tell the store proprietor to provide information when the new collection from a specific designer comes in. So, too, with push technology, customers specify what it is they wish to be informed about and under what conditions, and then they receive this information or entertainment as requested, when it becomes available. Push makes the computer seem more like television in that the experience can become more passive, but the information and entertainment will still have been

---

35 Find/SVP, 1996.

36 Intelliquest, 1996. Other sources place the figure between 21.5% (Yankelovich, August, 1996) and 27% (Advertising Age/Market Facts, September, 1996).

37 IDC prediction, 1996. Morgan Stanley expects 152 million users.

38 Find/SVP, 1996.

39 Forrester Research, May, 1996.

40 Clifford Lynch, "Searching the Internet," *Scientific American*, March, 1997, p. 53.

tailored to individual preference. Many people are familiar with the potential inherent in using pull technology, the basis of most Internet storefronts and Web sites. Using this approach, customers enter terms in a search engine at sites such as Yahoo or Alta Vista. The engine goes out on the Web and locates sites that may meet the parameters entered. Push may offer much more opportunity to the Relationship Marketer as it makes more use of technology to learn of individual preference and then acts on it.

Push Technology Examples

Examples of companies providing push technology include:

- Marimba provides software called Castanet to companies such as Lehman Brothers and PeopleSoft to allow these firms and others to provide information and software updates to individual customer requirements.[41]

- PointCast gives customers free software to download over the Internet. Using this software, users can choose what information channels they wish to receive, including CNN and *The Wall Street Journal*, whether the information should be from the US or the world: on politics, show business, weather, sports, stock quotes or lifestyles, and how often to provide the information. PointCast uses a standard that allows third parties to Web cast information to browsers.[42]

- BackWeb allows software to be distributed over the net. It embeds code from the customer's client system in the server to permit user profile information to be updated.

- AirMedia uses push technology to send current information over the airwaves to a device that customers attach to their computers.

- Netscape's Netcaster also uses push technology to allow the customer to select from among alternative content providers.

- Microsoft is working with companies such as PointCast and BackWeb to enable Internet Explorer to have a push capability.

---

[41] Steve Hamm, "Can Marimba's CEO Keep the Beat?" *Business Week*, September 1, 1997, p. 86.

[42] Judith Hurwitz, "Pushing and Pulling," *DBMS*, August, 1997, p. 12.

- Other companies working in this area include Lotus, TIBCO and Wayfarer. Lotus Notes V5.0 will likely include a window for receiving content. TIBCO has a broadcast feature as well as a point-to-point communications capability. Wayfarer allows information from individual employees from the Intranet to be combined with information from the Internet.

Giving the customer an opportunity to shop in your store when they want, how they want and with no direct vendor intervention appears to be of great interest to the time-starved, affluent, technologically literate North Americans. Among the products that are being sold in ever higher volumes over the Internet are computer products, travel, entertainment, apparel, gifts and flowers, in that order.[43] The Internet disintermediates distribution channels. That is, it provides the customer with an opportunity to buy direct, or through fewer layers in the channel. The Internet replaces labor at the customer interface with capital in the form of equipment, software, knowledge and process.

Successful Virtual Storefronts

One of the major Web success stories has been Auto-by-Tel (ABT), a car-buying service started by a former car dealer that is experiencing explosive growth.[44] In a single year, its revenues grew from around $6.5 million to about $30 million. The company invested $50 million to establish a network of around 2,000 car dealers across the US to whom leads are channeled by qualified buyers from the Web. Customers access the ABT Web site (autobytel.com) and, with a click of the mouse, enter their new or used vehicle preferences and requirements for financing and insurance. Buyers get the car they want at a low, no-haggle price, and dealers get a much lower transaction cost. Dealers pay about $12,500 for the right to associate with ABT, an annual fee based on the car brands it handles, a monthly fee and a fee to have their inventory in the ABT listing. In short, dealers pay a lot for the opportunity to be with the network. But they can also make a lot and benefit from ABT advertising to secure customer visits to their Web site. ABT was the first Web storefront to advertise on

---

[43] Forrester Research, May, 1996.

[44] Edward O. Welles, "Burning Down the House," *Inc.*, August, 1997, p. 66-73.

the Super Bowl, for example. Together, dealers and ABT are changing the face of the auto retailing industry, reducing greatly the traditional advertising, marketing and personnel expenses in the process and providing a real alternative to the national network of new and used car sales, renting, leasing and servicing put together by Wayne Huizenga's Republic Industries (at a cost of about $1 billion).

There are many other Web-based success stories, selling products from CDs to software and groceries. CDnow started in a basement, presently sells around $6 million of CDs. Netscape sells $1.5 million of software a month on the Web. Companies selling groceries over the Internet include Peapod, NetGrocer, Home Runs and Streamline (previously mentioned).

Peapod, headquartered in Evanston, Illinois, near Chicago, has about 35,000 customers in five cities and derives income from a monthly fee, a surcharge on each bill and by selling customer information to suppliers.[45] Even then, Peapod, which uses their runners to locate and choose merchandise from supermarket aisles, and then deliver it to the consumer at a typically higher charge, has yet to demonstrate that their financial model works. They have yet to make a large profit. Perhaps Peapod's links in its early days to the traditional grocery industry — it was associated with Jewel Food Stores in Chicago and Safeway in San Francisco — may have caused it to employ processes at higher than desirable cost. Nevertheless, Peapod can demonstrate enviable rates of customer retention, largely the result of saving women time in shopping,[46] and also by giving customers more product and pricing information, faster than otherwise available.[47]

Other grocery firms may have even more difficulty in generating sustainable profits where they charge less or provide a less informative Web environment. For example, Home Runs, a smaller player in the Boston area has no fees. According to the definition of Relationship Marketing employed in this book, mutual value must be continuously created and shared. If consumers are unwilling to eventually pay more for the additional value inherent in on-line grocery shopping, either the virtual stores need to educate consumers as to the value

---

[45] Scott Leibs, "Shop, Don't Drop," *Information Week*, August 18, 1997, p. 72.

[46] Most of Peapod's customers are women.

[47] For example, customers can obtain information about nutrition, kosher, cholesterol, sodium, prices and much more, and sort according to criteria such as these.

they are now receiving (always a costly and challenging approach to building value) or they need to reduce their costs, change their business paradigm or find another arena. Less than 1% of the people who are on-line currently buy their groceries this way, so there may be significant opportunity for virtual stores to increase their share of Internet, particularly because most grocery shoppers want to obtain their purchases without visiting a store. Information will be a key dimension for adding value, as retailers learn what their customers want and what they do not usually choose, and use this information to help the customer take time out of grocery shopping, one of the more tedious buying experiences.

Companies small and large are developing opportunities on the Internet with new and existing customers. And some companies are failing. Those companies that succeeded in securing business over the Internet have had a few things in common: they offered a product customers understood and valued, at a price better than retail and with great service. Their home pages are well designed and user- and commerce-friendly. Some have had the promotional benefit from directory services such as Yahoo! and Alta Vista. Consumers remain a little skittish about supplying their credit card numbers over the Internet, so companies marketing over the Internet need to have paid special attention to the security of the credit card numbers and the perception of that security by its customers.

To illustrate a small business success, let's look at a tiny coffee store. Hawaii's Best Espresso Company[48] went on the Internet to market coffee to consumers directly. Their success led to the closing of the physical store in favor of the virtual one. On the other hand, Beverly's Home Crafts[49] tried to sell home-made puzzles and crafts on the Internet but, even though they received about fifteen hits on their site per day, no one placed an order.

Some companies use the Internet to provide information and improve customer service. Fedex's Internet site, for example, provides pricing software to help the customer establish the cost of service for specific weights, distances and speeds of shipment. They also offer a track-and-trace capability so customers can establish the location of their package. Companies such as Fedex increasingly will be adopting advanced technologies in addition to, or in association with, the

---

[48] Roberta Furger, "Gold Rush," *PC World*, October, 1995.

[49] Ibid.

Internet to provide even more information to the customer. So, for example, instead of having every package bar-coded, to be scanned and read by a computer, a small, disposable computer chip may be glued on the package and ride along with it. Now the courier company — and the customer — can have all the information they could possibly need about where the package is, where to deliver the package, the time when it must be there, the method of payment, whether there is a fierce dog at that location, and much else. This is not science fiction — National Semiconductors is one company that provides a similar computer chip. More generally, computer chips are now so cheap they can be embedded almost everywhere and in products that have nothing to do with computers, such as the packages just mentioned. There are 200 million computers in the world, but six billion computer chips, and the volume of these is growing much faster than computers themselves. There is much potential for companies to provide each customer with new value by using these technologies.

Some Internet sites also focus on investor and stakeholder relations. For example, the United States Postal Service (USPS) offers their annual report on the Internet as well as free software to read it. Companies that have to file with the Securities and Exchange Commission (SEC) may as well put their annual reports on their Web site, since these reports are readily available over the Internet via the SEC's Edgar database.

A set of rules seem to be emerging that can help companies succeed with virtual retail storefronts:

- Provide information to engage the customer and move them through their purchase cycle.
- Help them bond to the organization by doing the unexpected. For example, a hearth products company provides an electronic coupon to take to the dealer to increase the likelihood that their brand will be specified.
- Make the environment easy to find. Perhaps advertise it.
- Make it simple to operate and provide superior value than is otherwise attainable.
- Change the processes typically used in the retail context to serve the customer. Grocery retailer Streamline puts freezers in their customer's garages or basements, and stocks these when the customer is out, saving the customer further time.

2. Computer Telephony Integration

In the CTI industry, like much of the technology landscape, it is like the Klondike Gold Rush all over again as telecommunications and computer companies vie to capitalize on the new media opportunities associated with integrating computers and telephones. CTI workstations allow clients to receive and respond to multiple voice mails, e-mails and faxes in one step with just one software system. CTI capabilities such as videoconferencing, information display on incoming calls, automated dialing and simultaneous voice and data transmission are also becoming more common in the workplace.

CTI offers promise for Relationship Marketing because it marries the power of processing vast amounts of information and presenting it at the point of contact for handling via telephony. One recent manifestation is the growth of telephone banking.

The market place is crowded with telecommunications equipment companies with the hardware, software and expertise to provide computer telephony integration solutions. Companies such as AT&T, Northern Telecom, Mitel and Rockwell are focused on making the telephone and computer one another's best friends.

There are also a number of standards[50] that make the selection of a CTI solution more complex. The two most popular standards are sufficiently well supported that both will likely see market adoption. The list of suppliers is becoming lengthy and the opportunity exists for customers to obtain CTI well tailored to their requirements. First, computer companies such as Compaq, Hewlett Packard and Apple have begun to respond to client demand for integrated computer and telephone services, primarily by providing telephone-enabled workstations. On the other side of this coin, telecommunications equipment companies including AT&T, Comdial Corp., Mitel Corporation, NEC Corp., Rockwell International and Rolm/Siemens are developing or have developed CTI solutions.

At the pizza chain Pizza Pizza, CTI is used not only for order management, but also for customer-relationship management. When a customer calls Pizza Pizza, that customer's name, telephone number, home address, favorite pizza toppings and the customer's entire

---

[50] Including TAPI and TSAPI, Telephony Applications Programming Interface and Telephony Services Applications Programming Interface, respectively. TAPI is being driven largely by "Wintel" — Microsoft and Intel, and TSAPI was proposed by Novell and AT&T.

account history flash on a sales agent's computer screen before he even takes the customer's call. When the agent picks up the line, he can now greet the customer by name, and avoid wasting time asking the customer such basic information as address, telephone number, the last time they called and whether the delivery is to be made to the back door, lobby or office floor. All that and more information is already right at the agent's fingertips, leaving him free to process the transaction efficiently while adding to the information value the customer wants. "Would you like 7-Up with the order?" knowing that this is the customer's usual choice. That's better customer service, enhanced productivity and increased revenues, and just one example of how CTI is changing the way companies relate to their customers.

3. Data Warehouses

The engine that enables Relationship Marketing, particularly for businesses marketing to consumers, is the database. This section considers selected issues concerning data warehousing, but obviously cannot provide sufficient detail on setting up a data warehouse. Rather, the intention is to provide the reader with some pointers that can help with an understanding of the warehouse and related matters, sufficient to prod and help direct the designer and manager of IT. In this section, we also consider database types and marketing content that could populate the databases.

Customer data warehouses can be defined as large repositories of information about the customer, from sources both internal to the company and from the customer and third sources, such as the government, credit bureaus and market research firms. Data can include behaviors, preferences, lifestyle information, transactional data and data about communications with the firm before, during and after the sale. It may include information about customer profitability, satisfaction, retention, loyalty and referrals.

Data-Warehousing Layers

More generally, data warehouses can be described in terms of the processes and layers needed to automate and add value to communications with the customer and to facilitate mass customization. This broader definition is summarized in Figure 26 on page 196, which shows the six layers of a data warehouse, selected processes by which the customer is often engaged and the outputs of the warehouse and mass customization.[51] The data warehouse comprises the following layers:

- Transactions, the layer at which level the customer interacts with the company, including the on-line transaction processing system, Internet, call centers or plain old telephony.

- Migration of data from the transaction-based system to the database. This could include retrieval, conversion, transportation and validation of the data.

- The database itself, which may comprise metadata — data about data — and data files and elements. Metadata may include data about the names of the data, its age, definitions, table structure, origination and standards for creating and using the data. The data elements that could be captured are discussed later in this chapter.

- Middleware is the connectivity layer that lies between the applications and the database and manages access to the data and communication of the data on the network.

- Applications comprise the various tools used for making the data into actionable information, including software for analysis, modeling and predictive tools, and applications that assess and help manage the performance of customers, the offer (the total value bundle of product, service and promotion), and which tracks and helps guide the various mass customization processes, functions and components. Production, logistics and procurement are three areas of associated requirement.

- The presentation layer is the set of standards established for the hardware, operating environment, user interface and locally resident software, among other components.

Data warehousing enables companies to extract information from the underlying data to develop a better understanding of the most profitable relationships, for example. Data mining relies on statistical modeling and the other tools discussed below to model customer information from the data warehouse into rules and patterns.

---

[51] For a thoughtful review of mass customization beyond that presented here, see Sean Kelly, *Data Warehousing*, John Wiley and Sons, New York: 1994. Selected concepts from Kelly's book were incorporated in Figure 26.

FIGURE 26: Data Warehousing

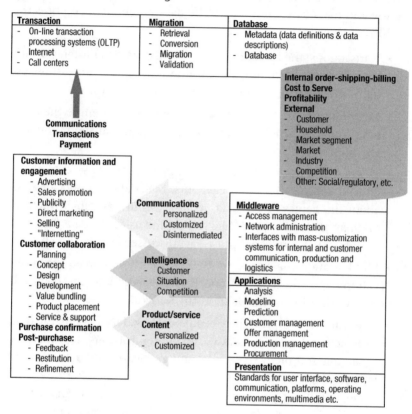

Data Mining

Data mining is a process that employs information technology — both hardware and software — to uncover previously unknown patterns of behavior, trends and issues arising from assessment of warehoused data.

Using data mining, companies may employ massively parallel computers and task-appropriate software to search through large volumes of data. Often the data is about customers and their purchasing behavior, and companies are looking for patterns that describe the behaviors and permit them to segment their markets in new ways, retain customers and become more relevant, by designing products and services to meet the needs of customer "clusters," communicate with them more effectively and earn their loyalty.

We worked with one mass merchandiser which discovered through data mining and clustering that one segment of their customer base comprises self-indulgent female consumers who buy both cosmetics and candies, leading them to place the cosmetics and candy sections of their stores closer together to accommodate such purchases. Is the US, convenience stores have found that many of their diapers are sold to men who often buy beer, at the same time. Using that information, some have placed the beer and diapers closer together in their stores.

Database queries are enabled by front-end tools such as FastStats and Rapidus to speed intelligent data review and response to inquiry. Data mining differs from database queries. Queries answer specific requests for information, either simple requests or ones that need multidimensional analysis or on-line analytical processing to provide the required answers. For example, if you want to know the names of customers that bought two crimson Chryslers in Cincinnati last year, the database could be queried for the information.

Data mining, on the other hand, employs tools that look for meaning, find patterns in the data and infer rules that may be causal, predictive or descriptive. This can lead to better management decision making in areas such as planning, matching inventory to customer requirements, customer targeting, and improving marketing and operating processes more generally.

Data Mining Tools

The main tools used for data mining include[52]:

1. Neural Networks
2. Decision Trees
3. Rule Induction
4. Data-Visualization Software

1. Neural Networks Neural networks use "rules" learned from patterns in warehoused data to construct hidden layers of logic. For example,

---

[52] Julie Ritzer Ross, "Data mining: Digging deeper for information treasures," *Stores*, v78n5, May 1996, pp. 66-68.

by reviewing patterns of a customers' calls, the neural network might understand that a specific customer only complains about poor quality at the end of its fiscal quarter when the customer wishes to return "defective" merchandise. This may lead the company to wonder if the customer is reducing quarter-end inventories of unsold product. This may result in closer attention to returns and the value of the customer.

2. Decision Trees Decision trees divide data into groups based on the values of variables which are classified according to the potential outcomes of decisions. For example, lifetime value could be seen as a potential outcome and grouped. The underlying variables which impact lifetime value could be assessed as a decision tree. For example, do customers with specific ranges of customer satisfaction that result in high purchases but with a high cost-to-serve for the company also result in a "best" customer designation of high lifetime value customers?

Tools using decision trees have difficulty handling continuous sets of data, such as customer age or sales, and require that information such as this be grouped into ranges.

3. Rule Induction Rule induction tools create non-hierarchical sets of conditions which sometimes overlap. So, for example, if the company wishes to maximize lifetime value of customers, which among the following factors should it focus on: customer satisfaction, customer complaints, returns, slow or disputed payments or customer favorability?

These conditions are easier to understand than the approach adopted by the decision tree model. Some rule induction tools generate partial decision trees, and use statistical techniques to choose which trees apply to the input data.

4. Data-Visualization Software Data visualization presents a picture for users to see and for them to make sense of the data, but does not automate the mining process. Visualization aids identification of underlying trends or patterns. Software such as this is a component of the presentation layer of the data warehouse, to which reference is made in Figure 26. New software provides visualization of several dimensions simultaneously, allowing the viewer to not only make decisions from the data presented in this concise manner, but also consider additional analysis that might be performed on it. In this, the visualization approach can be more powerful than statistical tools, such as regression analysis, that do not use human cognition. For example, software from a property management company shows, in graphical format, which among its buildings have high levels of vacancy, which buildings are unprofitable and which tenants are delinquent in their payments.

Some vendors combine various approaches to data mining including products that combine some of the above-mentioned approaches, or suites that offer options to the users. DataMind is working on a program to combine neural networks and decision trees. Thinking Machines has a suite which facilitates development of models with neural networks, decision trees or visualization and memory-based reasoning (a classification method that matches cases to similar records whose outcome is already known).

Examples of Data Mining Companies, Products and Services

In addition to some of the companies mentioned, the following are selected vendors with positions in the data mining and warehousing industry:

- Parallel computers: IBM, Unisys, Cray Research, Siemens/ Pyramid, NCR, HP, Sequent Computer

- Database software: Sybase, Informix, Oracle, Red Brick, NCR/ Teradata, IBM

- Data preparation software: Prism Solutions, Innovative Systems

- Analytic software: Cognos, SAS Institute, Prodea, Brio Technology, Arbor Software

- Visualization software: Visible Decisions, Belmont Research, SAS Institute, SPSS/Diamond

Widely-used enterprise software applications, such as the SAP, BAAN and MFG/PRO systems, already automate many of the relevant business processes that can facilitate mass customization, and have databases integral with them. Unfortunately, some of these databases are very complex for the non-technical user. In part, this is the result of databases being designed by people familiar with the complex approaches associated with OLTP (on-line transaction processing).

Databases from Oracle, for example, may have over a thousand tables, and SAP R/3 around 10,000. If the marketer has to be able to find his/her way through this, a technical assistant will likely be required. On the other hand, if the marketer is participating in an initiative to build a data warehouse, demand four things from the architect of the database: simplicity, completeness, real time data and ease of use for the non-technical user. Such databases can and are being built.[53]

Technology is advancing rapidly to help marketers mine the gold in the slurry of data they have in their warehouses, and firms are adopting the technology in ever-increasing scale and complexity to build their capability for Relationship Marketing. The following are examples:

- IBM has recently announced products and services such as:

  – The Intelligent Miner Toolkit, a compilation of advanced algorithms and processing tools, that will allow developers to write applications that analyze, extract and validate data. The kit's algorithms can spot data trends and patterns, whether the data is stored in flat files, relational databases or parallel databases. The Intelligent Decision Server is a LAN-based advanced decision-support server.

  – Three customizable data-mining applications are: customer segmentation, "market-basket" analysis and fraud detection.

  – A new data-mining service targeting small to medium businesses. Companies can send the records to IBM, which are then cleaned up, deduplicated and formatted, before being returned to customers via the Internet.

- Companies making increasing use of data mining and warehousing are creating opportunities for mainframe vendors with high performance or task-specific computers, typically of a parallel processing nature, such as IBM and NCR/Teradata, and the software vendors that provide the databases, such as Oracle, Sybase and Informix. Related partnerships are also emerging: one was recently announced between Pyramid (a manufacturer of massively parallel processors and a division of Siemens) and Informix for supporting very large databases.

---

[53] See, for example: Ralph Kimball, *The Data Warehouse Toolkit* (New York: John Wiley & Sons), 1996.

- Many companies are building large data warehouses, believing that these provide a competitive edge and "information beyond the product," allowing a lifetime of value creation with that customer. Examples include:

  – Fingerhut Company is expanding its collection of mail-order customer data from about 600 billion characters today to about two trillion characters — two terabytes — potentially overwhelming any traditional mainframe. In total, it has six terabytes of information on its customers.

  – Johnson and Johnson's finance department employs a data warehouse to enable managers in fifty countries to slice, dice, and analyze information from computers all over the company on many financial matters, from accounts receivable to inventories. Right now, J&J is considering dropping one product line that this process suggested. The company may use data warehousing for value engineering, developing a real time "virtual financial statement" to help make capital allocation decisions earlier and cut the number of hours required to do this and related work.

  – McKesson Corp., a wholesale distributor to drugstores, is using a data warehouse to improve operations. Each day, the company receives orders that break down to more than one million line items, each one of which refers to one of the 100,000 stock units it keeps on hand in 30-plus warehouses, at prices individually negotiated. Their Pyramid computer consolidates data from each of three mainframes and lets managers throughout the company analyze any or all of it as they choose.

- Some companies are moving from large data warehouses into gigantic databases, comprising terabytes of data, with trillions of bytes in storage.[54] Many of these large databases are in the telecommunications industry[55]:

  – AT&T has two data warehouses (HP9000/Red Brick; NCR5100) — one of 1.5 terabytes and another of one terabyte, which has allowed them to cut their costs of customer lead generation from 65 to 70 cents per lead to 4.5 to 6 cents.

---

[54] A terabyte can store one billion business letters, taking up 150 miles of bookshelf space.

[55] *Information Week*, September 30, 1996.

– Ameritech has a 2.3 terabyte warehouse running on Tandem equipment.

– BellSouth has two terabytes on Digital/Red Brick.

– MCI has a three-terabyte warehouse on Informix/IBM/Microstrategy and is adding 100 gigabytes of data per month. MCI sifts through the customer phoning data to fine-tune its marketing campaigns and formulate new discount-calling plans. The MCI data warehouse solution, called warehouseMCI, contains up to 3,500 characteristics associated with each customer among the over 100 million it considers current and potential users of its service. Information collected and warehoused includes spending patterns, product usage, demographic and lifestyle information.

• Beyond the telecommunications industry, other major users of terabyte databases are companies such as UPS, Sears Roebuck, Reuters, Tandy/Radio Shack and Wal-Mart.

 for💧

The data warehouse will likely co-exist with the pre-existing, so-called "legacy" systems. If the promise of the data warehouse is to be realized, more than just great technology and big budgets will need to be deployed. Processes will need to be engineered to permit each individual to be served independently, with their preferences, prior experience, attitudes, prior company "touches" and demonstrated behaviors, included previous purchase and return patterns, recognized whenever they interact and especially, when they are ready to buy. The information that supports this capability needs to be gathered and remembered, and the intelligence needed to use this data to advantage needs to be added. Finally, the skills required to deploy this technology need to be revisited and likely altered, so that customers can be taken through the purchase process in the way they want. And if a mistake is made, the data needs to be logged, so that the same mistake is not repeated.

In an extreme situation, perhaps a sales person who sells Alfa Romeos has reacquainted himself with an old customer and has begun to work with this person to be available when the customer wishes to buy. And so it comes to pass that the customer's old jalopy rusts out and a new vehicle is needed. Alfa Romeo makes the strategic set and the salesperson's (data warehouse enabled) responses are remembered and rewarded. The customer enters the showroom and is guided to the new Alfa Romeo 164, a high-end sports sedan. Disaster strikes. The customer is from Hong Kong. In that country, 164 means symbolically "road to death." Next time, the salesperson will need to be more sensitive to numbers, perhaps removing the numerals from the car or even encouraging Alfa to market the vehicle as a 168 model: "the path to good luck!"

The data warehouse has the potential to restore customer sensitivity in a manner that has all but been lost. My tailor knows me and my (forever expanding) measurements. He is willing to throw in a tie when I buy a suit or two. My hairdresser takes care not to comment on the declining density of my follicly challenged scalp, providing instead the same haircut I have always had, which is exactly what I want. I certainly do not wish to be reminded that I had a full head of hair when I first started with this cutter. In much the same way, a mass merchandiser can deploy data warehousing, intelligence, mass customization and reskilled point-of-sales staff to give me suits that reflect my measurements and purchase preferences, all the while engaging me in the tone and manner I prefer, making me feel special to the company, and for that moment, important.

The Database

Database design need not concern most marketers. But databases will be very much in our future, and there may be some debate as to the alternative choices.

Databases are collections of files organized in some manner, such as those discussed next. Files, such as a customer's purchase history, are groupings of records. Records, such as a customer's profile, are compilations of data fields. A field, such as that used for your last name, street name etc., is an item of data comprising one or more bytes or characters. Finally, a byte is used for a letter, number or character and comprises eight bits — zeros and ones.

There are three main types of databases:

1. Hierarchical

2. Network

3. Relational

1. Hierarchical

Hierarchical databases arrange fields in a series, structured not unlike a family tree or organizational chart, with the data usually becoming progressively more detailed or descriptive as one proceeds. Thus family name might be followed by first name, then gender, age etc. The fields or records that are further down the tree are subordinate to the ones above it. This means you need to start at the top to find a record. If a high level record is deleted, so are all the subordinate ones that link to the originating node. This is not a very desirable situation for the Relationship Marketer. Consider a firm which has discontinued a product and wishes to remove this product from its database. If the database is organized by product, all customer information is subordinate to it and would be lost on deletion of product fields.

Hierarchical databases were among the earliest to be implemented and may still be found in applications for high-volume processing.

2. Network

The network structure is similar to the hierarchical arrangement except that a number of additional linkages are made between records. Thus, the resulting structure looks like a family tree or organization chart with ladders linking selected fields. As a result, there is more than one way to reach a node. Several applications can simultaneously use the same database.

3. Relational

Increasingly, relational databases are being deployed. Data elements are stored according to their relationships with one another, in two-dimensional tables. For example, a video store retailer may set up these tables such as telephone number with name of primary renter, telephone number with address, telephone number with titles of movies rented, titles of movies rented with categories of movies and so on.

Relational databases facilitate cross-referencing, automatic retrieval and presentation of the data and the relationships in a manner the user considers natural, rather than according to the design of the database at the outset. As such, it is more flexible and easier to understand than the other alternatives, but it can take longer to search the database. This last issue is becoming less of a problem as processor speed increases, memory costs decline and massively parallel computer design proliferates. But, then again, the size of databases is expanding at a rate fast enough to offset some of these benefits.

Databases can be centralized for common usage, distributed locally or widely for access by multiple users, and can apply to a single user on the desktop. Relationship management cannot readily prosper in companies with "data hogs," people who establish and manage databases personally or even departmentally. The database is a capability of the firm. Its value comes from having access to its elements and looking for associations with other databases, or historical data sets. For instance, what would happen if every manager in a chain of stores or hotels kept a customer database that was retained at the local level. Clearly, the firm would not have a complete view of their customers and would not be able to create additional value for them by using the data for mutual advantage.

The Customer Information File

In the book, *Aftermarketing*, Terry Vavra notes the benefits of a customer information file:

- Marketing effort becomes more efficient and more effective because the marketer is able to identify her most important customers and then present to them the right offer, product, or service at the right time.

- Computer technology is harnessed to manage the vast amounts of data the marketer requires to interact with her customers in a truly personalized manner.

- A true "dialog" can be maintained with consumers by tracking interactions over time, identifying changes in purchasing, and allowing the marketer to anticipate future changes.

- New product development is facilitated by knowing who has purchased a product, how satisfied he or she is and whether any changes would enhance the performance of the product.[56]

---

[56] Terry G. Vavra, *Aftermarketing*, Business One Irwin, 1992, p. 36.

A list of the types of information that could be included in a customer file for building relationships with consumers appears in Table 9[57]. Considerations for building relationships with business-to-business customers follows in Table 10 on page 209.

TABLE 9: Selected Fields for a Customer Information File

IDENTIFICATION
- Account or identification number
- Name
- Telephone number
- Customer has reviewed company's data procurement, disclosure and archival policy: Y/N

CUSTOMER RATING
- Customer categorization in terms of value to your company
- Bonding continuum position currently
- Bonding objective

BACKGROUND

Demography
- Household
  - Size
  - Family structure
  - Spouse
  - Children
- Age
  - Date of birth
- Geography
  - Home address
  - Business address
  - Shipping address
- Income
  - Salary income or range
  - Asset or wealth estimate or range
- Education
  - Highest level of education achieved

---

[57] Ibid. p. 44.

- Affiliation
  - Educational institutions attended
  - Memberships of professional associations
  - Memberships of other organizations: leisure, community, religious or other personal
- Other
  - Height
  - Weight

Consumption habits or preferences

- Products and Services owned or consumed
  - Brands — consumer durables (e.g., automobile)
  - Brands — semi-durables (e.g., clothing)
  - Brands — non-durables (e.g., food and beverages)
  - Vacation destinations and frequency
  - Reading preferences
  - Color preferences evident in items of fashion, non-fashion
- Purchase locations (where are purchases made — location, intermediary type — i.e., what type of distribution channel intermediary
- Timing of spending (e.g., any noticeable skews by time of day, day, week, month when heavy or specific types of spending occur)

Segment affiliation

- Lifestyle categorization
- Psychographic segment
- Leisure pursuits

PRE-SALE COMMUNICATION

- Number of "touches" or contacts prior to purchases
- Types of information sought
- Channels of communication initiated by customer (telephone, Internet, interactive voice response, etc.), by type of information sought
- Offers and promotional material sent directly, by date
- Sensitivity to different media, assessed according to response to specific offers, promotional material, advertising
- Sensitivity to different media, assessed according to respondent's stated preferences in magazines, television, etc.
- Medium which contributed to first purchase (telemarketing, Internet, referral, television advertising, in-store promotion, direct mail solicitation, coupon etc.)

PURCHASE BEHAVIOR

Specific items
- For first purchase and all subsequent purchases: specific items or services bought by categorization code, such as SKU number, by department

Recency
- Date of customer's first purchase
- Date of all subsequent purchases
- Date of last purchase

Frequency
- Frequency with which purchases are made (per day, week, month, year)

Monetary value
- Amount spent on customer's first purchase
- Amount spent on all subsequent purchases
- Amount spent on last purchase
- Margin derived from customer's first purchase
- Margin derived from all subsequent purchases
- Margin derived from last purchase
- Average expenditures
- Average margin on expenditures

Financing
- For first purchase and all subsequent purchases: method of payment for goods or services bought: cash, credit card, store card

POST-PURCHASE BEHAVIOR

- Items returned
- Condition in which returned
- Purchase amounts of returned product
- Tone and manner of return, customer
- Customer complaint frequency, recency
- Customer satisfaction with issue resolution
- Elapsed time between product purchase and return

PREDICTED BEHAVIOR

- Product or service expected to be bought next
- Purchase location where product may be bought
- Media of primary influence
- Level of expenditure or price range of product
- Ancillary services which customer may purchase together with the product

CREDITWORTHINESS
- Bad debt history
- Balance on account
- Default on minimum payments on account
- Credit scoring and rating

ATTITUDES AND PERCEPTIONS
- Key selection and patronage criteria, company overall
- Key selection and patronage criteria, specific departments or product lines
- Perceptions of the company in respect of criteria
- Perceptions of competitors in respect of criteria
- Opportunities to improve positioning, by major area of purchase
- Opportunities to improve positioning, overall

(Data are derived directly, from questionnaires or merging external databases with internal ones, for example, or inferred through demonstrated behavior and preferences.)

TABLE 10: Selected Customer Information File Fields for Business-to-Business Relationships

IDENTIFICATION
- Account or identification number
- Company name
- Main telephone number
- Customer has reviewed company's data procurement, disclosure and archival policy: Y/N

CUSTOMER RATING
- Customer categorization in terms of value to your company
- Bonding continuum position currently
- Bonding objective

BACKGROUND
Business Demography
  - Industry classification code (SIC)
  - Employment levels

History of Company
- Date first incorporated
- Date first started making relevant products
- Corporate affiliations and interownerships

Geography
- Head office
- Regional offices
- Manufacturing locations

Sales, Profitability and Cash Flow
- Size — total sales
- Growth rate — total
- Size — relevant products
- Growth rate — relevant products
- Profitability — overall
- Profitability — relevant products
- Cash Flow, overall

Financial Position (relevant ratios, from financial statements. Could include:)
- Return on Investment
- Operating profit on net sales
- Asset turnover: sales/assets
- Current ratio: current assets/current liabilities
- Stability ratios, such as debt/assets
- Overhead: general, selling and administration/net sales
- Coverage: times interest earned
- Growth: sales growth/asset growth

Market position
- Market size for customer's products
- Market segment participation
- Market share
- Customer's major customers

Suppliers
- Major suppliers to this company
- Duration of relationships with major suppliers

PRE-SALE
- Number of "touches" or contacts prior to purchases
- Types of information sought
- Channels of communication initiated by customer (telephone, Internet, interactive voice response etc.), by type of information sought
- Contact history — non-personal
  - Offers and promotional material sent directly, by date
  - Sensitivity to different media, assessed according to response to specific offers, promotional material, advertising

- Sensitivity to different media, assessed according to respondent's stated preferences in magazines, television etc.
- Medium which contributed to first purchase, such as telemarketing, Internet, personal referral, television advertising, direct mail solicitation etc.
- Call history — personal sales calls, by date, by audience
- Call reports

PURCHASES

Purchase Behavior

Specific items
- For first purchase and all subsequent purchases: specific items or services bought by categorization code, such as SKU number, by department

Usage
- Rate
- Application

Recency
- Date of customer's first purchase
- Date of all subsequent purchases
- Date of last purchase

Frequency
- Frequency with which purchases are made (per day, week, month, year)

Monetary value
- Amount spent on customer's first purchase
- Amount spent on all subsequent purchases
- Amount spent on last purchase
- Margin derived from customer's first purchase
- Margin derived from all subsequent purchases
- Margin derived from last purchase
- Average expenditures
- Average margin on expenditures

Financing
- For first purchase and all subsequent purchases: method of payment for goods or services bought: cash, credit card, store card

DECISION MAKERS
- Names
- Titles
- Our staff who have relationships with these people
- Scoring of quality of relationships we enjoy
- Relationship scoring we plan to achieve, by person

DECISION MAKING

Process

- Decision initiators
- Decision influencers
- Decision makers
- Decision confirmers
- Executors of decision

Purchase cycle

- Time required to make decision, by type of decision:
  - New buy
  - Modified rebuy
  - Rebuy
- Month when decisions are initiated, by type of product
- Month when decisions are final

Criteria and Positioning

- Vendor selection criteria
- Product selection criteria
- Key selection and patronage criteria, overall company
- Key selection and patronage criteria, specific departments or product lines
- Perceptions of our company in respect of criteria
- Perceptions of competitors in respect of criteria
- Opportunities to improve positioning, by major area of purchase
- Opportunities to improve positioning, overall

Style

- Process by which business is contracted
  - Formal proposal development
  - Informal relationships
- Receptivity to proactive value addition

INFLUENCES

- Factors influencing level of business contracted
- Business cycle
- Derived demand dependencies

POST-PURCHASE BEHAVIOR

- Services required
- Items returned
- Condition in which returned
- Purchase amounts of returned product
- Tone and manner of return, customer
- Customer complaint frequency, recency
- Customer satisfaction with issue resolution
- Elapsed time between product purchase and return

CHANNELS
- Intermediaries used for product, type and name
- Intermediaries used for service, type and name
- Customer satisfaction with channel intermediaries
- Opportunities to enhance aspects of intermediary performance

PRICING
- Pricing history
- Pricing expectations
- Win/Loss assessments: prices of winning vendors
- Pricing structures preferred

PREDICTED BEHAVIOR
- Product or service expected to be bought next
- Decision maker for next purchase
- Value of purchase
- Decision maker's expectations of supplier preceding purchase:
  - Call frequency
  - Benefits
  - Presentations
  - New value to be mutually created
  - New value we are expected to create
  - Process changes
  - IT linkages
  - Training
  - Other
- Media of primary influence
- Ancillary services which customer may purchase together with the product
- Vendor preference, if any
- Current incumbent, if any

CREDITWORTHINESS
- Debt history
- Receivables on account
- Payment schedule
- Credit scoring and rating

SELECTED RELEVANT INFORMATION
- Customer's customers
- Business strategies
- Key initiatives
- Account planning

‽

The data warehouse is a key component of a learning relationship and its updating is important if real time insight is to be derived from the data. Increasingly, customers are themselves party to keeping the data current. Companies can give their customers direct or indirect access to data warehouses through Internet access[58]. While some IT managers oppose the sharing of customer information in this way, others argue that opening up the company's database to its customers is a way to increase bonding and aids differentiation if competitors are unwilling to share. Customer access to the data also can help ensure data are accurate and current.

Customer Privacy

Lurking in the background of all this potential is one nasty little drawback: customer privacy concerns. By monitoring customers' behaviors and linking this with other data, a company can know much about customers that can add value to the relationship. In the right hands, this information can be helpful to the customer. But in the wrong hands, or when used inappropriately, the customer's interests could be compromised. For example, before issuing life or disability insurance, a friendly representative of the insurance company stabs customers with a needle to draw blood for analysis. Eating too many french fries? Cholesterol measures are there for all to scrutinize and for inferences to be made. Telephone companies watch long-distance calling patterns and customize call plans for the particular caller. So an employee of the phone company might recognize that you call South East Asia often. He might phone your home to offer a deal on such calls. Your spouse answers and begins to wonder about the calls, which may have been of a private nature. Or the representative of a lingerie company calls your wife to inquire whether she likes the prior purchase you made and asks if she would like to buy more. You somehow forgot to mention to her that you bought the lingerie!

---

[58] For a thoughtful review of some of the technology implications, see Mark Madsen, "Warehousing Meets the Web," *Database Programming and Design*, August, 1997, p. 36-45.

Sounds far-fetched? Consider that your bank account files, credit charges, post-office-box numbers and contents, Social Security earnings, safe-deposit-box contents, phone call logs and IRS records are all available as commodities, from private investigators and others willing to obtain this information for you — or someone else[59]. And much more information can be obtained perfectly legitimately. Companies can and do buy your motor vehicle records to get your address, birth date, height, weight and the model of the car you own. And the firms need not be just the big ones. Speedy Car Wash, in Panama City, Florida, inputs license plate numbers to identify customers, understand their preferences regarding cleaning and vacuuming, for example, and to provide frequent user rewards — before the customer asks[60]. If you have moved, change-of-address information is available from the post office. Your creditworthiness is available from credit bureaus. Your shopping habits and the goods you buy are known to retailers with scanners at the checkout. Your reading habits can be obtained from the subscription lists of publishers. Loyalty cards can tell the marketer much more about where you fly and where you stay. Call-detail recorders let the hotel know who you called when you last stayed there. They also track the movies you watched. Big brother — or an unscrupulous company — really could be watching.

If you recently received an advertisement with a yellow sticky handwritten note attached to it, inscribed: "Try this. It really works!" and signed "J," you would not be alone. The ads were printed to look as though it has been torn out of a magazine, with a ripped edge down one side, inviting the reader to purchase advice on public speaking. J — John? Jack? Jim? Janet? Jane? — seemed to know you, by taking the time to send you a personal note. The reader, thinking this was sent by an unimpressed but caring colleague, may have been tempted to buy the product. After receiving one of these apparently personal missives, I called the company to find out if they had sent it. Sure enough, they did. "Why," I asked, "would you do business this way?" "Because we have found that it works," came the Machiavellian response. The only thing worse than being the receiver of this was being the poor person required to sit all day and scrawl these mindless notes.

---

[59] Jerry Rothfeder, "Invasions of Privacy," *PC World*, November, 1995.

[60] Susan Greco, "The Road to One-To-One Marketing," *Inc. Magazine*, October, 1995.

Protecting Customers' Privacy

If the customer's privacy is to be protected, the company's policies must be geared to this end. Access must be limited on a need-to-know basis. Data inducted into the system should be incorporated for specific application, and could be destroyed thereafter. Legal advice should be sought regarding the building of any database, particularly those of a sensitive nature, such as those in which law enforcement or other authorities may have interest. The customer typically has a legal right to see the databases you maintain on her. You might as well let her see her file so that errors she thinks you may have made or her fears of your nefarious purpose can be addressed directly. And applications of the data may need to "dumb down" the communication to avoid revealing too much information or information not pertinent to the customer. Sending the customer a newsletter including both standard and customized, but not personalized, content is one way to help avoid the appearance of knowing too much. And it may help eliminate the potential for a situation such as the lingerie example described above. There is nothing like an angry spouse to damage a supplier relationship.

ॐ

As we have seen in this chapter, technology has the power to add significantly to the relationship a company can forge and maintain with its customers. Technology can be used to advance each of Relationship Marketing's 11 Cs: Customer; Categories; Capabilities; Cost, profitability and value; Control of the contact to cash processes; Collaboration and integration; Customization; Communications, interaction and positioning; Customer measurements; Customer care; and the Chain of relationships. By providing the Relationship Marketer with strategic options in the choice among each of the 11 Cs, technology has the potential to improve customer bonding, by making processes consistent, focused and customer-specific and by providing the basis for real time interaction and management control, customer memory and learning regarding the relationship so that each customer experience can be made progressively better.

In the next chapter, we review the fourth major change that has elevated the role of technology as a strategic capability — mass customization. We will discuss, in context, how this important component of the 11 Cs can be advanced to improve the customer relationship.

CHAPTER EIGHT

Customizing for the Masses

Underneath all, individuals,
I swear nothing is good to me now that ignores individuals.
Walt Whitman

Mass customization is a key dimension of Relationship Marketing. As such, it also affects the entire organization. This chapter considers components of mass customization relevant to Relationship Marketing. Mass customization can be defined as the process of providing and supporting profitably individually tailored goods and services, according to each customer's preferences with regard to form, time, place and price. Mass customization need not involve changing a company's production line, although this may be necessary. Mass customization includes customization of services and communication. For some customers, being treated individually for services and communication may be more important dimensions than individualized production.

Mass marketers have historically viewed mass customization as interesting in theory but too expensive to implement practically, particularly if a plant was to be radically overhauled. Until recently, this was the case for many companies. Now the words mass customization are no longer quite as paradoxical as they once seemed. Mass customization is becoming more practical as a result of declining costs of technology, increasing flexibility of business processes, creating the potential to communicate individually and interactively with customers. Companies are now willing to see the customer relationship in general, and customer data in particular, as strategic and worthy of investment.

If a company is to commit itself entirely to Relationship Marketing, mass customization, as a concept, is not an option. It is a necessity. But the practical reality is that few firms can afford to implement mass customization in the extreme — where customer choice is infinite. While IBM may make computers to order, they do not custom-design every chip to the unique performance preferences of the customer. Neither IBM nor the customer can afford this. Full compliance with mass customization would be absurdly expensive for most companies and result in products being priced beyond the reach of customers. It may be more appropriate for companies to think in terms of the extent to which they mass customize, to provide the customer with an expanded array of choices — and attempting to do this without increasing the product line or building inventory.

This challenge could cause companies to consider increasing production, distribution, service and organizational flexibility to provide an increased array of offerings suited to individual preference. To illustrate, Morrison International of Sarasota, Florida, has reinvented the way eyeglasses are made. Traditionally, eyewear has involved custom-grinding lenses for differently shaped frames. Morrison fits premolded lenses into snap-together frames that adjust to fit any face. By rotating the lenses to any of 180 positions in the frame, 26,000 prescriptions can be filled using a stock of just 152 lenses[61]. The potential exists for the cost savings in this approach to revolutionize the retailing of glasses, while providing customers with choice and accelerated delivery.

Some firms have long built their businesses around mass customization. Firms in service businesses understand the importance of customization. The challenge is for more companies to do likewise and for those that have employed mass customization to extend and deepen their implementation.

There are many approaches to mass customization, some more appropriate than others for a given industry and firm. Buick's slogan "Can we build one for you?" required that Buick secure individualized

---

[61] Amy Borrus, "Eyeglasses for the Masses," *Business Week*, November 20, 1995.

information and develop processes to build some uniqueness into their vehicles. But Buick has made no attempt to build fully customized cars. If you want an ten-cylinder engine with 480 cubic inch displacement, manual transmission, red upholstery, side airbags and fins, forget it. Like most companies producing capital-intensive goods, Buick seems to establish core functionality for their products. They identify modules which can be mixed and matched, to allow the customer some choice. In so doing, they have made some trade-offs on the degree of uniqueness they are prepared to offer, preferring to provide individualized products rather than truly unique ones, to balance the costs of uniqueness with production and other constraints.

Opportunities likely remain for car companies, like many other firms, to further extend their thinking with regard to mass customization. One area where most companies have a huge opportunity to advance their mass customization is in the area of service. While it may not be economical to custom-design and -engineer an automobile engine, there is no reason a leasing package for the customer cannot be custom-designed for that customer alone. If you wanted to buy a car by making a down payment of the cash in your wallet, not pay for three months, then make a balloon payment of whatever bonus you receive this year, then pay a minimum of $50 a month until next year's bonus and so on, why not? Systems and processes should allow this to occur, and front-line people should be appropriately trained to help the customer achieve whatever each wants.

In addition to service customization, there are likely further opportunities in most companies to extend and deepen the mass customization of their existing technology and processes. Continuing the example of the auto industry, let us consider a dimension which is an important consideration in vehicle selection and which reflects personal preferences — color. At present, car companies allow customers to choose whatever color they want, as long as it conforms to the modest palette of alternatives their colorists have dreamed up. If the company were more committed to mass customization, it could allow each customer to choose virtually whatever colors he/she wants, both inside and out. Of course this would mean additional investment in technology and in process, such as in the dealer's showroom, in the assembly plant, with suppliers of paint, upholstery and interior trim and in the aftermarket repair facilities. Car companies and their suppliers would immediately say that the costs of allowing for a much expanded color choice are too high. Perhaps. But those who forget history may be condemned to repeat it. Ford used to be the pre-eminent car company before GM challenged the idea of black as the only color of cars.

Just as consumers can choose to customize products for their requirements, so can business customers. When American Cyanamid invented glow-in-the-dark green chemicals, they invited businesses to identify applications for the product, and soon firms were packaging and marketing Cyanamid chemicals for photolabs (it will not expose most photographic film), fishing lures (fish race to the lure like venture capitalists to deals), runway lights to outline rural landing areas, safety lights for kids to wear at Halloween, and who-knows-what lights for older kids to use at rock concerts. In developing the unique chemical technology and supporting it with custom engineering processes, Cyanamid created a mass customized approach to allow their customers to market a value-added chemical to a number of micromarkets.

Preconditions for Mass Customization

There are five preconditions for mass customization:

1. Individual Needs and Preferences
2. Assembling Unique Offerings
3. Customer Appreciation
4. Adaptable Technology and Processes
5. Support of Intermediaries and Suppliers

We discuss each of these issues below.

1. Individual Needs and Preferences

Individuals have needs or preferences that are specific to themselves. That is, each person or company should be a segment unto themselves. Even where customers' attitudes and behaviors are so alike that it appears as though the market cannot be served through mass customization, companies should look again. If the underlying needs or preferences differ, the level of bonding between the customer and the mass marketing supplier will likely be low, giving the customer little reason to continue doing business with the company.

In extreme cases, such as in monopoly markets, customers may have no choice but to buy what is provided. When they do have choice, they exercise it. Do you remember the ways of the old Ma Bell? (The vision of Lily Tomlin playing the long-distance operator with an attitude still echoes through my mind.) With the Consent Decree that brought the break-up of AT&T came numerous competitors, and far more customer switching than any had anticipated. The same thing occurred after the electricity industry in the United Kingdom gave customers choice. With the stampede of customers for the exit, the formerly docile and moribund monopolists become better at serving customers uniquely. Companies such as MCI and Sprint would not exist had AT&T done before what it does today.

2. Assembling Unique Offerings

Unique offerings can be assembled by customers or by the company on their behalf, or a combination of both. If unique offerings cannot be made, as in the case of the automobile engine referred to earlier, an opportunity for mass customization is limited to customizing only service and other intangible dimensions of the product.

A furniture manufacturer may establish mass-customized processes to produce sofas to individual preference, allowing customers to choose among such things as fabrics, styles and quality levels and charging a premium for this choice. Alternatively, a manufacturer may provide standard knock-down kits of unfinished furniture for customers to assemble and finish to individual taste. Another possibility is that the manufacturer provides the retailer with the ability to customize certain aspects for the customer, such as custom cut shelving for wall units, assembly of manufactured furniture modules, providing relevant brochures, literature, expert advice or videos and running training sessions on furniture finishing. The furniture manufacturer can then produce a standard product, while the customer receives a customized one, with the retailer playing the mass customization role.

The manufacturer has a responsibility to play in owning the processes for mass customization and for individually tailored communication. Had the furniture manufacturer understood which customer bought which styles of furniture, it could communicate with each, resulting in complementary purchases. And it would need to put the technology and processes in place within the company and in the retailers to provide the benefits each customer wants. For example, Andersen Windows has kiosks which allow customers and retail salespeople to collaborate on the design of a window and see how it would look. Taking this information, the system develops manufacturing specifications, communicates with the plant and provides pricing information, among other benefits.

3. Customer Appreciation

Customers will value and respond to a unique product/service bundle tailored to their requirements, and will reward the company for having mass customized.

If the manufacturer decides to provide a mass-customized solution to customers, it should target those needs that are key purchase criteria, not "nice-to-have" components of the product or service selection decision. For example, the customer with a bad back might want a vehicle manufacturer to provide seats contoured to the individual's shape. A company offering this will find new customers, additional revenues and potentially increased margin. Back sufferers will pay almost anything for more comfort. But if the car company chose to offer custom colors for trunk interiors (to pick one rather absurd area), few customers will derive sufficient new value from this to warrant the associated investment in technology and process.

In the previously mentioned furniture example, there are a number of customizers of sofas that have survived and grown over the years while some segments of the more standard sofa industry have been in decline. Apparently, there are enough particular and fashion-conscious customers who will pay the premium to make the customization of a sofa economic for the builder. The incremental revenue from mass customization should not only be profitable, but more profitable than existing business to warrant the effort. If this is impossible, at least it should provide the company with revenues that can be sustained in the face of competitive threats.

Mass customization can also reduce costs. When Compaq computer announced that they would be producing computers to order, this was not just a commitment to mass customization. It signified an intention to reduce costs from the combined processes that include Compaq, computer resellers and component and subassembly providers. The opportunity exists for Compaq and other companies producing to order to cut inventory carrying costs and write-downs associated with out of date products.

4. Adaptable Technology and Processes

Technology and processes are sufficiently flexible and adaptable to accommodate mass customization. Firstly, the company should have made investments in the necessary data and other technology underpinning a mass customization initiative. This means that the company should see the architecture of technology as being a key component of the infrastructure needed to mass customize processes. That is, the choice of the architecture determines what is feasible in mass customization.

In particular, the data warehouse should be central to the architecture, and all other processes for mass customization of production, communication and customer care should be linked to this warehouse. Without a data warehouse, a company will never know what it doesn't know and will continue trying to reach its destination by running faster, but on the wrong road. And if it has the knowledge, but not the processes to make the warehouse the engine of mass customization, each customer will be denied their personal solution.

5. Support of Intermediaries and Suppliers

Channel intermediaries and suppliers must be amenable to customizing their processes. Typically, mass customization processes will need to involve others beyond the walls of the company. If distribution channel intermediaries and suppliers need to be involved, they too will have to appreciate the value to be derived from modifying their technologies and processes. For example, if Chrysler is to provide customers with choice in the interior trim of minivans, it will need to change not only the processes by which customers order in Chrysler's stores and assembly processes in the plants, but the processes and technologies which link Chrysler to Magna, the company that supplies the interior trim for the minivans. If Magna is unprepared to allow customized selection of interior trim, Chrysler would have to abandon the project or get another supplier. And if Magna agrees to the changes, it, in turn, would need to secure the agreement of its suppliers of fabrics and other materials to any required changes in processes and technology. All these changes will need to be underpinned by sufficient new value being created for each customer so that new revenues and margin can be derived and shared among the entire chain of relationships.

A Range of Approaches to Mass Customization

Mass customization can take many forms and it is not always easy to decide which approach should be adopted. The following discusses specific alternatives, reflecting some of the choices companies have as they decide which combination of customization to employ.

Figure 27 suggests that the main dimensions for customization are in terms of:

- Product
- Service/non-product
- Communications

While companies within specific industries may position for mass customization in terms of any or all of these three dimensions, in practice some industries lend themselves to mass customization in specific areas more than others. Firms within the accounting industry, for example, compete to provide services at costs considered fair by the customer. As seen by the customer, the "product" may have limited customization. Even though the accounting firm may see it

FIGURE 27: Customization Versus Standardization

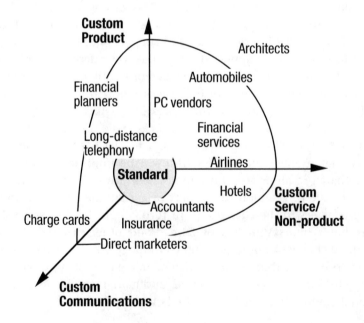

otherwise, the client considers accounting services as more or less a standardized commodity required for regulatory compliance or other reasons. However, if accounting firms wrapped a customized layer around the basic service, and included services such as consulting advice, prediction, industry context, management know-how, implementation assistance and access to the firm's network of relationships, new value can be created for both the firm and the client.

Customization Versus Standardization of Product, Service and Communications

Some of the main choices available to companies include customization of product, service or other non-product dimensions and communications. The principal combinations companies adopt may start with personalizing and customizing communication with the customer, then providing either customized service or product, before potentially customizing all dimensions. The main customization options reviewed below, are:

1. Standard Product, Standard Service, Customized Communication

2. Standard Product, Customized Service, Customized Communication

3. Customized Product, Customized Service, Customized Communication

Obviously, as levels of customization increase, so too, does the cost of providing such benefits. These costs must be offset by increased value in the market place or reduced costs, as previously discussed for Compaq.

Each option discussed below will have different implications for customer bonding. The firm's best customers will be able to provide additional perspective on the implications for bonding, and should be consulted. Additionally, each option will have cross-organizational impact which the Relationship Marketer will need to manage in the context of each specific business. For example, while customized communications may be limited to the functions historically found in the marketing department, customization of service and product are far reaching, and would likely involve people from design, development, engineering, operations, customer service, installation and so on. Because of the complexity of the challenge for the Relationship Marketer implementing mass customization, a team-based approach to implementation is necessary and should include senior staff from the affected functions. At a later date this may be less necessary if the organization is shaped according to the customers with which it collaborates and the capabilities and processes it employs, rather than the functions it performs.

1. Standard Product, Standard Service, Customized Communication

This applies, for example, to direct marketers who tailor their communications to the audience without changing their product or service offering. Some companies personalize the communications, but add little custom content. Firms such as Publishers' Clearing House mention your name prominently in their information literature, but do not acknowledge your reading preferences and offer you incentives to obtain a magazine which would fit your profile, interests or lifestyle. Had they done so, they would be customizing the content, adding more value to the reader and perhaps increasing response rates.

Any card you drop off at a trade show can stimulate a sales process that incorporates personalization, listening and customization of communication, without changing much about the product being sold or the services wrapped around it. Many of the loyalty programs to which you might belong also fall into this category, providing mass customized communication for everything from books to air travel.

The main implications of a company following this approach is that the investment in process and technology is focused at the customer interface and on the communication processes that support this interaction. The company is spared major investment in other internal processes and technologies. Companies customizing communications will see this as a key dimension of differentiating each customer and that new value can be created for and with customers through this communication alone. For example, when a division of TRW began offering the public an opportunity to see their individual credit reports over the Internet, TRW modified primarily the front-end of the customer interface without having to change materially the back-office functions associated with gathering, managing and storing current information.

2. Standard Product, Customized Service, Customized Communication

Going beyond mass-customized communication, companies can provide unique, non-product benefits for their individual customers. Technology is often the core capability that enables both personalized and customized communication. By coming between the company and its customers, technology also allows service delivery to be mass customized. In the previous example, should customers identify an error in their file and wish TRW to change it, TRW would be providing a mass-customized service that could create three-way value: for the customer (now able to benefit from a more accurate rating), for TRW (able to serve its corporate customers with accurate information) and for these corporations (able to apply better information to assessments of risks).

In the case of long-distance telephone, data warehousing and mining is a key, unlocking customer usage patterns and predicting future calling for each individual. If your current usage results in higher costs than you need to pay, data mining should allow vendors to offer you better options. Before this was possible, the companies with the largest market share may have been tempted to overcharge their customers. But now, any telephone company worth your business is calling to advise which plans are preferable, thinking as do you — from your perspective. In so doing, they are wrapping mass-customized service around their standard product to add value uniquely to you and to retain your business.

Banks and other financial institutions are able to do this too, but some continue to milk customers rather than do everything in their power to add value to the relationship. I have made this point to my local bank, which dominates the regional market. I have this mental image of my banker on the other end of the line sitting with her fingers placed securely and firmly in her ears while taking my call. Yes, she is aware I sometimes have funds in low yield deposits. And yes, she could be advising me of cash sweeper or other ways to enhance my value. But she would really prefer customers to go away so that she could really get organized.

Going beyond the product to mass customize other dimensions takes us into the realm of the intangibles that differentiate and make a competitive difference. If cars all work well and many look the same, perhaps financial terms customized to the earning patterns of the buyer might make the difference in getting them to buy your car. If home audio products have limited differentiation, perhaps in-home set up and testing of the product will be important to customers who cannot do these things themselves or those concerned about optimum acoustical performance. If personal computers have similar performance, perhaps in-home set-up, software installation, training and other related benefits could affect the purchase decision. I consider myself reasonably literate as a computer consumer, but would still benefit immensely from the understanding a vendor could provide to improve my productivity, such as with printing, duplication and binding facilities. This would provide mass-customized service to companies such as mine, when printing proposals and reports.

Companies with high levels of inflexible capital assets often cannot easily accommodate shifts in product customization, but can customize service and communications to add value to the product. Hotels rent rooms. I do not expect them to custom-design the room for me, but by using their guest history files and customer profile information, they may be in a position to customize the service that appears to customize the product. For example, by knowing I do not smoke or use the room's minibar and that I carry a laptop computer, they could give me a non-smoking room with telephone outlets and connection cables for my computer, offer me printer rental, photocopy and other business services of the hotel, but not a key for the bar (and not inquire as to what I consumed when I check out). All these are easily possible using industry-standard vertical-market software packages. The difference among hotels is not the technology — all have comparable packages. The difference is commitment to the use of innovative, customer-specific processes and then aligning the organization and its people to deploy the technology.

The mass customization of service requires that companies invest in human capital, in addition to the investments in technology, process and knowledge. People, for the most part, will still be required to deliver some components of service and manage customer communication and feedback.

3. Customized Product, Customized Service, Customized Communication

Full implementation of mass customization, taken to its logical conclusion, comprises customization in all three dimensions of product, service/non-product and communications. There are relatively few industries where companies generally deploy complete mass customization, in part because business processes and IT implementation are costly and difficult to achieve, and also because historical investment in fixed plant may not fully facilitate mass customization. Of course, as mentioned previously, there are firms which have pioneered some of these dimensions, such as Andersen Windows, where unique windows are made to the specifications of individual customers, and then people and technology mass-customize service and communications.

One industry where mass customization is fairly common is the management consulting business, particularly as practiced by firms that are focused on content consulting such as marketing research service providers. Content consultants know that they must deliver unique, fact-based, independent and objective analysis to resolve a specific business issue and provide exceptional service in the conduct of this work. Sometimes this means they must go far beyond "client service" to address the client's issues, business and personal. Even process and IT consultants, such as the large, general management consultancies, have developed non-product dimensions of their offer, wrapping around their services the political acceptability and other benefits inherent in using a major firm. Executives know that they can justify using a brand-name, major firm better than specialized consulting practitioners. Some of these major firms are challenged to develop brand equity beyond the functional benefits expected from the assignment, to include the benefits of interpersonal relationships and bonding — the feeling that the firm looks after their clients with special caring while still providing competence similar to that of specialists.

Companies customizing all three dimensions of product, service and communications will be expected to have the closest customer relationships and be most open to the customer, at every stage at which value is created for the customer. The other approaches to mass customization previously mentioned had more standard components to the business processes and technologies. There were fewer choices and combinations. Complete customization requires that virtually all investments link to customization and that the best customization engine of all — the human mind — be active at the customer interface, knowing what is possible, what can be made possible and how to help give the customer what each wants. Complete customization increases the complexity of the business and raises its scope of operations. It will require that suppliers and channel intermediaries themselves are integrated into the initiative and committed to the direction.

Complete customization is the most difficult to fully conceive and implement, and it is the most costly. But, precisely because it is difficult, opportunity remains in most industries to achieve advantage by adopting this approach. By expanding the array of options at the outset, rather than by providing an infinite customer choice, the company can manage its costs and progress without collapsing under the weight of change.

Developing a Mass-Customization Strategy

Mass customization has come full circle within a century from full customization of products and services through mass production, to doing this again, as suggested by Figure 28. In the era of cottage industry and the corner store, the proprietor saw each customer as important and served them well — as individuals. "M'Lord wants a suit with one arm longer than the other and bright red fabric for liner? No problem." In the time of Bell and Edison, products proliferated in industries as diverse as telecommunications, electric lighting, power generation, steel, tonics and colas. With Henry Ford came mass production to satisfy a burgeoning primary demand. When that demand tailed off, the sales era arrived, geared to thrusting products upon customers more effectively than competitors did. When companies began listening to their customers, the age of marketing had arrived, first serving the mass market, then focusing on the needs of groups of customers — market segments. Continuous improvement sought to do this better and better, and reengineering sought to make this structurally more efficient.

Now, along comes Relationship Marketing, with its allied requirement of mass customization, and the potential exists for much of the company to be turned upside down. Any CEO worth her options could resist the full implementation of Relationship Marketing because the capital costs previously incurred may be still insufficiently depreciated. Ford still has mass production at its core; there has been no headlong rush into fully mass customizing its production and assembly plants. IBM still has a sales culture at its core. It was not first out the gate to mass-customize PCs, and certainly not

FIGURE 28: From Customization to Mass Customization

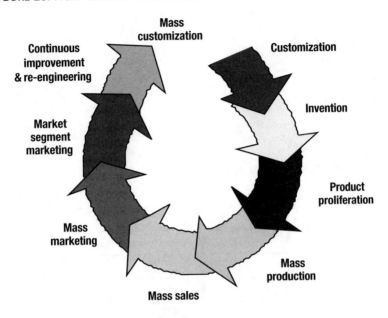

the larger and more differentiated RS6000 or AS/400 series computers. And Procter and Gamble still has market-segment-driven marketing and advertising at its heart. While it is breaking new ground with customer information systems, and has the potential to begin mass customization of communications, it is unlikely we will see full mass customization from P&G, at least not as fully customized products for the consumer market.

Assessment of Mass Customization

How then are firms to capture the value inherent in Relationship Marketing through mass customization? The challenge is to develop a mass-customization strategy and implementation plan that recognizes the current state and seeks to migrate to this new era. Important components of this plan include a review and transition plan for the dimensions of customization.

As mentioned, companies can choose to customize in terms of some or all of product, service (and other non-product dimensions) and communications. How then do you decide in which dimension(s) to apply mass customization?

Five assessments as presented in Figure 29 can help with the evaluation:

1. Mandate Fit
2. Customer Feasibility
3. Competitive Advantage
4. Operational Feasibility
5. Financial Feasibility

FIGURE 29: Mass-Customization Evaluation

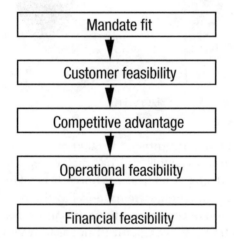

1. Mandate Fit

A firm's mandate and mission should provide some guidance about which dimensions would be suitable for mass customization and even if the concept is to be entertained. If the commitment to mass marketing of standardized product is firmly entrenched in the mandate, the company must either follow the mandate and exclude itself from mass customization, or adjust the mandate and mission. Many Canadian subsidiaries of US multinationals find themselves in just such a quandary. A major computer company recently considered mass customization dimensions and the level and nature of value-add for its Canadian operations. A strategic plan was presented to US executive management, describing how the company would capture mass-customization opportunities by focusing on individually tailored convergence solutions. This was to be done through strategic alliances and localized initiatives with, for example, content providers, telcos, cable television companies and kiosk vendors. This approach was geared to raise the level of value-add in Canada, market this value domestically and beyond and build overall margins in the face of increased pressure on hardware profitability. The company's operations in Canada could not be sustained at the levels then in place, so that the other option was that the business in Canada would need to be integrated with that of the US. The very clear and obvious preference of Canadian management was for the domestic operation to add more value. US management weighed the mandate of the Canadian operation, and concluded that this business should take standardized product from US inventory and add little domestic value beyond government and language requirements and mass communication. No new value was to be created in Canada. The president of the Canadian operation said, "they have asked us to fly our plane into the ground." The domestic operation has since been substantially merged with that of the US and the plane is in free fall.

Other planes are flying high. One retailer has placed Relationship Marketing in a key role in its mission statement. And much change has followed, in part the result of a renewed commitment to making this statement a reality. The board has agreed to the change, a new VP, marketing and competent professionals from the direct marketing industry were hired and the company is allocating scarce resources to the initiative. Even the previous president, focused more on the financials and IT operations of the business than on its marketing, has been replaced. The Relationship Marketing initiative has identified its most profitable customers and the focus has been on mass customized communication with those customers. The firm employed clustering techniques — a software-aided statistical approach — to group customers according to behavioral similarities. Each cluster was placed on a strategic grid, comprising purchase frequency on one axis and customer profitability on the other. Objectives were established and programs designed for customers in each cluster to increase visit frequency, customer bonding, upsell to higher profit items, sell complementary add-ons, sell substitutes of a higher margin and cross-sell other products. Focus groups were held prior to program design and after. Early indications are that the firm is on track to improved performance.

2. Customer Feasibility

Research should be conducted with customers to assess how best to focus mass customization for customer retention, business development and gross margin or margin mix improvement. One approach to this research might involve grouping or clustering existing customers according to their behaviors, as the retailer mentioned above did. Then, for each significant behavioral cluster, customization dimensions can be inferred from a research program geared to identifying the needs and preferences that could affect customization. This could be done by reviewing answers to questions asked directly or in response to indirect questions which seek to draw out these answers to fundamental issues such as:

- Concerning Product
- Considering Usage of the Product
- Reviewing Engagement with the Product
- Considering Communications
- Going Beyond the Tangibles and Functionality of the Product

Concerning Product

What does the "product" actually mean to the customer? That is, considering both physical/functional and abstract/intangible/emotional issues, what is the product to them and how do they value specific components of it? What is their ideal product? What is the gap between the current and ideal product that the customer, through his/her actions or communications, now bridges on his/her own? Do they want consistency or should the product be different each time?

Considering Usage of the Product

How do customers use the product that differs from what they think was the intended use of the product or how their neighbors use the product? How would they like to use it in ways that differ from others? What stops them from using more of it? What stops them from using it differently from their previous behaviors? Why do they not use it at different usage occasions or time of day? Why do they not use it in combination with other products they own or could buy? What do they do with it when not in use?

Reviewing Engagement with the Product

What is it about the design, packaging, product appearance, texture, aroma or appearance that they now personally change or would like to modify, to make it more acceptable for this individual consumer?

Considering Communications

What information do they need in advance of product use, concurrent with use and after use? Do individual customers actually know what they don't know? Do they have information needs that are not now being met for their personal requirements? If they had this information last time, how would their behaviors have changed? How would they like to interact with the company personally and with what media, content, style and manner?

Going Beyond the Tangibles and Functionality of the Product

What does the individual customer want in terms of service and other non-product dimensions before purchase, during purchase, immediately after purchase and throughout the ownership of the product?

"Higher-order inferences" would be derived from the available data on the lower-order issues evidenced by customer response to questions such as those above. That is, one would not attempt to ask a customer about his/her assessment of the mass-customization potential inherent in the non-product dimensions of the product or service. This is to be derived from responses to questions focused on their individual assessments, use, behaviors and perceptions associated with specifically identified non-product dimensions. The attributes to be gauged may have been framed in exploratory qualitative research with focus groups, comprising members of the specific clusters under examination. Mass-customization options can then be framed from this data, perhaps jointly with consumer panel advisory groups, explored in focus group research and quantified in mass research with specific clusters.

In business-to-business markets, joint work teams struck for the purpose can define issues and options for both firms to consider implementing, subject to the other assessments each will need to make.

More typically, customer feasibility is often delayed until management wants to push through a specific action plan and simply wants validation of what it already believes to be true. Marketers would do well to bring some balance to the mass customization debate by driving an "outside-in" dialog, seeking the views of the customers and others such as channel partners who are outside the company, and then ensuring that these perspectives are heard inside. And this must be done early on, before IT and operations seize and frame the agenda, and conduct operational and financial feasibility assessments.

3. Competitive Advantage

Mass customization has the potential to deliver competitive advantage for three main reasons:

- In many markets, customers want a solution which addresses their unique preferences, but suppliers may have been unwilling or unable to provide it.

- Competitors have yet to segment most markets to the ultimate segment — that of the individual. Very few firms currently have a Relationship Marketing plan and an implementation plan for mass customization.

- The specific focus of mass customization can be difficult to define and even more difficult to secure approval and alignment inside the organization to undertake the initiative. Precisely because full mass customization is hard to do and even harder to do well, an opportunity often exists in specific markets to seize the opening and do what others have not.

The competition for customers is described by Figure 30. The strategic triangle shows the types of information companies obtain to assess their position in the minds of individual customers and relative to competitors, behaviorally and financially. In this context, it will obviously be much easier to obtain the information needed for mass customization for business-to-business customers than for individual consumers since the cost of doing this with the latter group would be very high.

Once the dimensions of benefit have been identified with customers and the firm's current and potential positioning have been

FIGURE 30: The Strategic Triangle

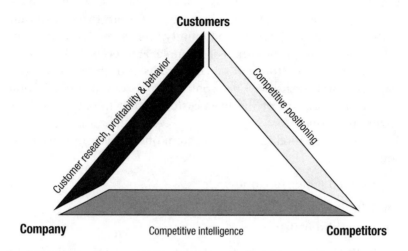

charted (based on research with customers), the company should assess how competitors are seen to perform in respect of these same criteria. Once competitor positioning has been assessed, customers may identify specific competitors who perform well along some of the same dimensions of mass-customization that your firm is seeking. Take this to mean that competitive intelligence should be gathered to assess how these competitors have been able to achieve the perception that they deliver the mass customization benefits customers want.

Competitive intelligence is the process of obtaining and analyzing publicly available data to develop business strategies that will retain or increase market share and shareholder value. There are a number of books that describe how to perform competitive intelligence, so this subject will not be pursued at length here.[62]

Your initial reaction may be that information about competitors' specific approaches to mass customization is not readily nor publicly available. Since the public availability of information is important for the ethical practice of competitive intelligence, you may indeed

---

[62] For a review of the straightforward competitive intelligence techniques that are becoming widely applied in most companies today, see, for example, Ian Gordon, *Beat the Competition: How to Use Competitive Intelligence to Develop Winning Business Strategies*, Basil Blackwell Publishing, Oxford, UK, 1989.

be right, as it is rare for competitors to openly divulge the key issues that have allowed them to mass customize. But sometimes companies do go public, often because management wants to gain exposure with their peer or investor community, and sometimes there are other leakages from the firm. For example, at a recent industry conference on mass customization, consultants and professionals, perhaps not fully sensitized to competitive issues described some fundamental aspects of the mass-customization initiatives of their clients and firms.

Competitive intelligence comes from one or more of three main sources:

1. required public disclosure;
2. information the firm chooses to disclose; and
3. from third parties.

In the case of mass customization, much of the intelligence a company needs will come from third parties, such as customers, channel intermediaries, suppliers of hardware and software, and vendors of industrial machinery. By piecing together what competitors have done, you have an opportunity to cost their program and to assess this cost in the light of your available budget. And, in so doing, your firm should have learned pitfalls to avoid and be able to plan a mass-customization program that is more likely to succeed.

4. Operational Feasibility

Once the options have been identified and validated with customers, and it has been confirmed that successful implementation will deliver competitive advantage that can be significant and sustainable, the next issue to be addressed is whether or not it is practical to implement these options. Clearly, every assessment will be different and each will depend on the options under investigation. In each case, specifications should be written to confirm the desired outputs of the implementation. Then the implementation should proceed under close monitoring to ensure that the specifications are being followed. I recall asking software developers to execute according to well-defined customer needs and competitor differentiation requirements. Off went the key developer to crunch code each night until the wee hours. At an internal unveiling of the implementation, key functionality was absent. "Well, one evening I needed to make a choice," he said in an edgy tone, "and I decided to do this instead." Operational feasibility should include review of:

- Information technology, considering issues such as those reviewed in Chapter 7.
- Business processes, recognizing that, to a very real extent, the data warehouse is reengineering. That is, thoughtful consideration of the IT architecture and full implementation of a data warehouse has the potential to change or transform the firm's business processes.
- People and associated knowledge and training issues (recruitment, training, motivation, management, retention for delivery of mass-customization benefits).
- Customer and channel interface issues (which may be linked to technology and business processes in areas such as call centers, interactive voice response (IVR), computer telephony integration (CTI), Internet, kiosks etc.).
- Approaches to engage the customer in a learning relationship, using a combination of the foregoing, so that the same questions need never be asked twice of the same customer.

Operational feasibility should clearly identify the one-time capital equipment that needs to be purchased and the processes and activities that need to be changed. The costs associated with the initial purchases and changes should be identified, and the ongoing costs described.

5. Financial Feasibility

Of course, the business case will depend heavily on assumptions associated with, for example:

- the lifetime value of customers;
- your ability to upgrade the margin of specific products and services, and margin mix of your product line overall;
- cost reduction in areas such as finished goods inventories;
- reduction of end-of-life product write-offs;

- new revenues from additional customers; and
- the response of competitors to your initiative.

Even though the benefits of mass customization can be immense, so too can the costs. In addition, mass customization may make existing investments in plant, process and technology obsolete, further causing the green shade brigade to weep. So, obtaining passage of the business case and securing capital expenditure approvals may well be an issue.

Although the potential investment may be large indeed, it should be recognized that the IT portion of this — including incremental bandwidth, memory, processing and storage — will become substantially less expensive in the future[63]. If, after weighing costs and benefits of financial feasibility, the numbers still do not work, do not give up the mass-customization business case yet. Seek a cost at which implementation will become feasible, and be prepared to watch the cost curve of technology and other factors until this can be done. Your issue may then become one of timing rather than whether or not to implement.

A Mass-Customization Plan

As mentioned, the costs of mass customization can be high. One challenge may therefore be to undertake just some customization, somewhat less than the full extent you and your customers might prefer. Develop a plan for full mass customization, and then select specific modules for fast tracking. The best ones to choose will obviously be those most desired by customers and those which make the most significant competitive difference.

Suppose you made off-the-rack suits. Recognizing the aging of the baby boomers, their declining interest in strenuous exercise and witnessing how some are cramming into their overstuffed trousers, would you not consider how best to produce suits in lot sizes of one, instead of longer runs? Perhaps you would focus first on the processes for training and providing incentives to sales staff, ensuring that customers are sold on the benefits of made-to-measure, then getting customers measured, transmitting measurements to the plant,

---

[63] I offer this mostly to challenge the constraints some may place on the initiative by saying it is too costly to mass customize.

implementing technology to produce in unique runs and processes to ship suits back to customers pronto. Later, you might focus on opportunities to expand the range of fabrics, develop customer data warehouses, expand the range of clothing for which you will mass customize, develop a distribution outlet further afield, serving more remote stores, and so on. Such costs as these can wait.

Insource or Outsource Each Component of Mass Customization?

Another way of reducing cost is to consider whether your firm should undertake the mass customization, or if third parties, such as channel intermediaries and end-customers, have a role to play in this process, too.

Dell Computer pioneered mass customization of personal computers, which they sell direct. But, if you want to buy a computer after they close their switchboard, or if you want specific software, you may still go to a computer reseller to obtain the service you want. The reseller often provides the customer with extended utility by assembling a total benefit bundle for the customer, integrating hardware, software, networks, delivery and installation and offering financing, service contracts, evergreen programs, repurchase of existing computers and training, among other non-product related benefits. And companies such as Compaq and IBM benefit by selling through this channel that firms such as Dell and Gateway 2000 have bypassed.

Before deciding who will perform specific components of mass customization, you could ask questions regarding four areas:

1. Customer Involved Directly
2. Customer Involved Indirectly
3. Custom or Standard
4. Supply Chain

1. Customer Involved Directly

Should the customer perceive that the product or service has been mass customized for him/her, or should they simply be delighted with the benefits they receive? If they are to perceive that customization has taken place, they will likely need to be involved in the customization process, requiring changes to technology and processes.

Customer involvement in customization will require that the firm develop a formal customer learning process and put in place the necessary infrastructure, including the data warehouse. The firm should emphasize four levels of customer learning for employees: individual employees learning more about the customer in the context of their role in the firm; team learning within the enterprise; team learning between the company and other firms with which it does business, such as suppliers and distribution channel intermediaries; and team learning with customers, using formal processes for interaction and management of the customer relationship. This makes eminent sense for the business-to-business marketer. Consumer marketers may find they need to invite the customer in, perhaps by establishing customer advisory groups, and/or move production close to consumption and mass customize service, as well.

In a 1988 report,[64] we noted the emergence of "shop-plants," where production was increasingly being moved closer to consumption. We described how muffins, photolabs and eyewear retailers were facilitating more immediate consumption and anticipated a time when fashion goods retailers would incorporate the customer into varied images of their products to facilitate the sale in-store, with production occurring in short succession. This is now under way. Paris Miki, a Japanese eyewear retailer, involves customers in a collaborative approach to review frames that are "right" for each individual. After taking a picture of the consumer's face, analyzing its attributes, and combining this with the customer's statements regarding preferred appearance, the screen displays glasses for the customer to review. Then the customer and the optician collaborate on the details of the frame, before the glasses are produced on site.[65] Many products in the fashion industry could be similarly customized.

On the other hand, my local Ford dealer sends me personalized and customized letters reminding me of the next date when my car should be serviced. I have no involvement in the process, but remain happy that they are tracking the service history of the vehicle closely enough to ensure that it receives proper maintenance.

---

[64] "Tomorrow's Customers," *Woods Gordon Management Consultants*, 21st edition, 1988.

[65] Abridged from James H. Gilmore and B. Joseph Pine, "The Four Faces of Mass Customization," *Harvard Business Review*, January-February, 1997, p. 91.

2. Customer Involved Indirectly

If the customer is not to be directly involved in the mass customization, how should the processes be designed so that they are acceptable to the consumer?

There is much potential in the process of gathering and analyzing data for the consumer to become startled or upset. As we have seen, Americans prize privacy and mass customization has the potential to be seen as a violation. Processes need to be designed with this in mind. Thus, rather than greeting a customer with "happy birthday" at the checkout, it would be better simply to send the customer sales literature, customized with content applicable to relevant birthday presents and cards a few weeks before the birthday.

By involving the consumer in mass customization, perhaps indirectly, the product may receive greater acceptance. Duncan Hines produces cake mixes that do not require much participation by the home baker. Among what little the baker does need to do is add an egg, which is not really needed — egg substitutes have been available for a long time. Homemakers feel guilty when serving kids products they see to have little food value. Perhaps the people at Duncan Hines feel that, by adding an egg, the homemaker can overcome guilt. Opportunities may exist to extend this thinking into other areas, such as icing, toppings, home-baked cookies, breakfast cereal and other consumer products.

3. Custom or Standard

Will the product or service be fully custom, or will some components, modules or subassemblies be standard, with customization occurring in selected areas only?

There are many different approaches to mass customization, well described in the literature.[66] The basic concept often involves definition of modules that can be shared in different ways within mass-customized products. Modules may involve the sharing or swapping of components and they may be assembled-to-order from submodules and components.

Considering the case of General Motors to illustrate the concept of component swapping and sharing. Perhaps GM's first discussion

---

[66] See, for example, B. Joseph Pine II, *Mass Customization—The New Frontier in Business Competition*, HBS Press, 1993.

in this regard should answer two questions: "What is a car?" and "What is a brand?" Resolving these apparently simple questions in the context of mass customization for their best customers for each brand may lead them to conclude, for example, that a car is a set of benefits a consumer expects, including such things as reliability, safety, comfort and affordability. A brand may focus more on the components of functionality and emotion the customer wants from that brand alone. If Pontiac "builds excitement," as their slogan claims, then the consumer would expect to pay most attention to the style, power, handling and driver experience of the vehicle, with secondary attention to the other dimensions.

Now if GM were to design vehicle functionality as modules and pool all these components from which customers can select — all their engines, all their transmissions, all their braking systems and so on, then a customer could start with a platform and add more of what they individually want in a car. Cram GM's powerful Northstar V-8 engine into the small Grand-Prix — why not? You might need to take the heavy-duty brake package and improved suspension, and you may have to pay quite a bit more, but if you want a family rocket sled, it is ready and waiting. The customer could have an expanded array of options, were GM to view all their divisions as platforms and housing for customer selections. And GM may be able to streamline the range of options, cut inventories of parts at all levels of their logistics system and in the aftermarket and eliminate production where there is duplication. Perhaps.

Another example comes from the technology industry. Software developers often produce their product as a series of modules which "talk" with one another, when enabled. It is not uncommon for customers wanting only certain parts of the software, say the financial package, to also receive payroll and benefits modules, since the customer only has access to the financials, the product resembles a solution built for him/her alone. This is taken further by the installer, which charts the purchasing company's processes and appears to customize the software for the individual customer's needs. Software packages actually make this a more or less routine implementation, but the customer thinks they are getting something far more custom than is in fact the case, and often pay a premium for this benefit. And, if the company ever wants the payroll and benefits, a simple key (number) can unlock access to this previously prohibited area.

Bally Engineered Structures, in Bally, Pennsylvania, produces refrigerated buildings such as walk-in coolers and freezers. It uses a standard panel of steel or aluminum with urethane as the core insulating component that can be assembled, Lego-like, into individual products.[67] This allows Bally to give their customers more options, design quicker and to make changes faster and ship more rapidly, all at less cost than previously.

4. Supply Chain

Is there an opportunity to disaggregate the value chain so that different companies produce mass customized components, or should the primary creator of the value deliver the total customized solution?

The historical view of production and supplying customers was called a supply chain whereby suppliers operated according to a process described by Figure 31 on the following page, once the standardized design and development processes had been completed.

A supply chain could be viewed as "inside-out" thinking that sees the customer as the end-point of consumption of a more-or-less standardized product. Mass Customization calls for a rethinking of this process of creating value for customers, because the process really starts with the customer, not with suppliers and manufacturers. It may be more accurate to think of the supply chain as a demand cycle among some of the members of the chain of relationships, presented diagramatically in overview in Figure 23. The implication of this figure is that the process of mass customizing for the customer never ends.

The individual customer interacts with the company and is engaged by the firm's capabilities: people, processes, knowledge and insight and technology. That engagement typically comprises involvement in the product design or configuration and a commitment to purchase a specific product and volume. Once this has happened, the firm procures raw materials, packaging and subassemblies on behalf of the customer, before assembling the modules in the configuration the customer specified. The process of making something for a customer may be triggered by the customer, or by the company applying its knowledge and insight to define an opportunity to add

---

[67] B. Joseph Pine II and Thomas W. Pietrocini, "Standard modules allow mass customization at Bally Engineered Structures," *Planning Review*, v21n4, Jul/Aug, 1993, pp. 20-22.

FIGURE 31: The Supply Chain

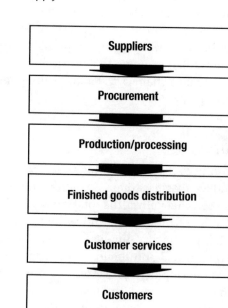

value with the customer. Either way, this leads to an order to make a product and provide services which, in turn, leads to procurement and production for the make-to-order product. As previously mentioned, after the product is made, the company wraps individualized service around the product and places it with the customer in the time, place and manner the customer expects. And so the process continues, without end.

A mass-customized product is not distributed in a "channel," which has a mass-standardization aura associated with it. (Channels sound to me like pipes that carry water to your house. Few products have this same commoditization, so most should go through something other than a channel.) Mass customized products are "placed" as, where and when the customer requires. Through a process of customer collaboration, the purchase decision is evaluated and the performance of the firm and its offering assessed so that both can continue to meet customer requirements. The suppliers to the manufacturer or service producer involved in this process, either throughout or at key milestones, are also evaluated collaboratively to ensure that they create the value the firm is seeking to achieve.

If mass customization means the value chain increasingly resembles a demand cycle, is outsourcing and subassembly production counter to the intent of the mass-customized company? More generally, and taken to the extreme, can a virtual company — a firm that produces little but lends its name to the product produced — also be a mass customizer?

This is an intriguing question and one that will be highlighted in the auto industry, which has long been a battleground of mass customization. Volkswagen's new plant in Resende, Brazil, produces VWs — nothing remarkable in that, except that the plant has just one Volkswagen employee in the entire facility. All the others are employed by, and machinery is owned by, suppliers that have essentially bought space in the plant to be in proximity to the other vendors' operations. Workers from Brazil's IochpeMaxion assemble the chassis, Rockwell incorporates axles and suspension, Cummins Engine adds motive power, Bridgestone/Firestone provides tires, and so on.[68] When a customer now specifies their preferences in a VW, all the sub-assembly suppliers must make it happen. Volkswagen owns the processes for car manufacture. They own the responsibility for the customer, dealer and supplier relationships. And they own the brand equity of VW. Beyond this, they have been astute enough to realize that they need not own much more.

&⊙&

Mass customization is risky and can prove challenging. Full mass customization can be expensive to implement unless margins and customer lifetime value is high, unless there is potential for significant additional value creation or create a breakthrough in the market. Spectacles are one such area, where margins have historically been higher than many other industries, where customers treat the product as a fashion good and are buying more often than their eyesight appears to require, and where the potential for longer-term value creation could be high. In the longer term, the merchant or "shop-plant" owner may be in a position to lever their customer knowledge by selling bi-focals as the buyer ages, expanding the range to include contacts, marketing consumables for keeping glasses clean, services for maintaining the glasses, insurance against loss or damage, offering

---

[68] *Toronto Star*, May 31, 1997, p. 21.

laser surgery through a linked facility and so on. All this, and the current economics, may make it viable to invest more heavily now to provide the customer with the unique appearance each wants.

For vendors in categories where some of the drivers are different, the results may not be economic and may not warrant the heavy up-front investment. And the executive who does not fully appreciate the underlying key success factors for industry participation can become a victim. Recently, the heir apparent to the presidency of a major US office furniture company, decided to push forward a make-to-order mass customization initiative for the firm. The program bogged down and the executive actually broke down, spending considerable time in recuperative care before returning to much lighter duty.

While mass customization can be challenging to implement, it is the skeletal structure for Relationship Marketing (the customer provides the heart and soul for the initiative). Without mass customization, or with too little, Relationship Marketing becomes nothing more than a catch phrase, a slogan of this week and an opportunity for competitors to do the real job. On the other hand, with too much mass customization, the company may go broke trying to give the customer more than they can afford. The job of planning for more mass customization in a company should go to the czar of Relationship Marketing, working in a multidisciplinary team to assess issues such as:

1. Do our best customers want a mass-customized solution? Will they pay more for it? Will they pay more for it from us (how are we positioned with them)?

2. What are the key dimensions of the solution that must be mass customized, from the perspective of the customer?

3. Will our existing capabilities — people, processes, knowledge and insight and technology — allow us to deliver the mass customization customers want? Do they have the right context, content, skills, flexibility, willingness, focus, structure? In particular, do we need a major make-over of the processes and technology in the company, from design/development, to production and onwards through the demand cycle? Can we save money through mass customization? Can we do mass customization in steps, according to what we can afford and what is necessary, rather than implementing a full-scale initiative at once?

4. What do we have to change about ourselves to deliver the mass-customization benefit? Will our existing organizational structure accommodate the change? Will our capital base? Will our culture? Do we have the leadership commitment? Importantly, is there a business case for the initiative?

5. If we implement a mass-customization initiative, what will be the competitors' response? How will we, in turn, respond?

6. What are the barriers to exit, should we implement a mass-customization initiative? What have we burned, what have we built by going down this road?

Mass customization and Relationship Marketing with customers more generally, will require the support of other stakeholders. Their contribution to the value that will be created and shared is critical for Relationship Marketing to work. The next chapter considers the chain of relationships with these stakeholders, including investors/owners, boards of directors, management, employees, labor unions, bankers, knowledge capital suppliers (such as ad agencies and consultants), equipment suppliers, raw material and consumables suppliers, IT vendors, channel intermediaries, customers, media and political stakeholders in government.

CHAPTER NINE

&∞

Building a Chain of Relationships

Victory shifts from man to man.
Homer

So far we have noted that Relationship Marketing has the potential to change everything in the company and its interactions with its customers. We have focused mainly on relationships between the firm and customer to add the value each wants. We have considered the unique value individual customers often want and the impact of this on relationships and on the capabilities internal to the enterprise. But the value customers want, whether individually or in aggregate, is not created by the company acting alone — it requires contribution from other stakeholders. This contribution comes from stakeholders committing to, and aligning with, the same relationship the company is trying to create with end-users. In other words, each stakeholder, whether employee, supplier, distribution channel intermediary, service company, banker or investor, has the potential to strengthen the company's relationships with its end-customers by seeing the complete picture, understanding their role and working with the company to continuously build mutual value.

If any one of the stakeholders do not advance the company's end-customer relationship, they limit or detract from the shareholder value the firm is trying to build. Worse. If the relationship between a stakeholder and the company differs in intent, intensity or nature, the outcome of the relationship between the company and its customers can be in doubt.[69] The end-customer relationship depends on the effective alignment of the company's capabilities with their expectations. In turn, for its capabilities, the company depends on the mutual value it creates with stakeholders other than the customer. So, if companies and customers are to continuously create and share mutual value to advance the interests of each, the company should expect and seek alignment with its stakeholders on the same basis. For example, if IT is to be a key capability in serving individual customers uniquely, the company should be aligned with IT resources that deliver the human and infrastructure capital needed to make the customer investment pay off. The firm thus depends on relationships with internal IT staff, external suppliers of computing, software and communications technologies, project managers and external consultants.

As another example, if a car company decided to make cars in any color an individual customer wanted, they will need help in areas such as the paint, painting systems, information technology and customer interaction and information processes, among others, within the assembly plant, in body shops and on the dealer's sales floor, to make this mass customization possible. Companies, such as paint supplier DuPont, will need to facilitate the process. If they do not, and the car company wants the custom paint capabilities badly enough, the relationship between the company and the supplier will be weakened, particularly should another firm step up to the challenge.

Relationship Marketing thus may be seen as a "chain of relationships" that are created by the company on its behalf and that of the customer, and are maintained and built by the company. The concept of a mutually rewarding relationship will not be hard for the company to communicate to its suppliers, many of whom are probably receptive to the concept of deepening or extending the relationship. Suppliers always seem more interested than customers in a meaningful relationship. It is the wise customer that understands that a supplier can contribute much more to the company's future than the lowest price, and that this contribution requires a relationship.

---

[69] Schneider and Bowen showed in 1985 that there is a link between relationships internal to the organization and the satisfaction of the company's customers: B. Schneider and D. E. Bowen, "Employee and Customer Perceptions of Service in Banks," *Journal of Applied Psychology*, p. 70.

Thus, while the concept of a chain of relationships may receive rapid approval among the various stakeholders, the specifics may be harder to achieve. It is no easy matter to bring capabilities into alignment. Companies such as Wal-Mart, with enormous purchasing power, were challenged to have their suppliers implement IT systems that are uniform. But IT is just one of four categories of capabilities, and even companies with clout like Wal-Mart cannot secure alignment of every capability with their thousands of suppliers. Having obtained IT alignment is an important step but not the end of the journey, as this chapter will discuss. Here we review relationships with stakeholders other than the customer. We consider how to improve relationships with these various stakeholders so that the company's share of the mutual value created with customers in turn is available for sharing with other stakeholders. The end-customer relationship is seen as the economic engine that provides for the company's other relationships. The deeper and more meaningful the end-customer relationship, the more will be available for sharing with others, leading to the potential for greater alignment with various stakeholders.

It is fairly common for companies to talk in terms of relationships with their stakeholders, and how the company sees relationships as important. But inherently the word relationship has no more meaning than quality, service or innovation, without being more specifically defined, and a commitment to relationships with all stakeholders is a commitment to clean air and all things nice. The challenge for companies is to see relationships as an explicit and fundamental component of their strategy and consider how to add value through relationships to all the stakeholders who together comprise the chain of relationships that develops value continuously with customers. In Figure 32, a chain of relationships is presented, showing graphically that all relationships must link and remain intact if the relationship important to the customer is to endure. This chapter considers the establishment and growth of relationships with stakeholders with this end in mind. Stakeholders include those mentioned in Figure 32. In this chapter, we pay attention to relationships with:

- Investors/Owners and Financial Institutions
- Distribution Channel Intermediaries
- Employees

FIGURE 32: The Chain of Relationships

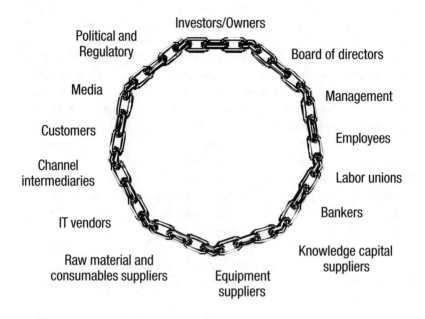

- Suppliers
- Co-venture Partners

  We also discuss:

- Management and Control of the Chain of Relationships
- The New Role of Management

Customers cannot be effectively integrated into a value-based relationship unless these other stakeholders are aligned in this same pursuit.

The chain of relationships between the company and its stakeholders should benefit from the same core principles as the relationship desired between the company and its customers, which would likely include:

- mutual benefit;
- continuity of effort and continuous improvement;
- long-term time horizons;
- real time and teamwork based issue resolution;
- knowledge sharing;

- systems integration;
- open communication;
- dispute resolution mechanisms; and
- identification of the conditions under which the relationships will change or dissolve and, as noted, the processes by which change will be managed.

The challenge here is to identify the values most important to customers and the role each category of stakeholder has in delivering that component of value. For example, if customers value on-time delivery as a critical basis for their relationship with a company, the relationships the firm develops with its suppliers and internal labor pools should reflect this. If there is asymmetry in the relationships — such as customers valuing knowledge content in the product to make them more competitive in their markets, but the firm, on the other hand, focusing on cost reduction with their suppliers — it is likely that the company will not be able to sustain a customer relationship in the long term. They will not be able to deliver to all their customer's expectations.

Relationships with Investors/Owners and Financial Institutions

Owners and management determine the relationship orientation of the firm. In closely held firms, owners have considerable influence and would need to be committed to this program for Relationship Marketing to become more than just another phrase of the month.

In more widely held companies, management may play a relatively more important role than owners in bringing a Relationship Marketing program to fruition. Publicly traded US companies have ownership that is characterized by numerous, relatively transient owners of stock, who manage by the value of each transaction, who each may have modest stakes, who use available public information to make rational, economic buy-sell decisions, and whose influence in the company individually and in aggregate is low.[70] In this context, management wields considerable power. Even in companies where institutional investors have significant stakes on behalf of

---

70 Michael E. Porter, "Capital Disadvantage: America's Failing Capital Investment System," *Harvard Business Review*, September–October, 1992.

pension funds, and investment companies have material commitments through mutual funds they manage, it is not common for either category to be aggressively represented on the board of directors. And without the owners and managers of long-term, patient capital providing strategic rather than transactional advice, the company may lack the will to invest sufficiently in the capabilities needed for long-term customer relationships. It should be no surprise that relationships between companies and with customers in the market place are most advanced in Japan, where capital is more often permanent and investment is relationship driven, with specific firms having significant investment stakes.

The reasons for this are rooted in history. Before the Second World War, the Japanese economy was dominated by the *zaibatsu*, ten family-led companies, including Mitsui, Mitsubishi, Yasuda and Sumitomo.[71] Although attempts were made at the conclusion of the war to ensure that the stock in these companies was widely held, before long the firms bought back much of the public distribution and set about their business relationships as beneficial owners and relationship managers. Today, the family-like structure of member firms, the *keiretsu*, some of which have the same names as their *zaibatsu* predecessors, make for strong associations and mutual value creation. There are three main types of *keiretsu*: those aligned with banks, those linked to industrial companies and those tied with trading companies. In all cases, patient capital is assured, as is the long view and a relationship orientation between companies. Among other benefits, the *keiretsu* structure benefits the members by lowering the cost of capital, ensuring markets and loyal suppliers, giving preferential access to buying departments and group projects.[72] The *keiretsu* are often held in place by cross-ownership, common company directors and significant on-going investment on the part of the lead company in the group, buying back stock to secure the position.

In all likelihood, the US system of investment will not be transformed over any meaningful time horizon and, in any event, there is little pressure to change. Particularly with regard to innovation, the performance of the US system has been much more effective than in international capital markets, which can be more rigid and structured, as noted in the case of Japan. But the issue remains that fleet-

---

[71] James C. Morgan and J. Jeffrey Morgan, *Cracking the Japanese Market*, Free Press, 1991.
[72] Ibid.

ing ownership geared to maximizing near term returns is not the best crucible in which to form long-term relationships, be they with customers or suppliers.

Conditions for Relationship-Driven Progress

Given these conditions, firms most likely to attain meaningful, relationship-driven progress will have as many of the following conditions as possible:

- patient, yet not undemanding, capital;
- narrowly held distribution of equity among stockholders;
- investors with similar investment profiles, with strategic investors preferred over near-term transactional ones;
- a board of directors which mirrors ownership preference, and which validates Relationship Marketing dimensions in thought and deed; and
- a process of governance at the board level which values Relationship Marketing, and ensures that management is focused on this issue by having its various subcommittees, such as the personnel committee, include Relationship Marketing in their terms of reference.

Certainly, in any company where the investor community is oriented to near-term results and rapid capital appreciation, and has a board that spends more time on current financials rather than strategic drivers of shareholder value, management will find it difficult to advance a Relationship Marketing agenda. In such an environment, the committed Relationship Marketer may be tempted to pursue opportunities elsewhere.

This need not occur. But for the company to commit to a series of strategic initiatives, it will first need a plan to develop strategic investors. The principles illustrated in this book can be put to work with the investor community, just as they can be for customers, and management can assess for which investors they will be creating specific value. Investor research is an emerging area of management discipline. Companies are now starting to assess the needs of investors as they previously did for markets, and seek to market their firms to specific segments in the investor community. At present, there are three main ways companies communicate with current and potential investors. Firstly, companies produce voluntary documents, such as extended detail in their annual reports, as well as file mandatory reports, such as the regulatory filings, requirements of the Securities and Exchange Commission and other regulatory agencies. Secondly, many companies seek to influence retail investors through communications intermediaries, such as the financial press and investment advisors with the trading and research firms. Companies use these interviews to help the investor audience gain a full appreciation for the value of the company. Thirdly, companies engage in extended discussion with the institutional investors, seeking to attract and retain them as investors. It is uncommon for companies to develop a detailed investor relationship plan, describing for example, the mix of investors the company seeks, the profile of investors to be targeted for retention and those to be secured as new investors, the measurable objectives the company has to assess investor relationships, the value each investor segment (and eventually, individual) seeks, the value the company plans to deliver, and the methods the company plans to deploy to bond with customers, including data warehousing and near real time communications, for example.

If the current mix of investors is not well suited to the key success factors of the industry, this plan can reshape the mix and position the firm favorably as an investment vehicle to investors with a preferred profile. In short, the investor relations function in many firms has received short shrift and represents an area of considerable opportunity for companies to build shareholder value.

Companies and Financial Value

In every industry, there are four types of companies. They are those that:

- build financial value internal to the company and externally for shareholders, with stock being fairly valued in the market;
- build financial value for shareholders, but have not been fully priced in the stockmarket;
- build share value for investors but have not created meaningful financial value; and
- do not develop either financial or shareholder value.

This mix of companies is shown in Figure 33. The largest opportunity for Relationship Marketing may be with companies which create real financial value, but whose shareholder value has not been fully realized in the market. This group is termed "realizable value." For these, there may be more of an opportunity to build shareholder value by assessing the underlying causes for the poor performance, be they ineffective investor communications, an inappropriate shareholder mix or other factors.

The group called "questionable value" in the diagram will need to be related to with great care in order to sustain the value creation already in the market. As for all groups, investors should be assessed for their investment behaviors. If investors in this group have been buying into a vision they expect the company to deliver, the firm will indeed need to make progress in its implementation or risk losing market value. Investor relations in firms with investors so behaving should focus on the progression of the company on the road to its promised destination.

In the group called "value stars," the company has already been successful in developing shareholder value that is more or less in line with its financial performance. Companies in this group can still develop and enhance relationships with these investors for a number

FIGURE 33: Relationships with Investors

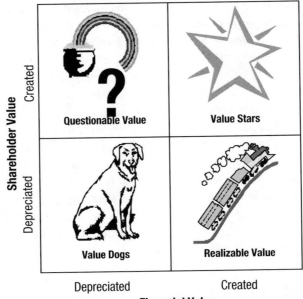

of reasons, including ensuring that their stock remains fairly priced and to help keep their investors invested, should the firm experience unanticipated shortfalls or disruption to their financial performance.

The group of companies called "value dogs" in the diagram also needs to focus on investor relations, but perhaps with different objectives in mind. These objectives may include ensuring that their investor-base is committed to the long term and will sustain the company as its financial performance evolves, restructures or takes other actions to improve.

Considerable research has already been conducted into shareholder value creation using approaches similar to the above.[73] For example, financial value could be measured as return on investment or return on net assets in relation to the cost of capital. Shareholder value could be assessed in terms of the change in market capitalization in relation to low risk investments in government-secured bonds. There is much evidence that, even in strongly growing stockmarkets, there are opportunities for companies to improve their investor relationships and continuously create the value individual shareholders want. In virtually every industry, there are companies that perform well in the stock market, those that perform poorly and those in between. And in every industry, there are some firms that merit a higher stock price and some that cannot justify the price they have. The Relationship Marketing company should not see investor relations as an isolated area to be staffed with functional professionals, but part of the business mainstream and a key process for which a Relationship Marketer should assume responsibility. The charge to that person could include planning the investor relationship, including understanding how and why his firm is valued as it is, and planning for implementation by employing the principles discussed throughout this book.

If you work in a firm where the investor relations function is weak or where senior management sees the role as peripheral — even a nuisance — to the conduct of its "real work," have management read this book and then start the debate. And if your firm is beholden to a bank or other financial institution, you will likely already have appreciated the importance of a close, open working relationship with your friendly banker. Here's hoping the banker will read this book, too, and place equal and real emphasis on the relationship.

---

[73] Andersen Consulting, Corporate Renaissance, Stern Stewart and Company, among others.

Relationships with Distribution Channel Intermediaries

A salesman from a major computer manufacturer announced to the management of a software, hardware and services company that he was pleased to recognize the company as a value-added-reseller[74] (VAR) channel for the manufacturer's products. On the other hand, the software company considered itself independent, certainly not part of any company's channel. The salesman described the computer manufacturer's unique vision and its differentiated products. The software company felt its customers did not see the manufacturer or their computers in that way. The salesman suggested hardware's critical role in the customer's decision to buy, but the VAR viewed software to be the principal driver in selling integrated solutions. With differing perspectives on many fronts, the meeting ended. In the period that followed, the hardware vendor did not establish a relationship with the software company, which went on to sell considerable volumes of other companies' hardware. The opportunity may have been there for the manufacturer, but it saw the intermediary as its conduit to market, not a customer. This was a real situation; I represented the software company at the meeting.

As important as the opportunity may be for companies to work together with their customers to create new business value, it is even more important for them to work together with their distribution channel intermediaries, and to treat them as they would their best customers, not just as "their" channel to market. It is important for three main reasons to have a real relationship with the companies that take one's product to market, reasons that the manufacturer may sometimes take for granted:

1. The battle for the customer first must be won at the channel level before the end-customer can be secured.

2. The intermediary adds value to the product that the manufacturer cannot easily or economically do.

3. The intermediary can be an enduring basis for creating new value with customers and for taking costs out of current systems.

---

[74] Essentially a company that takes the computer and, by incorporating software and services, provides an expanded solution to the customer.

The challenge for companies is to forge a meaningful relationship with distribution channel intermediaries, genuinely seeing them as having interests in common and making allowances for areas of difference. For example, both companies have an interest in advancing their financial position. But the vendor often wants the intermediary to operate according to a more "strategic" set of rules, while the company in the channel, often independently owned and managed, may see financial performance as a more personal and near-term accomplishment. The independent operator may think: "Sell more high margin stuff and buy a boat." The corporate channel manager may think: "These dealers are so short term in their thinking. I want more mind share and market share from them, so they will help us reach our plan objectives, so I will receive my bonus and buy a boat."

How to Build the Relationship

How then to build the relationship between manufacturers and distribution channel intermediaries, continuously and for mutual interest? The principles for continuously developing mutual value with channel intermediaries are the same as for customers, with a few twists. Here are ten steps on which to focus:

- Step 1: Mutual Respect
- Step 2: Establish and Own a Process for Relationship Development
- Step 3: Treat Distribution Channel Intermediaries as Customers
- Step 4: Recognize Distribution Channel Intermediaries as Independent Businesses
- Step 5: Plan Together
- Step 6: Innovate Together
- Step 7: Take-Out Costs from the Entire System
- Step 8: Align Operations with an End-Customer and Market Positioning in Mind
- Step 9: Bundle Services with Products
- Step 10: Be Consistent

We discuss each of these next.

Step 1: Mutual Respect

Mutual respect is a fundamental precondition for building the relationship. If either party considers the other to be weaker or inferior, or fails to accept differences, for example, with the other's management, culture, time horizons or business models, not only will new business value prove difficult and stressful for both to develop, but there is potential for existing value inherent in the relationship to erode. For example, there are manufacturers which consider intermediaries as short term in orientation (which is contrasted with the manufacturer's "strategic" view of the world — read "smarter") and even as "order takers" who may add limited value to the product. One supplier even refers to his distribution channel intermediaries as "box pushers." Manufacturers with such a poor attitude towards their dealers can experience persistent difficulty in growing their businesses through this distribution channel. Some even resort to making demands from their dealers, threatening them or insisting that they make more investments or commitments in support of the company, rather than working together in their mutual interest. Companies seeking these compliant behaviors before they have won the intermediary's commitment will make a quick trip down the road to confrontation and poor channel performance.

Step 2: Establish and Own a Process for Relationship Development

Vendors that wish to continuously build mutual value with their distribution channel intermediaries, will likely have adopted much of the advice provided throughout this book for other stakeholders. In so doing, vendors will have considered five main issues:

1. Differences in Relative Importance
2. Research of Relationship Quality
3. Formal Plan
4. Criteria for Measuring Performance
5. Process for Relationship Governance

   We discuss each of these matters next.

1. Differences in Relative Importance

Companies will understand the differences in the relative importance of distribution channel intermediaries by assessing their lifetime or long-term value. Companies will have selected among the intermediaries the best ones on which to focus.

2. Research of Relationship Quality

Companies will have independently researched the current state of their relationships with each of their distribution channel intermediaries. Included in this assessment, they will have reviewed the expectations of their best channel intermediaries, the current state of bonding and the intermediary's expectations and amenability for an advancement in bonding, alignment, performance and other mutual interests. The company will know what commitments the intermediary will make to the process of bonding with their supplier, including time, skill and financial levels of investment.

3. Formal Plan

The company will have developed a formal and explicit plan, objectives and process to work with each best intermediary to build the value both seek. The company will also explicitly state what they are and are not prepared to do to make the intermediary more profitable. For example, will the firm redesign its distribution channels so that there are fewer companies or types of channels competing for the available business?

There are a number of other dimensions to the plan that the supplier should address, including:

Channel member profitability This is typically the most important issue the channel intermediary wishes to address. Channel intermediaries need to control three factors to make money: product and service margin, inventory turns and "below-the-line" cost management. Below-the-line elements can include advertising, financing costs of inventory and receivables, overheads, inventory obsolescence and so on. If the vendor is to develop a serious relationship with the channel intermediary, it will need to help the company improve their performance in all dimensions. Perhaps a starting point for the relationship bonding is to engage in a diagnosis of the intermediary's business (subject to their approval, of course), assess areas of opportunity where the vendor might contribute and then work together to find ways to improve financial performance. It is likely that some of the approaches that will be adopted will lead to the companies aligning aspects of their businesses and redefining some responsibilities so that duplication of effort is reduced and the overall processes are streamlined. For example, the intermediary now handling all customer service may be encouraged to take only the first customer call, with more detailed service requirements being channeled to the vendor.

End-customer focus and management Channel intermediaries are often concerned about "who controls the customer" and like to keep customer information closely held. In the spirit of a partnership where both supplier and channel intermediary are focused on the same customer, it is not productive to think in such terms. If companies are genuinely working in the interests of one another and their own, they need to think in terms of assessing who will perform what role in adding value with the end-customer. The company and the intermediary need to develop a picture of the best customers, one that includes the total customer profitability, for the intermediary and for the vendor. With this assessment in hand, the companies can decide with which end-customers relationships will be forged, and what the implications are for both companies in terms of their processes, people, technology and knowledge and insight systems.

Training Many intermediaries have staff who will need to benefit from training in fundamental aspects of Relationship Marketing. The vendor should be prepared to provide this training, some of which may be formal, but much of which will likely be informal, with the channel intermediary's staff learning by doing — participating in joint teams to advance aspects of the relationship.

Planning A key aspect of the relationship between channel intermediary and the vendor includes mutual planning, starting with the establishment and synchronization of joint planning processes. It is not uncommon for intermediaries to have less formal planning processes and outputs than their suppliers, and for the plans to have content with limited usefulness to the supplier. Equally, the supplier's plans may have interesting information for the intermediary, but may not always be directly relevant. In addition, planning may occur out-of-phase, with one company planning according to a calendar year and another using their fiscal year-end as the basis for the planning cycle. The two companies will need to do their best to bring their planning cycles into alignment, so that joint planning is more relevant and timely. While this is not always possible, particularly in industries where there may be a large number of intermediaries with different fiscal year-ends, it may be possible for the vendor to have a "living" plan that is updated more than once a year to allow for mutual planning with important intermediaries, whatever their planning cycle.

Interenterprise information and communication systems The creation of mutual value with intermediaries will likely require that the information systems currently in place in the two companies communicate more freely. Each company should be prepared to open their databases — or several of their databases — to their channel partner. There are secure ways of doing this both on the Internet and using dial-up access. Sometimes the vendor's IT department may be in a better position to expedite and fund this initiative, a significant component of new value that the supplier can often contribute to the relationship. In the process, the customer may be better served, and the processes leading to this service can be streamlined.

Michelin North America designed an on-line ordering system, based on input from their dealers. They introduced their Bib Net system to automate routine transactions and to bond more closely with their dealers. Dealers can check inventory, order tires and process claims and do so outside of Michelin's regular business hours.[75]

Customer information systems In order to develop a total picture of the end-customer, the intermediary may need some help with their data warehouses, customer interface systems, software, data visualization or other issues where technical know-how is important. As for inter-enterprise information and communication, the supplier can contribute meaningfully to the intermediary by helping them adopt Relationship Marketing principles in their technology. For example, car companies can provide dealers with software for sales support in

---

[75] Nick Wreden, "Good Deal for Michelin Dealers", *Information Week*, October 20, 1997, p. 99.

ordering, pricing, product availability, financing and other areas. Hotel chains can provide software for travel agents to use not only to book accommodation, but to plan vacations, with considerable information on the destinations and hotels being considered by the traveler.

4. Criteria for Measuring Performance

Companies will have developed measurable criteria for assessing mutual performance and have a measurement and tracking system in place to manage and control progress to the mutual expectations.

5. Process for Relationship Governance

Companies will have a formal process for governance of the relationship, including dispute resolution mechanisms. They will also think of the relationship more broadly, not strictly in financial terms. Although financial considerations will obviously remain important, companies will have a wider array of measures to assess the mutual performance of the relationship, based on the key success factors for winning and keeping customers both supplier and intermediary consider to be attractive. These measures could include the level of resources focused by the intermediary on the vendor, intermediary share of best end-customers, growth in end-customer sales, end-customer satisfaction and favorability, and measures describing the alignment of capabilities to address the needs of best end-customers, such as the extent to which interenterprise information technology systems are in alignment.

Step 3: Treat Distribution Channel Intermediaries as Customers

We have noted the importance of customers as Relationship Marketing partners. Where the distribution channel is important to access and serve the customer, channel intermediaries are as important as customers. Companies fail to recognize this at their peril.

Whether they are retailers, dealers, resellers, agents or others, the intermediaries have many product and supplier options, and are often quite willing to exercise them, particularly when faced with onerous or one-sided policies from their suppliers. Yet some manufacturers still operate as though their firms and products command respect and have more or less monopoly power. Their policies and procedures, sometimes unchanged from the previous era, can be seen as arrogant by channel intermediaries. An applicable example was noted earlier for a computer hardware company that seemed to have missed customer focus and interest in the software they buy more so than the hardware in vertical markets.

Many computer companies make this mistake in some purchase situations and fail to recognize that the power of the computer company today is less than that of the software company. In making this mistake, they think they can still dictate the terms of the relationship, rather than earn it. One company that has absolutely got the point is Hewlett-Packard. For years they have focused on partnering with stakeholders, and today they have considerable depth and breadth of relationships. Their channel intermediaries are often more committed to the company than its market share would merit, in some sectors, likely leading the firm to yet greater heights. Apple, too, enjoys rabidly committed dealers, in spite of years of weakening financial health at the company and declining margins for both Apple and their dealers. Without the dealer affinity for Apple, perhaps yet other bites would have been taken out of that firm's market share.

Step 4: Recognize Distribution Channel Intermediaries as Independent Businesses

Many distribution channel intermediaries are not owned by large corporations, and are independent. These include dealers in the furniture, appliance, copier and office equipment, automobile and computer businesses and, of course, the many thousands of small retailers, restaurants and insurance brokers that dot the nation.

Problems with the relationship between the manufacturer and these independent intermediaries arise when manufacturers talk in terms of their channel, and attempt to attain objectives that may be at odds with those of the intermediaries. Often, the distribution channel intermediaries are owner/manager operated, and have the associated independent characteristics that might be anticipated from owner/managers. When vendors and channel members disagree about matters such as account control, making investments for the long term, loyalty and support for the vendor and its strategies, the issue of arm's length operation and the right to independent decision making is often at the heart of the disagreement.

Step 5: Plan Together

Imagine this situation. A channel intermediary deals with two main suppliers. One insists that the intermediary meet contracted volume commitments. The other works hard to build the business of both the vendor and their distribution channel intermediaries by openly sharing strategic plans as a prelude to joint tactical planning. All else being equal, with which company would you build your relationship?

A supplier's best channel intermediaries should be amenable to sharing mutually sensitive data and strategic plans and working together, prior to the next iteration of each's plan, to incorporate the other's interests. Planning in this way will require teamwork, executive participation and mutual commitment. The planning process should begin with a plan for a plan, identifying significant expectations, outputs, milestones and responsibilities.

Step 6: Innovate Together

There have been many innovative retailing formats and concepts that have come to the US market in the last decade. Examples include the warehouse club — such as Price Costco, Sam's Club (owned by Wal-Mart) and Pace (Kmart), specialized large-scale operations (Toys-R-Us, Home Depot, Circuit City), and specialized mall outlets (such as The Gap), as well as many others. Aggregations of box stores in so-called Power Centers have emerged to challenge the regional mall. And virtual storefronts are changing the face of distribution channels and even industry structures. For example, Met Life, Prudential, Nationwide and other firms and brokers are selling insurance on the Web. Fedex, UPS, DHL, Airborne and other courier companies are also on the Web to price and take orders, and track and trace parcels. Travel agents such as Epicurious, BizTravel and Travelocity have their services on the Web, as do the major airlines.

In the age of the Internet, it might be said that the Web makes Siamese twins out of retailer and customer. The retailer, learning about the customer's preferences and behaviors becomes reliant on the individual business of each. The customer, having invested in learning the retailer's processes and interface, and having disclosed data, such as credit cards, without ill-effect, is likely to remain glued to the supplier as long as the supplier values the relationship equally.

Are there not more opportunities for vendors to work with distribution channel intermediaries to improve their financial position, make their business model more workable or innovate together? Innovation could occur in new formats, new models within existing formats, new merchandising or financing models, new service categories, going on the Web with the supplier's product foremost, or opposing new Web-based retailers. The vendor may have a pivotal role to play in helping the intermediary improve its financial position or establish a basis for renewed growth. Car companies have allowed too much intra-channel competition by letting too many dealers compete in a local market. For example, in San Diego alone, there are about fifteen Ford dealers within a thirty mile radius of one of the dealers. If Ford does not make attempts to rationalize their dealers and establish a Web-presence for the remaining ones, the market place surely will. And then, the remaining dealerships may be in a position to dictate terms to the car companies. Watch Republic Industry and Wayne Huizenga in this regard.

Step 7: Take-Out Costs from the Entire System

The principles of improving business processes or reengineering aspects of an entire business have been applied by many companies, but opportunities remain to take out time and costs from the processes that cross traditional boundaries of ownership, and which involve suppliers and distribution channel intermediaries. This recognition alone could spur some manufacturers to look beyond their own business operations for cost savings.

For example, Apple implemented a technology solution called ARIS (Apple Reseller Information System) to enable distribution channel intermediaries to undertake on-line ordering of products and parts, review inventory levels in Apple's warehouse, and confirm pricing for all products. By doing this, Apple reduced labor content (and associated cost) compared to the manual approaches previously in place. Resellers cut working capital from inventory and discounting associated with obsolete inventory, while retaining a broad product selection on offer.

Step 8: Align Operations with an End-Customer and Market Positioning in Mind

As in the case of the auto industry, there may be opportunities for companies to rationalize their channel network to fit more closely with the actual volumes available in a market, the profitability of those volumes, the shopping patterns and preferences of individual and best customers and the services these customers expect.

If over one-third of small businesses are buying their computers by mail, does it make sense for companies to have total commitment to a distribution channel of physical storefronts? If the computer company is serving customers from among the remaining two-thirds, which end-customers have the potential to provide sufficient profitability for both intermediary and supplier, and what needs to change in the operations processes of both to make the end-customer happy? If customers want knowledge, for example, in areas such as computer networking, and the intermediary does not currently provide this, there may be opportunities for both intermediary and vendor to identify the service need and establish who will do what and who will pay for each area of capability or activity. In the Relationship Marketing era, there is a need to review roles and responsibilities in the context of an expanded scope of service, one of the main outgrowths of seeking to be more relevant and intense about bonding with customers.

If the distribution channel network for cellular phones was initially designed for in-car installations, does it make sense for cellular companies to maintain dealers in out-of-the-way locations, where today's customer for cellular would rarely venture? In short, manufacturers may assess how many distribution channel intermediaries are needed to go to market and focus their business building initiatives accordingly with those that remain. Perhaps they could seek to build a more intense relationship with fewer intermediaries similarly committed, rather than a fragmented series of initiatives with a large number. Any reduction in number has the potential to build the long-term business case of remaining distribution channel intermediaries and enhance their loyalty to the vendor.

Step 9: Bundle Services with Products

Many companies have witnessed declining differentiation of their products over the last decade, as the number of firms and products available in the market has swelled and markets have matured. There is research[76] evidence that, as markets mature, company performance

---

[76] Profit Impact of Marketing Strategy — PIMS database.

becomes more similar. Perhaps one reason for this, is that companies learn to duplicate successful moves and avoid pitfalls as information proliferates.

One way to improve financial performance, even in industries where some companies have more similar results, is to add value in something abstract, such as the shopping experience, the knowledge of salespeople in pre-sales consulting, after sales support, credit terms, evergreen programs or software. At present, the channel intermediary adds much of this value and takes much of this margin. Manufacturers able to create value for end-customers in non-traditional ways, and willing to bundle this value with the tangible product, will likely secure more attention and support. For example, rapid order fulfillment may enable distribution channel intermediaries to be more responsive to their business customers, but can also elevate inventory levels. Understanding this, manufacturers can work with their distribution channel intermediaries to develop processes and apply technology in support of their requirement.

Step 10: Be Consistent

A computer company may sell through many resellers, as it takes its computers to market. These resellers are competitors and each resents the fact that the computer company works with the other companies that deprive them of sales. This is a typical situation for many industries. If the manufacturer will not cut out some of its channel intermediaries or adopt other approaches to build the channel's business case, it may at least wish to be consistent in the way it applies its current policies. Inconsistency — just the smell of it — can lead some intermediaries to believe their suppliers favor their competitors, even if this is not the case. For example, one channel member was convinced the manufacturer did indeed have inventory when it said it was out of stock. He would tie up the manufacturer's order desk with multiple requests for product, and many of the manufacturer's employees would be contacted to establish if the product could somehow be sourced on a rush basis. Only when standardized policies were established and communicated to the resellers, and only after all calls were routed and tracked through the call center, could the intermediary be convinced that its supplier was operating consistently.

Relationships with Employees

For value to be continuously created for customers, the company must do the same with employees for they will manage the processes, provide the imagination, implement the technologies and derive the insight to help deepen customer bonding. And there will always be intangible factors that can help the customer with the value they seek, factors which will never be explicit in processes. For example, what process will make an employee consistently likable? What process will make them respond well under pressure? What process will make customers respect them? The employee is central to Relationship Marketing for, without their commitment, the initiative will fail. And some of the current employees are not suitable for Relationship Marketing and may need to be trained and upgraded or "traded" to firms which remain focused on mass marketing and product specialization.

Companies adopting Relationship Marketing as a key business strategy will need to consider their human resources in a new light. Just as companies are encouraged to see their customers as individuals with whom new value will constantly be developed, identify the best customers from among those they serve and align their capabilities in pursuit of customer expectations, so too should the company see its employees in much the same way. Employees can be considered as individuals with whom new value will be created, the best among the employees can be identified and the capabilities of the company, aligned to customer requirements, should accommodate the development of new value with employees, paying particular attention to those who do and can create most value for the company.

This implies the need for an employee-centric database, capturing the full value of the employee by describing and seeking to qualify the value each creates for the company, in relation to their total cost to the firm. The database should thus go beyond the HRIS (Human Resource Information Systems) employed in many firms. With Relationship Marketing, companies need to continuously develop mutual value with employees. It can be a huge challenge for the company to really help the employee find meaning from their personal journey and may require a change in culture and even mind-set of the leadership, especially for companies still locked into the traditional command and control paradigm worthy of F.W. Taylor. Relationships with customers will not typically be enduring and committed until the relationships with employees deepens.

The database is the component at the center of an employee relationship. It facilitates profiling of the person, understanding the meaning each seeks, knowing the barriers each faces, the level and nature of bonding with the enterprise, and learns more about the staff member as they make their personal journey. This means populating the HRIS with data crucial to the development of the individual, in terms relevant to each, according to the meaning each wants. The HRIS can become a key organizational capability, matching people to processes and functions, and, most importantly, to customers. End-customer relationships often depend on people to go beyond standard polices and procedures to make a big difference in problem resolution and the attachment a customer feels for the company. The suitability of the person to the job and to the customer personality, industry and other typology can be assisted by an HRIS geared to achieve this. The processes in support of the HRIS may sometimes need to change, such as giving employees access to their files.

Just as the company will pay particular attention to the needs of its best customers, so too should it focus on its best employees, and provide mass customized development for each, both in the functional nature of their current job and in terms of their intellectual and interpersonal development.

Employee Skills

A company focused on Relationship Marketing will likely find that the broadening of the scope of products and services they provide their customers will result in a need to simultaneously broaden the scope of knowledge of its employees. Now employees will need mastery of more processes, technologies and people with whom they must interact. For example, a customer calling to inquire about the operation of their new widget should be met by someone who has the information. The information will either come from the person directly or indirectly from data warehouses or people with the knowledge, which will require that the person be able to engage new processes to access, assess and communicate the information.

Companies will always require deep functional specialists, of course, for it is they who provide the knowledge to develop and improve product and service. But most firms need more employees who have a broader scope of knowledge, who are "broad" in understanding how everything the company does comes together for the customer as each expects. This implies a need for companies to do things right with respect to the relationships they plan to foster with employees, on behalf of customers:

1. Identify the Relationship Marketing skills required from employees who are to participate in all the processes that deliver customer value.

2. Assess the performance of employees in respect of these skills and determine any knowledge gaps, by working this through with employees and communicating effectively, often in real time, not just in a simple questionnaire or other impersonal manner.

3. Develop training programs and technology support to reskill and/or deskill processes where employees require additional knowledge or context.

This last point is important, for it has the potential to change the company's training processes. At present, many companies establish major training initiatives, putting vast amounts of information into three-ring binders and then attempting to drill this into the skulls of their staff. This approach can be expensive and is more likely to fail than one focused on just-in-time training, when appropriate for the employee to be trained, rather than when the company chooses to offer a particular program. Technology can be of much assistance here, as it has the potential to:

1. Provide training content to employees when they wish to be trained, or when they need to be, using multimedia approaches and training over the company's Intranet, Extranet (which dealers' employees can access) or Internet.

2. Provide information to employees to help broaden their scope of understanding or aid them in real time, such as by having a computer prompt the front-line clerk to ask a customer a certain question or offer a specific service. Even in a learning relationship, where the customer knowledge is being deepened and the directions to front-line personnel change, the employee has an opportunity to grow with the process and integrate into it with training and support of this type.

3. Interact with employees and adjust to their level of skill, advancing their capability as each grows.

Increasing Scope Challenges
Traditional Job Descriptions

Relationship Marketing, by requiring more scope of knowledge from employees, may also challenge the boundaries for the business function they have historically performed. A quick example follows. If a manufacturer of cast-iron wood stoves finds, in the process of working with a dealer, that this firm would like to carry both gas and wood stoves, how should the company respond if it does not now make gas stoves? What would be the implications of its response for its staff? End-customers want gas hearth products in their homes — they start quicker and burn cleaner — and are choosing gas in ever-increasing numbers. Entry into the gas hearth segment could be costly for this cast-iron stove company, which is undercapitalized, although many of its competitors are not. But ignoring the value the channel intermediary wants and the trends in the market could prove even more costly. Either way, the employee dealing with the intermediary could feel like a deer caught in the headlights of a truck. If the company decides to make gas stoves, it will be competing with stronger companies in that segment. If the company chooses to not make gas stoves, its dealers will probably migrate to companies with broader product lines. What, then, will cause the deer to move before it becomes road kill?

The strategic answer might be to have gas hearths produced under the company's brand name by other manufacturers, helping to avoid additional investment in plant and machinery, if not inventory and receivables. Another might be to comarket with a company that makes gas hearths but not wood stoves, distributing through a group of dealers common to both. Each option will have different implications for employees with the cast-iron stove company. In the first case, service personnel will need to learn how to maintain gas hearth products, for example. In the second, new processes will need to be established to bond with a company nominally in the same industry, to help avoid problems that may occur, such as if one firm wants to make hearths now produced by the other, or if a company wishes to terminate a dealer now fully supported by the second firm. Whichever path the wood-burning stove company adopts, it should be prepared to clearly identify process, knowledge and IT implications, and the requirements from specific employees in tending to these capabilities and broadening their individual boundaries.

Employee Trust Important

On the other side of challenges such as these, is the response by the employee to change. Proceeding on the basis of mutual trust, the employee must simply be prepared to willingly, knowledgeably and happily trust his/her future to the company and the company should treat this trust as an icon. The employer company must foster this, for it has no alternative because trust is the basis for new value creation in every company. As organizations become flatter and better informed, as knowledge proliferates, processes bind and throughput accelerates, no executive can review every aspect of the process of value creation. The executive should set boundaries within which employees are free to create value, framing the meaning of the word "trust" in policies and procedures. Recently, a salesperson in an Internet company committed the company to a comarketing venture for which he had no apparent authority, offering free Internet access in a cross-promotion with another firm. This venture had major financial downside but the company was forced to go ahead because the employee had committed it. If there are no reasonable limits, empowerment can sink a company, especially in the wild-west of technology industries.

One way of managing the increased scope of knowledge and responsibility expected from employees, without undue disruption, is to encourage self-managed work teams for key processes. For example, instead of senior software developers narrowly defining tasks so that individuals can write modules which will be integrated and then quality tested, a development team can simply be asked to make customers more competitive in their markets. The team will identify a process to develop the insight they need and their responses to this insight.[77]

Trustworthy Leaders

Trust can only be fostered by the trustworthy. Leaders must fall into this category and be seen to fall into this category. If they are to receive trust, respect and commitment, they must give it. A case in point: a multinational software company, focused on the financial

---

[77] There are many excellent books on the subject of teams, including Jon R. Katzenbach and Douglas K. Smith, *The Wisdom of Teams*, Harvard Business School Press, 1993.

engineering of shareholder value, has been unable to develop trust-based relationships with suppliers and staff. While there may be many reasons for the lack of trust, it mostly seems to come down to a breakdown of trust in the president, who attended the Josef Stalin School of Management and has withered all but the compliant and asbestos-clad. The culture has proven unacceptable for staff building for the long term and has resulted in an exodus, including the more talented software developers on whom the firm's new products depend. Such departures affect the company's prospects and erode longer-term shareholder value.

Trust can be further fostered by understanding personal values and doing more than the employee expects in this regard. The development of trust starts before the employee crosses the threshold of the company. Consider Microsoft, where employees can routinely work at 80 hours a week. Why would people move to Redmond, Washington, for an opportunity to work there? It comes down to personal values. Microsoft knows that good software can only come from good people, so they set out to find the best, reviewing more than 120,000 resumes and interviewing 7,400, to hire just 2,000 people.[78] And when they find the best, they go to unusual lengths to address individual requirements and demonstrate the early commitment of Microsoft. For example, they might provide flexible hours for people concerned about the sheer number of hours to be worked, they might find a suitable house and fax a picture to out-of-town candidates, they might even help with personal preferences, in one case locating a karate instructor for a candidate with this interest.

Unionized workforces represent a further challenge for continuous mutual value creation because value needs to be created at the union level as well as at the individual one. At a major company, the salesforce is unionized, which is not common. Unions tend to be seen as a more secure environment for the employees and some management would see this as anathema, preferring to lever the insecurities of some members of the salesforce into higher sales. But, at this company, the unionized salesforce is seen as a valuable component of account management, and has performed as such. In fact, management has encouraged the unionized salesforce by expanding their influence through a "Feet on the Street" program, which encourages

---

[78] "How Microsoft Makes Offers People Can't Refuse," *Business Week*, February 24, 1992.

unionized staff in other than sales positions to undertake some sales-related activities, some on a temporary basis and others as agreed with their management. In both cases, long term, four-way relationships are being advanced — between the company, individual employees, unions and customers. The experience of customers served by the unionized employees is positive. Deepening the bonding between customer and supplier, some customers have formed teams with account representatives and operations personnel to advance interests mutual to the respective organizations.

Relationships with Suppliers

Meaningful and continuous relationships with strategic suppliers can be fundamental to the success of a company. In the computer industry, for example, major producers of personal computers and software that have early access to chip makers plans and latest products, can have enormous advantage in an industry where products are obsolete before they are introduced. Microsoft and Intel have long had a symbiotic relationship to the advantage of both firms, so much so that some refer to them as "Wintel," an abbreviation for Windows-Intel, which together comprise the strategic heart for the vast majority of desk-top computing. Major desktop computer companies maintain close relationships with Wintel, or risk eroding their market position. IBM helped engineer and adopted a Motorola chip for a new generation of personal computers while Compaq was further fostering its relationship with Intel. Now Compaq is the largest manufacturer of personal computers in the world, aided by Intel's success. While giants such as IBM and Compaq are jockeying, the second-tier companies are faced with even larger challenges and must be seen by the chip companies as strategic customers if they are to enter the big leagues. In short, a sound relationship with suppliers is very important if value is to be developed and maintained with the end-customer.

Essential Ingredients

The company can treat suppliers as they would for any other stakeholder mentioned previously and in particular, as the obverse side of the customer-relationship coin, described in Chapter 6 and outlined in Figure 17. Essential ingredients in the supplier relationship include:

1. a data warehouse describing significant dimensions of the supplier and their performance;

2. assessing supplier contribution to company profitability and future potential profitability, then selecting strategic suppliers from among those that add relatively more value;

3. understanding how each company is currently bonded with the other, and what objectives might be established for deepening the relationship, particularly with strategic suppliers;

4. benchmarking suppliers relative to one another, in terms important to the company;

5. assessing the company in terms of its amenability and flexibility in implementing supplier relationships;

6. stating the opportunity that can be derived from increased supplier bonding, especially with the best or most strategic suppliers;

7. establishing a process to plan, implement, manage, measure and share the creation of new value;

8. putting in place a method of governance for the relationship; and

9. managing change between the company and its suppliers, in much the same way as discussed for change management with customers.

As with employees and indeed, all stakeholders, relationships with suppliers include and require the development of mutual trust. A precursor for a trust-based relationship is bonding on the basis of core values. If these values, business practices and objectives of the company and its suppliers do not align before forming a relationship, it is unlikely that the relationship will endure.

Once the firms are value and culturally bonded, then the respective leadership should establish and publicly commit to alignment and continuous mutual value creation. Finally, the firms will be in a position to align their strategies and capabilities, to ensure that the value the company has committed to the end-customer is delivered seamlessly and rapidly. When this has happened, essentially a *keiretsu* has been established.

The road to the *keiretsu* is paved with statements of good intent but also a mating ritual as companies seek to find the right alignment for them. Suppliers may be held back from a full relationship by feeling uncertain as to the repercussions if the relationship goes wrong. What will happen to the jilted suitors? Will they still be available and open for business? Marketers have always been told never to burn their bridges with customers or suppliers, but Relationship Marketing — if it leads to close alignment between companies that see one another as strategically important — may result in precisely that. If one chooses the right bridge to keep open and the right ones to burn, the company may not only survive but become stronger, particularly if relationships are forged with the first-tier companies before competitors fully appreciate the importance of Relationship Marketing and customer bonding.

The rules of competition are changing. In a previous era, companies competed with other companies. This is no longer true for many. Now, chains of relationships compete with other chains, like spider webs competing with other webs to trap a tasty morsel. Sometimes the network of relationships can be reconfigured easily when one company drops out. For example, a relationship between grocery stores and beverage manufacturers might fall in this category. Take away one grocery store chain and Coca-Cola will not fail. In the bike manufacturing industry, the fragmented nature of the industry means that retailers can be assured of replacement product should one supplier fail, and frame manufacturers can typically buy components from substitute suppliers, should there be a supply disruption further back in the relationship chain.

But sometimes, and not as common, the network is mutually and fully dependent, and an individual component of the chain of relationships cannot be readily replaced. Boeing may be highly dependent on General Electric for motive power in some of their jets, for example. If the alignment is very close and interdependent, companies may merge, as has happened in the Canadian photographic market, were Fuji has acquired companies in the consumer and industrial segments of the market.

Opening Up

One of the business challenges for this decade is for the supplier to open their companies to their customers, to make both more competitive. When successfully done, supplier and intermediate customer are bonded and able to work together to create the new value the customer wants, ultimately bonding the entire business processes with those of the end-customer's. Typically, technology needs to open up for the company to be fully open for business with its suppliers. For example, General Electric (GE) developed the Trading Process Network, which gave suppliers access to the firm's lighting unit, via a secure Web site. As a result, GE halved procurement times and reduced prices by up to 15%.[79]

The largest retailer of hardware and automotive aftermarket products in Canada is Canadian Tire. Locked in a competition with new arrival Wal-Mart, the firm is looking for every possible angle to improve its market position, including working with suppliers in non-traditional ways. Canadian Tire represents over one-third of the bikes produced by manufacturer Groupe Procycle, so Procycle is open to Canadian Tire's thrusts of cost management and logistics and service improvement. The two firms discussed how bikes are made — in modules, with parts such as seats and handlebars sourced from others coming together with the frames and assembled by Procycle. Once the process was established, Canadian Tire and Procycle discussed when Procycle needs to place orders with its suppliers and the dates when Canadian Tire must place its order with Procycle. This helped Canadian Tire push back the date of its final order commitment, and better meet changing customer demands. Canadian Tire is using technology to allow for better supplier relationships, including a planned-order function which will provide forty-two buying teams with Canadian Tire's forecasts of demand, updated weekly and projected for the next six months.[80]

Vendors of packaged software are important contributors to the opening up of a firm to its customers and suppliers. The largest vendors of such software include i2 Technologies, Manugistics, Numetrix, ILOG and Chesapeake Decision Sciences. Their software planning modules for manufacturing, demand, distribution and transportation. Companies adopting this software report that they are able to improve financial performance through inventory reduction and meeting changes in customer demand, even when unanticipated orders soar. But perhaps the major benefit is the closer working relationship and increased bonding, the result of bringing processes, technology and people into greater alignment.

The Internet can be another important method for interenterprise bonding, particularly when companies can access one another's databases and reports, and engage in secure communication, including

---

[79] Tom Stein, "Orders from Chaos," *Information Week,* June 23, 1997, p. 45.

[80] Gordon Brockhouse, "Supply-side Tactics," *Infosystems Executive,* July, 1997, pp. 10-16.

ordering. For example, Fruit of the Loom has established a capability called Activewear Online, that lets this company create and support personalized Web sites for 30 of its largest distributors.[81] These sites allow distributors to better meet the urgent needs of their customers, and for Fruit of the Loom to "become better business partners with our customers," in the words of the chief information officer.

Relationships with Coventure Partners

In some cases, a firm may wish to establish relationships with companies they have not previously done business with, as they seek to maintain and deepen the customer relationship. Perhaps a company that provides dentists with dental consumables, equipment and operatories, such as Patterson Dental Co., might wish to further expand their product line as they seek to become a one-stop dentists' shop. Patterson already markets equipment such as drills and chairs, consumables, including X-ray film, and provides financing for dentists' purchases. They recently bought a company to broaden their range of products to include stationery and print-to-order products for the dentists' front office. For companies such as Patterson, the future may hold even further growth in the scope of products and services provided, perhaps including software for the management of the dentist's practice and even personal services, such as financial planning for well-heeled clientele. Even for large companies, the broadening of scope creates new management, process and resource challenges.

To take advantage of the opportunities inherent in a customer relationship, the company may need to forge non-traditional relationships. In the above example, a distributor of dental operatory systems and services may associate with a company providing vertical market software and support for dentists. They may also associate with a company that provides financial planning services. And they may do all this under a single brand name or multiple brand names, cross promoted. Sears grouped a number of personal financial and real estate services under the common aegis of Sears and the originator's brand, such as Coldwell Banker, Allstate Insurance and Dean Witter Financial Services, creating an apparent opportunity for cross-sales to the same consumer. The assumption was that the customer could be cross-sold with multiple financial and related services and

---

[81] Tom Stein, "Orders From Chaos," *Information Week*, June 23, 1997, p. 52.

that various transaction and customer data could be shared. There may have been room for further improvement. In 1993, some of the companies in the financial services group had an initial public offering, and Sears reduced their interest in the companies at that time. Coldwell Banker was sold. Yet the opportunity was there for cross leverage of the underlying value of customer data, but perhaps not quite as Sears approached it.

A company need not own all the companies with which it goes to market, but the firm with primary customer responsibility must control the processes by which customer value is fabricated and managed. Of course, as in the case of the dental operatory distributor mentioned above, the company can own the various operations which control the processes. But, increasingly, technology will be used between companies to manage the flow of data to help ensure that customer value is created across a broader front and between companies that do not have interlocking ownerships.

Customer Access

Most companies want customer access and account control, and the opportunity to expand their businesses through increased scope. Few want to be serfs to the kingpin, who, with customer access, may have the perpetual opportunity to dictate the terms of a relationship the supplier needs to gain access. Thus, increasingly competition will be for access to the customer and the company most likely to maintain this access and manage it for strategic advantage will have:

1. a strategically important product or service — one that is vital to the future of the customer;

2. a capability to interact today as the company expects, with open people, technology and processes, and sharing of knowledge and insight;

3. an ability to propose and deliver a range of services to add even more value in the future, sometimes in non-traditional areas with non-traditional suppliers; and

4. control of the processes and technologies by which value is to be created with a network of suppliers.

Models for Collaboration

There are many models for working together to provided an increased scope of service or capability to the end-customer. Some examples follow:

- The company may already have some experience working with non-traditional business partners, such as in the area of comarketing, where a firm making breakfast cereals may promote an offer from a computer company, say.

- In some industries, it is also common for firms to spread their research and development (R&D) expenditures across a broad range of opportunity areas, to ensure that the risk of failure is reduced. This results in R&D being shared, sometimes with competitors, as happens routinely in the computing industry.

- Sometimes companies set up research consortia to help share R&D costs and limit the potential for competitors to breakthrough with proprietary expertise or patents. Again, there are numerous examples from the electronics, semi-conductor and computing industries.

- Companies can develop coventures with their competitors, assuming different roles on specific bids to help position both for success, such as in the aerospace and defense industries, where firms simultaneously cooperate and compete. For example, Sperry provided the computing capability as sub-contractor to RCA, which led the Aegis technology program for the US Navy. At the time, both Sperry and RCA had computing and communications capability, and these firms still could have competed on other defense projects while they were cooperating on the Aegis program.

In the context of Relationship Marketing, no longer will companies just sell what they make. In the future, firms will need to consider making some of what they sell, and have relationships with coventure partners to deliver the rest. The alliance may be formal or informal, with a designated firm being the lead supplier and "value integrator," and having ownership of the processes by which value is created for the end-customer. Where formal, the alliance may be captured in a legal format, such as a company with equity interests from investing parties comprising the beneficial owners.

Consider the case of auto companies that today are rewarding their suppliers for making components and subassemblies lighter.

Companies which provide various braces and housings will find that they cannot build these with traditional materials, such as steel, while reducing weight, and that alternative materials, such as aluminum, magnesium or titanium, may be required. Suppliers that provide solutions made from steel may be advised to consider production from other metals or simply to establish an alliance with companies already able to do this more specialized production.

Management and Control for the Chain of Relationships

Relationships with stakeholders have the potential to substantially change financial and operational processes when fully implemented, and may challenge the traditional management and control processes of the company. For example, some suppliers are able to assess customers' inventory levels — either electronically or in-person, and then top up the inventory by initiating an "order" to themselves, shipping and billing — all on their own initiative. Fastforms, a progressive business forms and printing company located in Guelph, Ontario, has established precisely these trust-based relationships, which have led to an expanded scope of service for its major accounts, substantial savings for the firm's customers and long-term contracts, as customers reduce the number of suppliers with which they deal.

Challenges

Traditional management has been guided by the centralization of planning, leadership, organization, command, communications, information and control. In this era of Relationship Marketing, these principles are challenged for a number of reasons:

1. Decisions need to be taken in real time, or near real time, and management involvement delays decision making.

2. Decisions need to be taken by people who are closest to the customer, not by more remote management.

3. Information systems have democratized corporations and shifted intelligence to where it can be used. Management's role has changed and is no longer the hub of all the company's knowledge. In many cases, management may not be party to all the

decisions being made as the bits and bytes whiz around without scrutiny or intervention.

4. Many of the people in the company are very knowledgeable, some with more depth and breadth of training that the people who nominally manage them.

5. Technology systems now in place produce more information than management can assimilate and the systems are advancing faster than are people — substantially faster.

6. Business processes take care of all but the exceptions, which can then be codified and incorporated in revised processes.

7. Bricks and mortar have been replaced by virtual environments. Libraries have become computer terminals with characters on a screen — the knowledge of man is at your fingertips, not managed by a control freak disturbed at the prospect of misfiled books upsetting the Dewey system. Banks are becoming virtual, too, with policies and procedures being captured in software. The potential exists for loans to be approved and managed without the intervention of someone who manages money as though it belongs to the Mafia.

8. In most industries, employees, customers, investors and suppliers have choice. Management that functions primarily by emphasizing command and control in their business dealings will find these stakeholders exercising their choice in a stampede for the exit.

Relationship Marketing, discussed above and throughout this book, can be seen to be quite different than the traditional practice of marketing. Traditional marketing meant aggregating — whether customers, products, distribution channels, investors, employees or even competitors. With Relationship Marketing, companies disaggregate and manage each individually, according to their preference, as long as the company can accommodate this. With Relationship Marketing, companies deploy technology more strategically, and in the service of the individual. Companies use this technology not just to expedite and improve efficiency, but to enhance effectiveness, predict customer preference and initiate the purchase. With Relationship Marketing, companies seek to continuously bond and to do so in real time and in an organized strategic framework. Without Relationship Marketing, companies are at the whim of whatever new idea comes along, making chaos from orders.

The New Role of Management

The new role of management is to develop, nurture and manage the underlying capabilities of the company and its access to the resources which constantly improve those capabilities. This, in turn, means developing a supportive company culture, a plan to improve capabilities, and an implementation plan for making it all happen and measuring performance.

Measurement Issues

The measurements will be non-traditional ones, too. Management will need to measure issues such as:

- the company's performance in terms of total expenditure by each customer, tracked over time;
- the equity competitors have in customers' minds and the components of this equity;
- customer satisfaction and favorability;
- competitive measures of the performance of key capabilities: people, process, technology and knowledge;
- competitive intelligence in terms of the network of relationships competitors are creating and developing and the state of these relationships;
- customer profitability, not just product profitability;
- number of current and new customers;
- purchasing by different purchasing units within specific accounts;
- customer expenditures by supplier and for all relevant products, not just what a company currently makes;
- customer contacts, by type;
- position of the account on the bonding continuum;
- customer loss, leakage, attrition and recovery; and
- share of spending loss, leakage, attrition and recovery.

Over a foreseeable time horizon, issues such as those presented in Figure 34 will be subject to measurement. Increasingly, therefore, management — and particularly, marketing management — will become the custodian of business processes; an advocate of the customer in these processes; a judge in terms of the balancing of the interests of the various stakeholders in processes, outcomes and benefits; and the keeper of the measurements to facilitate this, assess performance, reward and recognize staff.

Increasingly, Relationship Marketing will require that marketing management takes a process view of the organization, and break down processes into their subcomponents, assessing each for the potential to work with customers to continuously create and share mutual value. As management focuses increasingly on the management of processes, the charting and alignment of those processes to add value to customers becomes challenging indeed. To illustrate the complexity, one company considers each of the marketing and sales subprocesses, including developing customer awareness for its offerings, stimulating inquiries, qualifying leads, writing proposals, conducting demonstrations, closing the sale and activities to be performed by marketing and sales after the sale is concluded. For each of these, the firm assesses the role of a wide variety of channels to the minds of its customers, including mass, targeted and direct advertising, telemarketing, Internet, trade shows, telesales, channel member sales and direct sales. Then the firm considers how best to apply the channels to the processes, and assesses opportunities to engage the customer to advance the overall process.

FIGURE 34: Relationship Marketing Metrics: Selected Current and
Future Measurements

Cost	Time	Profit	Customer Value
Total demand cycle Delivered cost by module, and module assembly Costs by customer	Demand-cycle response time Order-to-customer delivery response time Response time in respect of key relationship variables	Return on demand-cycle assets Inventory coverage ratio Cash flow by customer Operating profit by customer	Perfect orders: reliability, availability, lead times, quality, delivery flexibility, information quality Customer loss and leakage rates Net present value of the customer

୨୧

This chapter discussed the importance of thinking about Relationship Marketing as a chain of relationships, each individually important and each potentially a source of new value to be created and shared, continuously. The chapter noted key approaches to managing each type of relationship, drawing on the central ideas presented in Chapter 6, which dealt with the planning of customer relationships. The next chapter builds on this and asks how a company should consider organizing to capture opportunities through Relationship Marketing. The book concludes with a review of core concepts.

CHAPTER TEN

ઝઉ

The Relationship
Marketing Company
of Tomorrow

*The mind of man is capable of anything — because everything
is in it, all the past as well as all the future.*
Woodrow Wilson

Before considering what a company fully adopting Relationship Marketing would look like, let's consider how work itself is changing and
the implications for relationships.

Relationships Determine Future Success

Relationships are the fundamental asset of the company. More than
anything else — even the physical plant, patents, products or markets — relationships determine the future of the firm. Relationships
predict whether new value will continue to be created and shared
with the company. If customers are amenable to a deepening bond,
they will do more business with it. If employees like to work there,
they will continue down their learning curve and produce more and
better. If investors and bankers are happy with their returns, they will
continue to keep their funds in the company and help secure its
financial underpinning. And so on for other stakeholders. Relationships are predictive. All else is history.

Everything you can touch is becoming worth less. And everything
that you cannot, everything abstract, is appreciating. Intangibles that

are becoming more valuable include intellectual property, such as patents and trademarks, the "soft" benefits associated with buying a product, such as the way you feel when you use a certain hair coloring, and services and know-how, such as installation and training. Intangibles also include rights and territories, such as the right to use a specific license or process, and the territory occupied in the mind of a channel intermediary, partner, employee or customer.

Behaviors stem from attitudes, which are, in turn, formed by many things, including friends, family, society, experience and learning. Attitudes can also be affected by what the company communicates to position itself favorably in the minds of its audiences. Attitudes drive the behaviors that lead to a purchase and the opportunity to work together to develop yet more value for one another. This is a relationship, and relationships are the most valuable of all intangibles.

Relationships are important and will become more important, for, in the end, when the means of production is fully automated, and when the knowledge of man is in databases, this is all there will be. Value will be created by relationships. People will exist in a world of networks. Each node in the network will be either a physical person or a computer. By linking people and computers together in real time, new value will be made, continuously. And the nature of work will change yet again, from a noun to a verb — from the *place* where we do things, to the things we *do*. Employment will not be a psychological contract between a company and its staff. It will be between people, using technology and process to create value.

Connections Will Become More Fluid

In this environment, much will be fluid. In the "Dirty 30s," the unemployed rode freight cars across America and Canada in search of work. They gave up their roots and connections in small towns across the land to find food and a future. Now, it will not take an economic catastrophe to send people on their way. With computers and videoconferencing and modems and telephone lines, people will more rapidly make and break connections to shape value for customers and find meaning for themselves. In short, connections have the potential to change on a more frequent basis, within the company, between enterprises, between clusters of companies who have chosen to associate, between the company and individuals beyond its borders and between individuals outside the company. Only value-creating relationships will hold connections in place, so the relationships must be continuous and mutual.

Relationships Can Extend the Duration and Value of Connections

Recognizing this, companies have just two choices. They can go with the flow and build the capabilities needed to enhance relationships. Or they can go against the flow and seek to lock down every current and valuable connection by increasing exit barriers with a contract, and then enforce contracts to protect the embedded value. In this way, they can profit from their past investments and use the funds to buy into other, similar situations. For example, some US utilities are considering imposing exit charges for customers switching to other energy suppliers, to compensate the original utility for investments they made in expensive nuclear plants or other costs that are now harder to recover. Other utilities are considering instead how to bond more tightly with their customers and increase customer retention in this way. It will not be easy for utilities to simultaneously raise exit barriers and increase customer bonding. They will need to do one or the other.

Relationships Will Increasingly Require More Investment in Strategy

Many companies that have too many fragmented, unaligned programs have already recognized the importance of investing more narrowly, earlier and to greater effect. But opportunities remain to have a strategic umbrella as a unifying concept, under which initiatives can be placed and aligned. When one looks at the capital budgets of some companies, they still seem to be investing without such umbrellas, and lack strategic integration of their initiatives, including and perhaps especially, in the areas of technology and marketing. The opportunity remains for companies to reassess their strategies as a basis for getting that most precious management preference: focus.

Relationship Marketing can be the unifier of strategic initiatives in the post mass marketing, mass production and mass anything age. Opportunities to advance Relationship Marketing include selected significant points made previously and emphasized here.

Customer Mix

Many companies still focus on developing competitively superior customer satisfaction. If they have the right customer mix, this can lead to increased market penetration. If they have the wrong mix, they are accelerating as they drive over the cliff.

Opportunities remain for companies to reconsider their customer mix, deciding with which customers they should do business, with which they should not, and what to do about those who are in between. Call these "best," "worst" and "average" customers, respectively. Making this call will require that firms assess customer profitability and categorize customers according to the current and predicted value each represents. This customer-value segmentation can help companies decide how much to spend on creating value with each customer.

Having identified best, average and worst customers, companies will develop strategies to build profitability from each category. Best customers will be researched and analyzed to explore how the firm can bond even tighter with them and become yet more strategic to the account. Their behaviors will be examined. Insight will be derived from their purchases and actions, with the data warehouse supporting much of the analysis. Among other benefits, the warehouse and associated mining and visualization tools can help the firm be ready to sell when customers are ready to buy.

While some customers will require investment for a deepening of bonds, others should be fired because they are not profitable today, never will be and have no influence on your market success. Customers who are in-between — the average customers — will need to be managed and disciplined to build company profitability. Many will follow the lead of the banks that push consumers out of the doors, to the automated teller machines (ATMs) for routine transactions. If they will not be managed, they will be disciplined, just as the banks charge higher service fees at the counter for standard deposits and withdrawals that could have been handled by the ATMs.

Banks are also deploying new technologies, such as PC-banking, for their average customers. This not only expands the range of service for which technology can substitute for people, it also deepens the bond between consumer and company, once the consumer has invested time in learning the software.

Focus

Focus has historically been seen as the holy grail of management. Focus to those who are financially trained often means cutting products or markets and bringing the organization into alignment to cater to the remaining most profitable or strategic sectors. This can lead to scale economies and improved profitability. This is an approach that works well in companies with too much complexity and those with too little competition. But now most companies have reengineered much of the complexity out of their businesses. The overly busy people who remain do not have too much appetite for further complexity. And no business today is immune from brutal competition, so simple focus and business alignment often open the door to those who are happy to have less focus and more business. Now the word focus should be redefined to mean focusing on the best customers and giving them everything they want, whether individual products or services are profitable or not. This will lead to an increase in scope — more products and services, rather than less — and lead some to charge that you are not being focused. Give them this book.

Access

In the Relationship Marketing era, competition will be fought primarily for customer access. Those who have it will be able to benefit from an increase in scope. Those that do not, will become suppliers to those that do, or perish. Companies that today identify the best customers and pursue their business with passion will be better able to earn access and put in place the processes to become kingpin.

A few years ago a small company printed forms and communications materials for its customers. Then it focused on its best accounts. It began to manage customer inventories of its own products. In so doing, it reduced the costs of the processes for ordering, while improving service. In turn, the printer received opportunities to supply much of the new business in the account, whether it could actually print the products or not. Now, other printers that want to deal with these accounts must go through the lead supplier. This is making this small firm much bigger and vastly more profitable, challenging the basis for competition in the industry.

Bonding

Every relationship could benefit from increased bonding. This means every supplier needs to know where they stand with their customers, where they want to be and how they plan to get there. Bonding is a continuum and it makes more sense for companies to think in terms of advancing a relationship to the next level than to consider vaulting all the way to the end of the spectrum. Who gets married on the first date? Speak to one another first. Enjoy one another's company. Seek common ground. Hold hands. And so on. A company needs a bonding objective and a strategy to achieve this — with every account and customer.

Collaboration

Relationships — business or personal — fizzle without continuous reinvestment to create new value. Collaboration is a key to building this new value and the closer this collaboration is to real time, the more opportunity there is to bond. One way to secure real time or near real time interaction is to use technology at the customer interface. Another is to blur the lines between customer and supplier, eventually inviting the customer into the innermost sanctums of the company, just as you might expect of them. Work teams properly structured, governed, managed and geared to mutual learning can help drive collaboration throughout the processes by which value is made. Companies need strategies for collaborating. But first, they need to overcome the notion that there is a "we" (our firm) and a "them" (the customer). Companies need not think of customers as kings, but they do need to think of them as peers in a process by which both customer and supplier are to benefit.

Chain of Relationships

Great customer value requires that even more value be created with suppliers. Some of the value the customer wants is lost along the way in the form of learning curves, inefficiency, profit margins and errors. This friction means that companies have to work even harder to align with all their stakeholders to eliminate the friction the customer does not want. Technology helps. Process formalization helps. But more than these, strategy is required to frame approaches to create and share mutual value with every category of stakeholder, without incurring the friction for which customers should not pay.

Novelty

Some years ago a company was rescued from the brink of bankruptcy by a banker sympathetic to its plight. Now, thirty years later, the firm still does business with the same bank. Only trouble is, the bank long since stopped investing in the relationship with this, by now, very successful company. The president asked himself, "they got me to where I am, but will they get me to where I want to be?" The answer caused him to switch banks. This is a true story and exemplifies the idea that companies must create current and strategic value. They need novelty and a strategy for giving this to their customers. Novelty means more than innovation. You can innovate the process for counter-balancing rotating camshafts in car engines, and be irrelevant to the customer. Novelty means giving the customer new, strategic value.

Customer's Customer

It is no longer enough to have strategies to add value with the customer. The company seeking an enduring bond will need to help the customer develop relationships with their customers, further extending the chain of relationships mentioned earlier. In short, the company needs an understanding of the customer's customer, the strategies of the customer in respect of each end-customer, and a strategy for advancing the customer's Relationship Marketing interests with their customers.

Relationships Will Also Depend More on Flexible Capabilities

Those companies seeking to build relationships and create new value will need to build flexible capabilities in their technologies, processes, people and knowledge and insight. Their technologies must allow for virtually any shift that can be foreseen, in areas such as technology and industry structure, considering scenarios for industry evolution, in areas such as the formation of buying groups, concentration of ownership or the disappearance of classes of trade, such as whole-salers. Technology must be open to customers and other stakehold-ers, and secure from competitors and predators. Databases must be broad and deep and companies should continue to make invest-ments in data through good times and bad, for it will be the data that provide the new ideas, insight and source of increased earnings. Data can only be mined if the ore body is rich.

The Customer Data Warehouse Is Only the Beginning

Databases should not be limited to customer transactions. They should cover the customer more extensively, considering their vari-ous interactions with the company and the communications of the company with them, whether or not an actual purchase or return has been made. And databases should be maintained for stakeholders in addition to customers, so that knowledge and insight can be devel-oped and new value continuously developed with each. While some companies have put in place data warehouses for customer data, the Relationship Marketing company of tomorrow will have data ware-houses for other stakeholders, and will manage these databases to create new value with each, be they investors, employees, channel intermediaries or suppliers. In many firms, databases are spread throughout the company. An opportunity exists to reuse much of the existing transaction, behavior and research data to create more value. The tools are here today to manage existing data more effectively.

New ways should be sought to exploit the data, such as cross-linking the various databases so that any resulting relationships can be even deeper. How deep would be the bonding between the com-pany and its stakeholders if the bonding occurred at multiple levels? Companies already encourage employees to become investors. Could customers be encouraged to become investors, or could employees also be customers, or customers employees?

Involve Users in Process Design

Processes, too, should be open, flexible and continuous. Processes should be mapped and framed by the users of the outputs and by those who manage the process. For example, strategic planning should not be a two-day exercise for the executives at a comfortable retreat. It should be a continuous process — one in which all stakeholders and best customers, in particular, participate.   There is an implicit warning here that Karl Marx might have issued. If processes are designed without the input of those tending them, and if we, the means of production, find the processes to be alienating, then we have a situation far more devastating than the worker alienation seen by Marx. We will become alienated from ourselves. The company with workers alienated in this way, will find that they are the most alienated of all. Employees disgruntled with the processes of the United States Postal Service who return with shotguns have been categorized as having "gone postal." In the future, and without user involvement in the design of the processes they must tend, widespread alienation may result in more business for therapists, pharmacists, gunsmiths and prisons — the extreme outcomes of really bad relationships with one another and oneself!

Structure Follows Strategy and Process

The strategy and processes of a company should determine its structure. Companies organized according to the mass marketing paradigm will now need to reorganize around its customers and also around other stakeholders who create value for end-customers. One way of thinking about this is described in Figure 35, suggesting the

FIGURE 35: Capabilities and Relationships as Cornerstones in Organizational
        Design

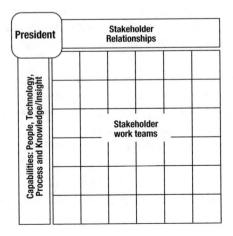

need for two main thrusts in organizing the company: capabilities and relationships with stakeholders.

The President's Role

The president's role includes five main components in the context of such structure:

1. To integrate — the capabilities with one another, relationship-focused work teams with one another, and the capabilities with the work teams.

2. To resource — ensuring that a sufficient flow of people, time, money and knowledge goes to the areas that need these.

3. To balance and prioritize the demands of the various work teams, capabilities and initiatives each wishes to pursue.

4. To lead, motivate, provide a compelling vision and keep the organization focused on creating value in real time, continuously and mutually with stakeholders.

5. To organize and control, ensuring that the results are there and that financial and operational controls are in place to limit any abuse of trust.

Relationship Managers, whatever their titles, will be in charge of integrating the company's processes and other capabilities that create customer value — right at the customer interface. The Relationship Manager should be a leader on a work team comprising individuals who manage the processes the customer values, and which are necessary to develop, nurture and control aspects of the relationship. Representatives could have responsibility for processes such as innovation, ordering, shipping and billing, customer service and so on.

Other work teams could be organized to address the needs of other categories of stakeholders such as employees, suppliers and channel intermediaries. Representatives on these teams would have responsibility for the principal capabilities, including processes, that develop value for and with these stakeholders.

Working with these Relationship Managers would be capability managers in charge of planning and implementing flexible and high performance capabilities to supercharge the customer relationship.

There should be a capability manager for each of people, process, information technology, and knowledge and insight systems. Process capability managers could be further classified according to the specific processes for which they are responsible.

Benefits of This Approach

A company organized along these lines will have a structure that recognizes four main issues:

1. It organizes the company around its stakeholders, with the customer being first among equals.

2. It integrates stakeholders into the business processes, and seeks to work continuously with them to create the value each wants. As such, it enables the definition of Relationship Marketing.

3. It understands the importance of specific capabilities in advancing relationships with stakeholders and that these capabilities should be key areas for investment.

4. It creates a series of trust-based relationships, which rely on the company's capabilities to indicate departure from the norm. If trust is abrogated, the various processes, people, and IT systems should bring the company back into line. A manager of culture and values would be responsible, in this structure, for ensuring that codes of conduct are appreciated and are enshrined.

This approach is modular. It allows the company to add work teams for different categories of stakeholders, such as for investors and government. It lets the firm structure teams for specific best customers and other teams to handle remaining customers. The same hold true for best employees and others. It even permits the company to blur its borders, and incorporate virtual work teams, some of which it may not directly lead but in which it could participate.

Stop Along the Road to the Future

Clearly, a company organized along these lines would differ fundamentally from the organization found in most of today's companies. A quick reaction to the above, therefore, may be that this is complex and unworkable. As the company moves from its current structure to

one more closely resembling the above, it will likely need some intermediary steps to allow adjustment of the employees to the changes,
and to learn what works and what should be avoided as the firm proceeds. The above structure should therefore be seen as a destination.
The company's bus will probably need to make some rest stops along
the way. Consider Figure 36, the more formal organization chart that

FIGURE 36: Organizing for Relationship Marketing

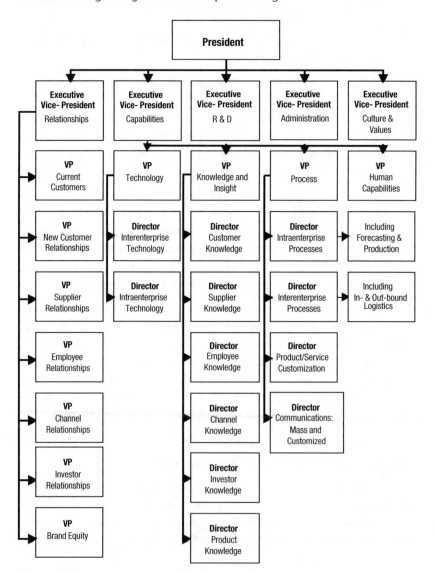

follows. Perhaps this could serve as a starting point for discussion in your company should it seek to make Relationship Marketing its cornerstone and structure itself accordingly.

The traditional functional roles change in a company organized primarily by capability and relationship. Some of the most important functional areas seen in today's company structures are underplayed or roles fundamentally changed in the above, especially for sales and marketing, but also for product management, plant operations and research and development. Sales and marketing, in particular, will increasingly be divided into two main roles: 1) those associated with identifying, securing and forming initial relationships with new accounts, and 2) retention, penetration and new value creation with existing accounts. Sales and marketing with new customers can include traditional roles and current structures most organizations use, while incorporating selected processes from Relationship Marketing, such as identifying prospects from the profiles of the company's best accounts. Reporting of sales and marketing can be through the executive vice-president of relationships, as suggested by the above chart, to help ensure an orderly transition in the management of an account when it is designated as a current customer.

Are companies organized this way today? Some are going down this road, taking breathers along the way. One new media company has a substantially similar structure, for example, and attributes much of its success to this. It has an internal relationship manager whose sole purpose is to manage the connections, culture and values and overcome any internal friction. Other firms, such as Hewlett-Packard, have senior management in charge of Relationship Marketing.

Clearly, a company serious about Relationship Marketing will need to consider how its organization must change to reflect this new strategy. A structure such as that presented above could be given consideration in the context of a firm's culture, leadership and other business strategies, as it seeks to continuously create mutual value with customers and other stakeholders.

જાજ

Today, management may feel that relationships are satisfactorily in hand with sales or marketing advancing the firm's interests with customers. For example, sales may be pursuing relationship selling endeavors and marketing may be driving initiatives associated with direct or one-to-one marketing. But, while sales may manage the relationship with individual accounts to generate near term sales, and marketing may seek to identify and satisfy customer needs for market segments and individual customers, neither typically deal with ten main issues:

1. Changing Customer Expectations
2. Segment Customers, Not Markets
3. Best Customers Deserve Best Value
4. Value Provided to Customers Depends on the Chain of Relationships
5. Data, Data, Data
6. Technology for Mass Customization
7. Board and Investor Support Needed
8. Recognition and Reward for Teamwork
9. Relationships and Capabilities, Not Silos
10. Organize by Relationship and Capability

The book concludes with a brief review summarizing each.

1. Changing Customer Expectations

Customers' expectations of suppliers, products and services are rising and customers are becoming more sophisticated in their purchasing and more knowledgeable in the business of their suppliers. Companies seeking to develop new business by simply becoming better at what they have been doing might be trying to win tomorrow's war with yesterday's weapons. If the shifting expectations of customers are to be satisfied, new approaches will need to be adopted and implemented, sometimes at the expense of existing programs. If Relationship Marketing is to be successfully adopted, the importance and value of this approach relative to existing ones needs to receive common agreement and understanding.

2. Segment Customers, Not Markets

The old rules of customer segmentation rarely work because customers often behave in a manner not predicted by more traditional approaches to market segmentation. Opportunities exist in many firms to segment customers based on considerations such as their current and potential value to the company and their amenability to a closer working relationship with the firm, leading to categorization of customers according to best, average and worst.

3. Best Customers Deserve Best Value

Few companies have ever rewarded a customer for being the type of customer they want. Fewer have ever managed, disciplined or fired a customer. But customers are not equally important. The firm recognizing this and focusing on their best customers is more likely to improve all aspects of its business, not least of all its bottom line, than companies that neither differentiate among customers nor give their best customers their best value. Companies that give all customers similar value will end up satisfying very few of their best customers and will weaken their profitability by giving too much value to their worst.

4. Value Provided to Customers Depends on the Chain of Relationships

Companies rarely focus on strengthening the chain of relationships with all those who contribute to the performance of the end-customer relationship, including employees, suppliers, distribution channel intermediaries and complementary products and services partners. Many companies have an opportunity to assess existing relationships throughout the chain, set relationship objectives with each category of stakeholder and develop appropriate strategies.

5. Data, Data, Data

Few firms have the right types of data, integrated data warehouses or intelligent, real time customer and stakeholder insight needed to advance specific relationships. Opportunities exist for many companies to focus more on the data warehouse as an instrument for customer and stakeholder knowledge and insight. This means they will often need more data about each category of stakeholder and processes to manage this considerable amount of data without being swamped.

6. Technology for Mass Customization

Few firms manage the end-customer relationship in a series of mass-customized processes, aligning human resources, processes, technologies and knowledge systems to support all aspects of internal and external Relationship Marketing. Beyond the role of the data warehouse just mentioned, firms should recognize the role and applications of technology to improve the customer relationship, some of which may also relate directly to the data warehouse, such as giving customers access via the Web to data or reports in/from the warehouse.

7. Board and Investor Support Needed

Management needs the backing of a board of directors and investor community that will welcome a focus on Relationship Marketing because the attendant costs can be high and the returns will not be immediate. They, like others in the chain of relationships, will need to be individually addressed to advance the cause of Relationship Marketing in the firm.

8. Recognition and Reward for Teamwork

Internal reward systems are still geared, in many companies, to recognize the performance of the hunter who brings home the biggest pelt, be that a large sale, a major acquisition or a long-term contract. The quality of a customer relationship depends on teamwork, so rewarding the individual runs counter to relationship development and advancement. Internal incentive and reward systems need to be revised to recognize both the importance of the customer relationship and the role of teams in improving this. Essentially, recognition and reward should be geared to compensating for farming rather than hunting.

9. Relationships and Capabilities, Not Silos

Many large, fragmented or multi-disciplinary companies have diverse, but often unlinked initiatives, that touch the customer. These need to be integrated and the learning from each point of contact needs to be incorporated within the firm to ensure that the customer relationship is managed in a planned way. In turn, this requires that the company not only address relationships but the capabilities that allow them.

10. Organize by Relationship and Capability

Some companies are today organized with a product management focus, but view Relationship Marketing as important to their future. This is completely at odds with Relationship Marketing, because it focuses on the product rather than the relationship. Companies which view the customer relationship as a central component of their strategies will likely achieve closer bonding with customers by organizing according to relationship category and capability type. Relationship category can include stakeholders and groups within each, such as best and average customers and new account relationships. Capability types can include people, technology, process and knowledge and insight.

෯ඊ

INDEX

ȢȢ

TALKING WITH THE AUTHOR

If you would like to discuss any aspect of this book with the author, Ian Gordon would like to hear from you. He can be reached at the following locations:

Telephone: 416-920-8883
Fax: 416-515-2097
E-mail: Rel82ian@aol.com

Ian Gordon is with TCI Convergence Limited, a firm of management consultants whose eight Practice Leaders are former partners and principals with major management consultancies. TCI Convergence serves companies of different sizes in diverse industries. Its clients include three of the ten largest companies in America. TCI Convergence provides a broad range of Relationship Marketing consulting services including:

- Relationship Marketing strategy development
- Customer profitability analysis
- Customer relationship quality research and assessment of the amenability of customers to deeper bonding
- Customer data warehousing, mining and visualization review and enhancement services
- Marketing and general management competency assessments
- Organizational design
- Relationship Marketing program design
- Relationship Marketing strategy for stakeholders other than customers, including distribution channel intermediaries, suppliers and investors
- Training programs, including in-house seminars and speaking engagements

For speaking engagements, contact:

Mr. David Lavin
The David Lavin Agency
24 Duncan Street, 4th floor
Toronto, Ontario, M5V 2B8
Canada

Telephone: 416-979-7979
Fax: 416-979-7987
E-mail: david@davidlavin.com